# A Bio-Bibliographical Dictionary

of

# Twelve-Tone and Serial Composers

by

Effie B. Carlson

The Scarecrow Press, Inc.

Metuchen, N.J.          1970

## Acknowledgments

The author would like to thank the few hundred organizations, publishers, and composers that have responded to requests for information and material. This correspondence has been invaluable in the compilation of Chapter II. I regret that it is not feasible to provide a complete list of these contributors.

Several close friends and associates have taken time to read the manuscript and their comments and ideas have been most useful. In particular I should like to express my gratitude to Mrs. Ruth L. Fisher, and to my husband, Thomas A. Carlson.

A special note of appreciation is extended to Dr. Calvin Bower, a member of the music faculty at the University of North Carolina.

# Table of Contents

Chapter             Page

I.  Introduction. . . . . . . . . . . . . . . . .  9

  The Twelve-tone Concept Emerges . . . . .  10

  Arnold Schoenberg's Twelve-tone Technique  13

  The Piano Works of Arnold Schoenberg,

   Alban Berg, and Anton Webern . . . . .  21

II. Composers of Serial Piano Music

  Since the Schoenberg School. . . . . . . .  36

   Amy, Gilbert. . . . . . . . . . . . . . . .  36

   Apostel, Hans Erich. . . . . . . . . . . .  37

   Babbitt, Milton. . . . . . . . . . . . . . .  38

   Barce, Ramón . . . . . . . . . . . . . . .  41

   Barraqué, Jean . . . . . . . . . . . . . . .  42

   Baur, Jürg. . . . . . . . . . . . . . . . . .  43

   Bennett, Richard Rodney . . . . . . . . . .  44

   Berio, Angelo Luciano. . . . . . . . . . . .  45

   Blacher, Boris. . . . . . . . . . . . . . . .  47

   Boulez, Pierre. . . . . . . . . . . . . . . .  50

   Brown, Earle. . . . . . . . . . . . . . . . .  57

   Bussotti, Sylvano. . . . . . . . . . . . . .  59

   Castiglioni, Niccolò . . . . . . . . . . . . .  60

   Clementi, Aldo. . . . . . . . . . . . . . . .  61

   Copland, Aaron. . . . . . . . . . . . . . . .  62

   Dallapiccola, Luigi. . . . . . . . . . . . . .  65

   Decaux, Abel. . . . . . . . . . . . . . . . .  70

   De Kruyf, Ton. . . . . . . . . . . . . . . .  70

De Leeuw, Ton . . . . . . . . . . . . . . . 71
De Pablo, Luis . . . . . . . . . . . . . . 72
Dickinson, Peter . . . . . . . . . . . . . 73
Donatoni, Franco . . . . . . . . . . . . . 74
Fortner, Wolfgang . . . . . . . . . . . . 76
Fricker, Peter Racine . . . . . . . . . . 79
Goehr, Alexander. . . . . . . . . . . . . 81
Halffter, Cristobal. . . . . . . . . . . . 82
Hamilton, Iain Ellis . . . . . . . . . . . 83
Hauer, Josef Matthias. . . . . . . . . . 84
Henze, Hans Werner. . . . . . . . . . . 89
Jelinek, Hanns. . . . . . . . . . . . . . 92
Jolivet, André. . . . . . . . . . . . . . . 95
Ketting, Otto . . . . . . . . . . . . . . . 98
Klebe, Gisehler. . . . . . . . . . . . . . 99
Koechlin, Charles. . . . . . . . . . . . . 102
Koellreutter, Hans Joachim . . . . . . . . 104
Koffler, Josef. . . . . . . . . . . . . . . 105
Kohs, Ellis Bonoff . . . . . . . . . . . . 106
Křenek, Ernst. . . . . . . . . . . . . . . 108
Leibowitz, René. . . . . . . . . . . . . . 116
Lutyens, Elisabeth . . . . . . . . . . . . 119
Lybbert, Donald . . . . . . . . . . . . . 120
Martin, Frank. . . . . . . . . . . . . . . 121
Martino, Donald. . . . . . . . . . . . . . 124
Merku, Pavle . . . . . . . . . . . . . . . 125
Messiaen, Olivier Eugène Prosper Charles 126
Nigg, Serge. . . . . . . . . . . . . . . . 130
Pâque, Désiré . . . . . . . . . . . . . . . 132
Paz, Juan Carlos. . . . . . . . . . . . . 133
Pentland, Barbara . . . . . . . . . . . . 135
Perle, George. . . . . . . . . . . . . . . 137

Pousseur, Henri. . . . . . . . . . . . . . 139

Ramovš, Primož. . . . . . . . . . . . . 142

Rands, Bernard . . . . . . . . . . . . . 144

Reynolds, Roger. . . . . . . . . . . . . 144

Riegger, Wallingford . . . . . . . . . . . 146

Rochberg, George . . . . . . . . . . . . 149

Sakač, Branimir. . . . . . . . . . . . . 151

Schäffer, Boguslaw . . . . . . . . . . . 152

Schat, Peter. . . . . . . . . . . . . . . 153

Schibler, Armin. . . . . . . . . . . . . 154

Searle, Humphrey. . . . . . . . . . . . 155

Serocki, Kazimierz. . . . . . . . . . . . 157

Skalkottas, Nikos. . . . . . . . . . . . . 159

Srebotnjak, Alojz. . . . . . . . . . . . . 162

Stockhausen, Karlheinz . . . . . . . . . . 163

Tal, Joseph. . . . . . . . . . . . . . . 169

Tokunaga, Hidenori . . . . . . . . . . . 171

Urbanner, Erich. . . . . . . . . . . . . 172

Valen, Fartein. . . . . . . . . . . . . . 173

Van Vlijmen, Jan. . . . . . . . . . . . . 174

Vlad, Roman. . . . . . . . . . . . . . . 175

Vogel, Wladimir Rudolfovich. . . . . . . . 177

Wagner-Régeny, Rudolf. . . . . . . . . . 179

Weber, Ben Brian. . . . . . . . . . . . 180

Weinzweig, John. . . . . . . . . . . . . 183

Weiss, Adolph Andreas. . . . . . . . . . 184

Wolff, Christian. . . . . . . . . . . . . 185

Wolpe, Stefan. . . . . . . . . . . . . . 187

Woytowicz, Bolesław . . . . . . . . . . . 189

Zimmermann, Bernd Aloïs . . . . . . . . 190

III.  A Geographical Survey. . . . . . . . . . . 199

Bibliography. . . . . . . . . . . . . . . . . . 212

vii

# Chapter I

## Introduction

The main purpose of this study is to extract from the history of twentieth-century piano literature a framework for understanding the role of serial composition in contemporary music.

The study has been organized into four parts. The first discusses the emergence of the twelve-tone concept, the Arnold Schoenberg twelve-tone technique, and the Schoenberg School. The second contains eighty alphabetized entries which constitute a representative group of composers who have written twelve-tone, serial, or serially-oriented piano music; the entries provide addresses and some biographical information, stress the main features of each composer's use of serial ideas, and include lists of piano scores and selected bibliographical material. The third part provides a brief outline of the evolution of twelve-tone and serial music in those countries playing a prominent role in the musical culture of this century. The fourth part is a general bibliography listing the most important scholarly publications related to the emergence of serial composition.

The serial technique of composition has established itself as a major force in twentieth-century music. Chromaticism of the late romantic era was a major cause for the break-down of tonality at the turn of the century, but it also precipitated the "atonalism" from which Arnold Schoenberg's twelve-tone concepts emerged to indicate a challenging new path for music. About mid-century the feasibility of total serialization evolved from concepts of the Schoenberg School. In turn the exploitation of this extension of serial principles spawned a hybrid type of chromaticism that utilizes serial principles originally deduced from the atonality of the early 1900's as a means of disciplining this same chromatic gamut. This chain of events indicates that the fundamental principles of the strict Schoenberg twelve-tone technique only hinted at the vast new perspectives becoming available to the present generation of composers.

9

A desire to examine the role of serial composition in musical evolution prompted the idea of limiting this study to a single channel which could provide a representative cross-section of serial music. It would thereby be feasible to explore the fundamental aspects of the history of twelve-tone and serial music in this century in greater detail than a broader survey would permit. The most logical such channel to choose is the piano literature of the last half-century. No other musical genre is so capable of demonstrating the various trends of dodecaphonic and serial music stemming from concepts prevalent in the early twentieth century as they were clarified and formulated by Arnold Schoenberg. Since the conception of Schoenberg's Three Pieces for Piano, Op. 11 (1908), each transition to a new phase, or the extension of Schoenberg's ideas by other composers, can be exemplified by piano compositions of musical merit as well as historical interest.

Several reasons for the widespread use of the piano by serial composers can be given. A large number of contemporary composers are adept at the piano, many having the status of professional pianists. The piano is one of the most readily available equal-tempered instruments, an essential attribute for twelve-tone writing. It also possesses a tremendous potential for meeting additional demands of the extension of serial principles in that it is a percussion instrument, has a wide pitch range, can produce both vertical and horizontal structures, and is therefore receptive to efforts to exploit series of varied attacks, timbres, dynamics, intensities, or sonorities. The techniques of "prepared" piano have further enlarged the capabilities of the instrument.

## The Twelve-Tone Concept Emerges

The twentieth century has been marked by radical changes in the basic concepts of the arts and sciences which have had important effects on musical composition. The focal point at which these changes can first be most clearly distinguished is the turn of the century.[1] These years, unique for their stimulating intellectual atmosphere, initiated a veritable tidal wave of experimentation in the search for new means of artistic expression. The twelve-tone concept was a musical manifestation of this new evolutionary phase in man's creative thought. An event of primary significance in the musical world was Arnold Schoenberg's succesful formulation of a twelve-tone method, and the subsequent association of the three composers constituting the modern Viennese School:

Schoenberg, Alban Berg, and Anton Webern.

The rather considerable variety of opinions at the
turn of the century regarding the use of total chromaticism[2]
nurtured the ideas from which Schoenberg's concepts of
twelve-tone writing could materialize.[3]   As in other arts,
music was ripe for new means of expression.  New sounds,
new rhythms, and changing concepts of form were challenging
the composer's imagination.[4]  Freud had stimulated the urge
to delve further into the inner consciousness, and had fostered man's realization that the mind was capable of deeper
perceptions.  Creative minds sought to give vent to intellectual and psychological expression hitherto unexploited.[5]
This concept initiated a probe into musical source materials
which has not yet diminished in intensity.  Schoenberg's
search for ways to utilize the full potential of the basic
components of musical language   led him to experiment with
new ideas for musical expression of space and time.[6]  He
sought a new technique that would permit this extension of
musical perception.  Schoenberg's formulation of his twelve-
tone technique emerged with great impact on the musical
scene as it met the need for a stabilizer in a disturbed
musical aesthetic.

Suspicions of an approaching crisis in the realm of
tonality began to be detected in the mid-nineteenth century.
As early as 1858 or 1859, while composing Tristan und
Isolde, Richard Wagner[7] became aware that he was entering
a zone for which he was not yet prepared and he retreated
to a more diatonic style.  But as composers gained understanding of romanticist trends, it was possible not only for
Wagner, but others, such as Hugo Wolf, Gustav Mahler, and
Johannes Brahms, to accept and utilize the challenge of
chromaticism more readily.[8]  As music moved into the un-
charted areas of the full chromaticism, the melodic line was
subjected to extensive elaboration.  Daring asymmetries were
conceived in form and rhythm.  Exploitation of chromatic
harmony[9] led to the use of chords built on intervals other
than the traditional superimposed thirds.  Claude Debussy in
his impressionistic style, and Alexander Scriabin in his late
piano works, (Op. 58-74), were leading forces in the use
of chromaticism and its new chords as the final breakdown
of functional harmony approached.  The use of radical
chromatic sonorities was a crucial factor leading to the
emancipation of consonance and dissonance.  The disintegration of traditional concepts of consonance and dissonance

was essential to twentieth-century music employing the full chromatic scale with no "tonic" point of reference. [10] Schoenberg envisioned a vast new potential in these developments and the first major discipline which sought to utilize this potential was his twelve-tone method.

In view of the rapidity of serial evolution, it is advantageous to utilize as a guide a brief outline which divides the development into several phases. Six convenient stages are apparent within the piano literature. These are not arbitrary, but realistic divisions, based on the study of numerous representative scores. They can be stated most simply as formulation, assimilation, extension, re-evaluation, broadening, and diversification.

The first stage of serial composition constituted the discovery and formulation of Schoenberg's method of composition with twelve-tones related only to one another. The second stage, assimilation and spread of the Schoenberg technique, began with Schoenberg's two closest associates, Alban Berg and Anton Webern, and their students. The accomplishments of Webern initiated the third stage, the beginning of important extensions of the Schoenberg technique. The post-war years brought a re-evaluation of serial principles on the basis of their continued extension by key figures in both America and France. This renewal of activity was stimulated more by Webern's music than that of Schoenberg or Berg, and has been referred to as the post-Webern movement. It gained considerable impetus in the post-war years, particularly in the Americas, by the immigration of Schoenberg, and others who were enthusiastic about the potential of his twelve-tone technique. During this fourth stage the feasibility of extending the serial principles to any or all musical elements was realized. Simultaneously electronic music reached a new peak in its development. Interactions between serial and electronic music were of mutual benefit to both, and also stimulated some reassessment of atonalism. This merger opened the doors on a fifth stage that broadened the area of application of the Schoenberg principles by their extension outside as well as within their original domain. The compatibility of many radical trends, such as chance (aleatory, improvisational) or stochastic techniques, with serial composition has revealed a common bondage between serial, atonal, and electronic music. The association of radical but nevertheless compatible ideas has fostered the sixth and most recent stage, a

diversification of serial composition into several hybrid
varieties. The practicality of total serialization has met
with several stumbling blocks, the main one being the
problem of audibility. Composers found it more expedient
to specialize in the use of selected serial devices and this
splintering action has characterized the present decade.

## Arnold Schoenberg's Twelve-Tone Technique

The first stage of serial composition was Schoenberg's
discovery and development of an effective dodecaphonic technique. Features of the method tentatively emerged in 1908
in Schoenberg's Three Pieces for Piano, Op. 11, and assumed a tangible form in the Five Pieces for Piano, Op. 23,
of 1923.

In the early 1900's Arnold Schoenberg was well-
acquainted with the efforts of his contemporaries to solve
the compositional problems posed by conflicting concepts of
tonality and chromaticism. His own composition had gradually moved toward a manner of expression beyond the scope
of tonality. He was also aware of theoretical approaches
to these problems, particularly the harmony text of Simon
Sechter. [11] In this treatise Sechter sought to revise theoretical analysis in accordance with prevailing practice. Schoenberg's study of this text, in the course of his own teaching
and theoretical investigations, stimulated him to clarify
harmonic practice of his own time. Subsequently Schoen-     [12]
berg's two major theoretical works appeared, Harmonielehre
and Structural Functions of Harmony.[13] There were also
plans for other theoretical works, of which only a few were
completed.

In Harmonielehre, Schoenberg observed that the
complex harmonic phenomena of contemporary writing had
only a very remote relationship to functional diatonic harmony. But whereas others merely relegated these new structures to the extreme limits of traditional tonality, Schoenberg
perceived their value as the source of new developments if
successfully exploited. The book, Structural Functions of
Harmony, completed in his later years, extended and revised
his earlier text.

In his own composition before 1908, Schoenberg constantly stretched the limits of harmonic function. Roving

harmonies are characteristic, frequently in a contrapuntal texture; cadences are obscured; the whole-tone scale is employed to effect over-all construction, not merely for sound or harmonic unity, as in Debussy's writing, but more as a six-tone row. Independence between chord and melody occasionally suggests a form of polytonality.

In Style and Idea [14] Schoenberg emphasized the direct influence of chromaticism as leading to the change from a concept of tonality to one of extended tonality. In both Wagnerian chromaticism and the impressionism of Debussy, the two main trends paving the way for Schoenberg's theories, non-functional harmonies were increasingly prevalent. Schoenberg recognized that dissonance was thereby gaining in comprehensibility. He concluded that chromaticism, impressionism, and expressionism contributed to the emancipation of the dissonance. Thus was possible the development of a style in which both consonance and dissonance were comprehensible, and tonal center and modulation could be abandoned. The immediate result was atonality, which dominated contemporary trends for about fifteen years. In his atonal writing Schoenberg continued his experiments with the use of a twelve-tone scale, devoid of tonal functions.

Schoenberg established basic ground rules to discipline the twelve-tone scale, which marked a culmination of late nineteenth and early twentieth-century evolution, and initiated the first clearly defined usage of serial composition in this century. His twelve-tone technique became the main stimulus to new artistic concepts among musicians for several decades.

One of the most remarkable features about the groundwork which Schoenberg created was the allowance made for freedom within a strict method. Even his immediate disciples, Berg and Webern, found sufficient latitude, permitting them to adapt the method to their own creative styles in unbridled fashion. It is this very adaptability to any style which has partially clouded the true relationship between strict twelve-tone writing and other types of musical composition. [15] A lack of sufficient direct sources from Schoenberg's thoughts further explains why misconceptions often occurred in the interpretation of his method. He published very little explanation of his ideas. His main essay on the technique appears in Style and Idea. [16] The recently published letters, [17] a selection from over three thousand, contain enlightening remarks. The basic text [18] on which Schoenberg planned to collaborate with his former student, Josef Rufer, was only just published in 1952, and Schoenberg's ill health during his last years prevented his working with Rufer extensively. In the original edition of Harmonielehre some space was devoted to Schoenberg's new theories, but this was deleted in the English language edition. Erwin Stein, an ardent Schoenberg pupil and disciple, has paraphrased many of his teacher's statements in Orpheus in New Guises.[19]

The following enumeration has utilized the aforementioned sources and seeks to offer a condensation of Schoenberg's principles.[20]

1. Invention of a series consisting of 12 different tones:

    a. Basic row (Grundreihe) constitutes an ordering of 12 tones;

    b. Basic shape (Grundgestalt) constitutes the contour, or form of the basic row.

2. No tone in series repeated, except in special circumstances:

    a. As characteristic element;

    b. For sonority or articulation;

    c. For compositional devices (accompaniment figures, pedal point, trills, tremolos auxiliary tones, etc.).

3. Use of the series in four basic forms:

    a. O: original series;

    b. I: original series inverted;

    c. R: retrograde form of O;

    d. RI: retrograde form of I.

4. Use of 48 available forms through transposition of the four basic forms.

5. Use of available forms in horizontal or vertical dimensions:

    a. Melodic only;

    b. Chords only;

    c. A combination of melodic and chordal usage.

    6. Avoidance of octave doubling which would empha-
size individual tone.

    7. Octave displacement of tone(s) permissible.

    8. Subdivision of row into segments:

    a. Usually symmetrical;

    b. Preference by Schoenberg for hexachordal
structuring in which tones 7-12 were
inversions of 1-6, permitting use of one
hexachord as accompaniment to the other,
without repetition of tones of the series.

    9. Alteration in the ordering only within limits:

    a. To avoid suggestion of tonality;

    b. For specific compositional purposes.

    The preceding list indicates the scope of the original
Schoenberg theories but disguises the comprehensive nature
of these principles. The following supplementary discussion
clarifies how these principles embraced their future potential
from the beginning of the considerable metamorphosis that
has occurred, since the practice of the Schoenberg technique
began. The ordering of these comments is parallel to the
points in the preceding list.

    1. Invention of a series. Schoenberg's ideas as to
what constituted a good series were highly developed. He
did not consider theme (or melody) and thematic material
as synonymous. The basic row supplied the source material,
and was dependent on consideration of the basic shape. As
source material, the row provided motivic ideas which could
be disconnected or united as desired, while the basic shape
provided the inherent form or structure. In his teaching
he extolled the concept of basic shape (Grundgestalt) of the
source material as the very essence of form. As such, it

should be the fundamental consideration in the construction
of a basic row, for herein it served as the predeterminant
of the entire structure of any musical work. Schoenberg
applied this concept to the evaluation of any style or form
throughout music history. Ironically his emphasis of the
fact that this principle, both consciously and instinctively,
had permeated musical evolution, led to its disassociation
from his other principles of twelve-tone writing. Consequently many composers overlooked its consideration in the
construction of a series. The inevitable result, that some
series can only be characterized as contrived, was detriment-
al to the early acceptance of Schoenberg's twelve-tone technique. This misconception was partly due to the language
difficulty in translating the German terms Grundreihe (basic
row), and Grundgestalt (basic shape), and their consequent
confusion as identical terms.

One of the main ideas that led to twelve-tone writing
was the motivic principle of late romanticism and impressionism. The convergence in atonal music of the two ideas,
motivic construction and the use of the twelve-tone chromatic scale, suggested a thematic basis employing both.
The motivic concept led to the discovery that a twelve-tone
row consisting of a group of motives could serve as the
generator of vertical groups of tones and horizontal lines,
which, if used according to basic principles, could unify
the sounds of atonal music, and result in an aesthetically
satisfying form and style. Thus, the principle of motivic
combinations can be used to construct a basic row. On the
other hand, once the concept of a twelve-tone row was discovered, it was equally possible to derive motives from a
row. Both methods have been employed, but it would appear
that Schoenberg's major emphasis is on the fact that if the
basic shape has not been adequately considered, it is difficult
to derive combinable motives. Schoenberg was the first to
admit that he did not fully understand what he had discovered.
This admission only emphasizes the fact that his idea of a
serial ordering was not contrived, but derived from essential
phenomena. In Schoenberg's thought generally, everything
was derived from the twelve-tone row and principles of row
use could be amplified and clarified with experience. An
unexpected later discovery was that the statement of the basic
row could not only be delayed, but even omitted from a
composition for which it had provided the source material.

2. Repetition of tones. Simple repetition was frequent-

ly used from the beginning of twelve-tone composition and
was not considered a loosening of the method. A significant extension of this principle has gained increasing prominence: the idea of omission of selected tones in order to
create a tension allowing the deleted tone (or tones) to acquire a special function. One such concept, in which the
reappearance of a specific single tone is postponed, thereby
attempts to establish a sense of "tonic" peculiar to dodecaphonic music. A variant of this concept, based on the
omission of two or three tones in a basic series, attempts
to create cadential feeling upon their deliberate occurrence.

3. Use of the series in four basic forms. The
utilization of internal relationships that can affect structural intricacies is the most important extension of the
principle of the four basic forms. The number and kind of relationships that may exist between the four basic forms are
dependent on the basic order of the original series. For
example, the possibility of mirror forms exists if the
original row is constructed on the principle of hexachordal
symmetry. Much attention has been given to Schoenberg's
preference for a point of inversion at the fifth, which is one
interval that will guarantee that the mirror principle can
be employed. It is undetermined how well Schoenberg understood the potential of the point of inversion. Its selection
is so crucial to the type of row that will ensue that it is
surprising that he did not emphasize it or discuss it more
completely. Perhaps he intended to do so in writings he
never completed.

4. Transposition. Although the availability of 48
forms, through transposition, was recognized from the
initial formulation of Schoenberg's theories, it is to be noted
that many works fail to employ them extensively. Hill has
noted that the use of simultaneous transpositions by Schoenberg suggests an awareness of their potential as functional
modulations.[21] This feature is also developed in the work
of some of Schoenberg's students, but the extent to which it
was consciously understood is obscure. Many composers
have felt that saturating the texture with transpositions tends
to destroy, rather than reinforce, the unity of serial writing.
Utilization of the transposed forms has been more noticeable
in recent years, since clarification of the essential harmonic
principles of twelve-tone composition has begun to emerge.
This may foster more extensive usage of the available transpositions of a basic row by uncovering more effective uses

for them.

     5. <u>Horizontal</u> and <u>vertical</u> <u>aspects</u>. Twelve-tone
composition having been initiated primarily on the basis
of a linear ordering possessing ready adaptability to contrapuntal techniques, the vertical aspect came under investigation more slowly. So long as equal-tempered instruments were employed, no new melodic intervals were
possible and the freedom of consonance and dissonance in
the linear (horizontal) movement of twelve-tone writing did
not require as drastic an adjustment by the ear as vertical
elements. But in chordal (vertical) combinations many un-
familiar effects became commonplace. The vertical potentials of dodecaphonic writing have been clarified more gradually than the linear aspects because of the complexity of their
sound. [22] Apart from suggesting that the chords should be
related to the row, Schoenberg left it to the discretion of
the individual composer whether a more or less arbitrary
formation of the vertical structures should be derived from
the basic series or whether some degree of premeditation
should occur during construction of the basic row to determine the harmonic material to be made available. Both
procedures have been widely used.

     Opinions as to the essential nature of twelve-tone
harmony are varied, and also somewhat incompatible. For
example, one viewpoint is that twelve-tone music does not
have an underlying harmony, but is a completely linear
system. Accordingly, vertical structures would then be
thought of merely as "non-adjacencies."[23] Another attitude
is that a sense of harmony exists in twelve-tone music only
when it incorporates tonal principles.[24] Apart from attempts
to synthesize dodecaphonic and tonal writing, recent practices suggest important relationships between vertical structure and principles of transposition and segmentation.[25]

     6. <u>Octave</u> <u>doubling</u>. Schoenberg's eagerness to avoid
tonal implications led him first to stress avoidance of octave
doubling, although after a brief experience with it, he found
this prohibition unnecessary.

     7. <u>Octave</u> <u>displacement</u>. Respect for the original
ordering of a series was not broken by placement of a tone
or tones in another register. This simple concept permitted
experimentation with spatial effects from the very beginning
of the twelve-tone practice and became, as expressed in the

pointillistic style of Webern, one of the most significant
of the early extensions of Schoenberg's concepts.

8. Subdivision. Symmetrical division of the row
into six, or three or four note segments was common
practice during the initial development of the twelve-tone
principles. With the break-down of symmetrical form,
other types of segmentation (partitioning, fragmentation)
have since been exploited with increasing frequency. Simple
segmentation employs a consistent pattern in dividing the row
for either vertical or horizontal purposes and was, of course,
related to motivic construction. However, extension of the
segmentation principle has enabled the composer not only to
combine either symmetrical or asymmetrical sections from
within a single row but to combine complete rows themselves.
Further, this principle of extension facilitated the use of
sets (source-sets, set-complexes). Thus, along with the
emancipation of dissonance, and the emancipation of rhythm,
the exploitation of asymmetry should be considered an equally important influence in serial history. Composers and
theoreticians have begun to recognize specific types of rows,
whose characteristics lend themselves to certain kinds of
subdivisions and manipulations.

9. Alteration in the series. Alterations in the
ordering of the original row were instituted primarily to
avoid suggestions of tonality. Justification of greater freedom in linear ordering, apart from transferring tones to
vertical structures, began rather cautiously. Paul Brainard
has demonstrated that Schoenberg seldom employed any other
unorthodox treatment whenever he proceeded to employ alterations in a basic row.[26] But the realization that the unity
of the basic row could be maintained in spite of free re-
ordering or permutation of the series stimulated further
experimentation. Numerous techniques of alteration have
been employed, simple as well as complex. Utilization of
mathematical principles of numerical ordering has made it
feasible for a composer to control complex permutational
systems and maintain thematic unity throughout an extensive
work without undue effort.

The composite usage of these individual aspects of
Schoenberg's techniques has contributed to the realization
that the concepts of both inner and outer form can acquire
new and wider meanings. Further understanding of the inter-
relationship of Schoenberg's elementary principles emerged

at an accelerated pace once the extension of these principles
began.   A full theoretical discussion requires more space
than justified within this study.   But in the descriptions of
piano scores in Chapter II, typical examples of the fusion
and extensions of Schoenberg's principles are discussed.

## The Piano Works of Arnold Schoenberg, Alban Berg, and Anton Webern

Schoenberg's piano works span a quarter of a century,
from 1908 to 1932.   It is in piano composition that he
initiated each major change in the evolution of his style.
Op. 11 (1908) is the first of his atonal works,  Op. 19
(1911) contains his first twelve-tone writing,  Op. 23 (1923)
employs a basic row technique throughout,  Op. 25 (1925)
contains his first completely twelve-tone work,  and Op. 33a
(1929) and 33b (1932) reveal a well-developed row technique.[27]

Schoenberg's style contains a high degree of chromaticism, a predominantly contrapuntal texture, a tendency
to avoid tonality or to employ polytonality, use of classical
devices (forms, repetition, imitation, rhythmic patterns,
etc.), and a flavor of romanticism.   These general characteristics are apparent in Drei Klavierstücke, Op. 11 (1908),
Schoenberg's first atonal composition.   And, although elements of tonality are present, much in the general style of
the three pieces signals the emerging features characteristic of his twelve-tone technique.   All the thematic and
motivic ideas throughout the work are developments or
variations derived from the basic shape of the three initial
bars.   In piece No. 2, the original intervals of the basic
shape are found, as well as variants resulting from octave
displacement.   In No. 3, the basic shape is slightly elab-
orated.   Harmonic structures are based on the intervals
of the first two chords (bars 2 & 3).   Contrapuntal techniques, which became increasingly prominent in succeeding
works, vary the relationships of thematic material.   The
rhythmic movement is quite free, and devoid of strong
accents.

The first stage of serialism began with Schoenberg's
gradual movement from an atonal style toward experiments
with a row technique.   In 1911, Schoenberg completed his
Six Little Piano Pieces, Op. 19.   His first twelve-tone
composition is the fifth piece of this set.   The opus as a

whole is a striking example of the early trend toward brevity and economical use of materials of the twelve-tone idiom in its formative stage. Brevity eliminates the need for repetition and development. As Schoenberg has indicated, he was interested in exploiting single ideas in the search for form.[28] The form in this work is created by variations of the initial motive or parts of it. For example, in No. 4, the rhythmic structure is the basic element of the form. No. 6 is based entirely on a single chord, subjected to subtle variations of dynamics.

During the years between the Four Songs, Op. 22 (1914), and the Five Pieces for Piano, Op. 23 (1923), Schoenberg suspended publication of music in order to intensify his investigation of the new system. He stated that the first major problem was to develop a compositional technique that would achieve coherence and form without regression to traditional methods and yet would maintain sufficient freedom to nurture originality. Schoenberg sensed that he was penetrating into the realm of natural laws of order and form. He realized that to compromise, by perpetually synthesizing newly emerging ideas with traditional means, would be to suppress the opportunity for recognizing the potential inherent in the twelve-tone concept. He withdrew from the musical scene from 1915-1923 in order to intensify his investigations and to clarify and prepare his theories. He finally laid the foundation for a method of composing with twelve tones which are related only with one another. He later summarized the genesis in the following letter to Nicolas Slonimsky.[29]

> Hollywood, California
> June 3, 1937

Dear Mr. Slonimsky:

The 'method of composing with twelve tones' had many 'first steps' (Vorversuche). The first step happened about December 1914 or at the beginning of 1915 when I sketched a symphony, the last part of which became later the Jakobsleiter, but which never has been continued. The Scherzo of this symphony was based on a theme consisting of the twelve tones. But this was only one of the themes. I was still far away from the idea to use such a basic theme as a unifying means for a whole work.

After that I was always occupied with the aim to
base the structure of my work consciously on a
unifying idea, which produced not only all the other
ideas but regulated also their accompaniment and the
chords, the 'harmonies'. There were many attempts
to achieve that. But very little of it was finished or
published.

As an example of such attempts I may mention the
piano pieces op. 23. Here I arrived at a technique
which I called (for myself) 'composing with tones,'
a very vague term, but it meant something to me.
Namely: in contrast to the ordinary way of using a
motive, I used it already almost in the manner of a
'basic set of twelve tones.' I built other motives
and themes from it, and also accompaniments and
other chords--but the theme did not consist of
twelve tones. Another example of this kind of aim
for unity is my Serenade. In this work you can find
many examples of this kind. But the best one is
the Variationen, the third movement. The theme
consists of a succession of fourteen tones, but only
eleven different ones, and these fourteen tones are
permanently used in the whole movement. With
lesser strictness still I use the tones of the first
two measures in Tanzscene.

The fourth movement, Sonett, is a 'real composition
with twelve tones.' The technique is here relatively
primitive, because it was one of the first works
written strictly in harmony with this method, though
it was not the very first--there were some movements
of the Suite for piano which I composed in the fall of
1921. Here I became suddenly conscious of the real
meaning of my aim: unity and regularity, which un-
consciously had led me this way.

As you see, it was neither a straight way nor was
it caused by mannerism, as it often happens with
revolutions in art. I personally hate to be called
a revolutionist, which I am not. What I did was
neither revolution nor anarchy. I possessed from
my very first start a thoroughly developed sense of
form and a strong aversion for exaggeration. There
is no falling into order, because there was never

disorder. There is no falling at all, but on the
contrary, there is an ascending to higher and better
order.

Arnold Schoenberg

Schoenberg made conscious use of a tone-row for the
first time in Op. 23, 24, and 25, which were in progress
simultaneously from 1923-24. The <u>Five</u> <u>Pieces</u> for <u>Piano,</u>
Op. 23, contains Schoenberg's full realization of his twelve-
tone technique. The first four pieces do not employ complete
twelve-tone series, but basically the row technique is
applied. The principle of octave displacement and rhythmic
variation of the basic shape are the dominant means for
executing variation. The use of chords built from the melodic material is a feature of No. 2, but more significant
is the simultaneous use of row forms. No. 3 demonstrates
numerous ways for employing a short series as the foundation
of an entire piece. The simultaneous use of row forms is
developed into more complex relationships in the last two
pieces. A climactic stage in the usage of the twelve-tone
technique by employment of a complete twelve-tone row
occurs in No. 5. The basic row is clearly stated in the
first four bars. It does not recur in this ordering until
bar 17. Rather, it is characteristic of the piece that the
row frequently appears as two segments, but not necessarily
symmetrically,[30] as the first five tones are usually converted
into a chordal accompaniment for the other six or seven.
The complete form is found at the beginning of the second
and third sections (bars 17-23, and 100-105).

The <u>Suite</u> <u>für</u> <u>Klavier</u>, Op. 25 (1924), exemplifies
Schoenberg's development of the practice of perpetual variation in twelve-tone music. The row E F G D♭ G♭ E♭ A♭ D B
C A B♭ becomes the source of all the sounds. The same
row is the basis for each of the six movements. In this
work Schoenberg applied his discovery that the use of two
intervals of the same size (in this instance diminished fifths
appearing between the third to fourth, and the seventh to
eighth tones of the series) facilitated division of the row
into three symmetrical units of four notes each. This is a
more elaborate type of subdivision than the earlier types
of segmentation, such as the division of a row into hexachords, that were frequently treated merely as the equivalent of the traditional antecedent and consequent parts of a

phrase. As employed in Op. 25, the three units are over-
lapped, coupled, interchanged, and used in either vertical
or horizontal forms.  When, further, mirror forms and
transpositions are so manipulated, the principle of perpetual
variation emerges.  In the Praeludium, Schoenberg also used
differing row forms simultaneously; the transposition at the
diminished fifth accompanies the original series.

In the Gavotte and the Minuet, Schoenberg employed the twelve-tone row for melody and accompaniment
simultaneously but with greater attention to the inter-relationships of these two musical lines than in his earlier twelve-
tone style.  The melody-accompaniment relationships within
these particular pieces, however, still depend considerably
on the symmetrical structure of the row, although Schoenberg used the influence of one musical line upon another
to safeguard the basic shape during employment of rhythmic
variations.

In his last piano works, the Klavierstücke, Op. 33a
(1929) and 33b (1932), Schoenberg's concept of basic shape
is deployed in a unique manner.  He subordinated the linear
ordering to that of the vertical structuring.  Op. 33a begins
with three chords consisting of the twelve tones of the row.
Maintaining the basic shape of these chords, while they are
re-arranged, over-lapped, put in canon, or otherwise
developed, provides a sense of unity throughout.

Both Op. 33a and 33b are works of greater complexity
than most of the previous piano scores.  Although the harmonic principles of serialism have yet to be explained in
great depth or scope, Schoenberg's amazing flexibility in
these works, in controlling the complex relationships of the
vertical structures derived from a twelve-tone row, reveals
his considerable comprehension of harmonic principles fundamental to a twelve-tone technique.  Both scores anticipate
similar usage by other composers, and could well provide
a starting-point for a study of twelve-tone harmonic principles. [31]

Schoenberg continued the search for basic types of
row structure and their relationship to the over-all design
in the development of his twelve-tone style in his late works.
Tonal characteristics frequently played a part in these scores.

The assimilation and spread of Schoenberg's ideas
was carried on through his own students, and particularly
by his two friends and associates, Alban Berg and Anton
Webern.

Alban Berg was raised in a home atmosphere which
encouraged interest in philosophy, literature, and music.
In this environment he developed a strong urge to become
a poet, but in his teens this interest turned to musical
composition. In 1904 he met Schoenberg and Webern. A
close association among these three men continued throughout their lives, and has had important repercussions on the
evolution of music in this century. From about 1910 the
influence of Schoenberg and Webern caused Berg to alternate or mix his romantic lyricism with the new dodecaphonic
style. Henceforth, he frequently employed highly chromatic
writing, atonality, and twelve-tone techniques within the
same work and, not infrequently, tonal characteristics as
well. Such mixtures distinguish Berg's evolution from that
of Schoenberg and Webern and mark him as the member of
this triumvirate who most clearly linked the twelve-tone
system with the immediate past.

Berg's romantic background, combined with his six
years of study with Schoenberg, gave cause for many similarities in their twelve-tone styles. Thus Berg tended to
adopt condensed traditional forms and contrapuntal writing.
One of the most characteristic traits in his dodecaphonic
writing, however, indicates the influence of Webern. This
trait Berg referred to as "constructive rhythm,"[32]whereby
a rhythmic pattern would recur as a distinctive figure, much
in the manner usually associated with a melodic figuration.

Berg's only piano work is the Sonate für Klavier,
Op. 1 (1906-08). The sonata is romantic in style and harmony and basically is in the tonality of B minor, although
highly chromatic. Numerous passages defy the restrictions
of functional harmony. At this time Berg was concerned
with the same crucial problems which were confronting his
teacher, Schoenberg, in the development of a dodecaphonic
method. Berg's solutions show the influence of Schoenberg,
but his own originality dominates the musical expression.
Berg illustrated two major characteristics of row-variation
emerging in twelve-tone writing: one is the use of the
perpetual variation of the initial series as a means for
unifying the entire work and the second is the attempt to

employ extensions of the initial series as the source of new
structures. With these complementary ideas, Berg anticipated
such developments in serial composition after mid-century
as constant permutation of linear ordering and the use of
open forms.

Anton Webern studied music and philosophy at the
University of Vienna, receiving a Ph.D. in 1906 in musicology. His dissertation was a study of Heinrich Isaac's
Choralis Constantinus. The topic was in keeping with
Webern's interest in the contrapuntal techniques of the
fifteenth and sixteenth centuries and their usage in his serial
composition. Webern began to study composition with Schoenberg at the Vienna University and rapidly acquired a profi-
ciency in the use of the twelve-tone technique, which he
readily combined with his skill in contrapuntal writing.
Canonic writing became a major characteristic of his style
and of particular significance in the Piano Variations, Op.
27 (1936).

Throughout his career Webern taught composition
privately and conducted extensively. From 1918 through
1921 he continued organizing contemporary music programs
for the Society for Private Musical Performances, established
by Schoenberg.

Whereas with Schoenberg atonality was sometimes
only an obscured tonality, Webern sought absolutely to avoid
association with traditional forms and tonality from his
earliest work. Contrapuntal devices and the twelve-tone
system were the basic tools with which Webern began the
realization of his creative ideals. He extended Schoenberg's
method and in many ways anticipated the total serial concept
and other late developments in the evolution of serial music.

It had been possible for Schoenberg to initiate the
basic principles of his method by focusing on the ordering
of the linear sounds, with utilization of tones from the
series in vertical structures serving as a by-product of
this ordering. It was Schoenberg's belief that understanding
of new shapes and functions of rhythm, harmony, and form,
would emerge as application of the row principles proceeded.
Webern recognized that the interdependence of all elements
constituted the crux of the new musical concepts and that
the essence of this relationship was form itself. Thus his
music assumed a more radical nature than that of Schoenberg.

The changing concepts in musical art eventually embraced
all fundamental aspects of expression, with the matter of
form constituting the central core in this evolutionary
phase.[33]

Webern concerned himself first and foremost with
expressing his material with the utmost economy in order
to create music of absolute purity. The brevity of his
work is accentuated by the fact that his life work of thirty-
one compositions can be performed in approximately three
hours. As Schoenberg expressed it, Webern placed a whole
novel in a single sigh.[34]

Webern's compositions are highly organized structures.
His concept of form broke completely with the traditional
molds which Schoenberg never fully abandoned. Webern
extended Schoenberg's concept of basic shape, not only by
extensions of separate devices of the twelve-tone technique,
but by their combined usage. Constant change of relationships between all musical elements expedites the movement
of musical events through space and time. Musical space
and time acquired new significance in Webern's compositions.
In the execution of the pitch lines Webern emphasized the
time-space relationship with extreme pointillism, consistently
exploiting Schoenberg's device of Klangfarbenmelodie.[35]
Counterpoint is employed almost exclusively to insure the
audibility of each sound in the transparent pointillistic texture. Not only the execution of each sound itself, but also
the interval between that sound and another, is considered
in its relationship with all other elements in Webern's work.
Certain intervals (6ths, major 7ths, minor 9ths, major 2nds)
are favored as a means for creating a sense of time and
space through their use to control tension.

Webern's Piano Variations, Op. 27 (1936), marks a
culminating point in the possibilities for variation technique
in twelve-tone writing. The potential of this substitute for
the forms of functional writing was apparent in Schoenberg's
twelve-tone piano works. But in his Op. 27, Webern finally
realized the adaptation of the perpetual variation technique
to the twelve-tone idiom devoid of traditional bonds. Pitch,
duration, dynamics, and attacks are constantly varied in a
contrapuntal texture. In each movement variation is based
on one structural element. Mirror forms (Spiegelbeld),
favored by Webern are predominant, but the score contains
all the major features of Webern's style. Thus the first

section of the first movement uses mirror forms divided
into hexachordal segments, as well as smaller mirror
structures, frequently extended by meaningful interpolations
of silence. The second section is based on a variation of
the initial row. The notes are freely rearranged, but the
basic shape is always maintained. Frequently a motivic
cell reappears in one of the variants of the row as a
characteristic figure. The final section employs the basic
shape and plan of the first section. The row is a transposition at the minor sixth. Mirror forms are still in
evidence. The eight bar coda uses a variant on the transposed row.

The second movement is a development section. The
entire movement is a strict canon in contrary motion, with
the thematic material consisting of a row, its variation,
and variants of these two. Webern discovered a basic row
of canon in his work, applicable to any twelve-tone row;
the superposition of any of the row forms, and its inversion,
will always produce the intervals of the whole-tone scale if
the initial notes of both forms constitute one of the intervals
of the whole-tone scale.[36]

In the third, and longest movement, Webern is
credited by Leibowitz with not only attaining the culmination
of his own style, but that of Western musical language.
The theme continually undergoes both transformation and
variation. Both inversion and retrograde movement contribute greatly to the structuring. The work ends on its initial
note.

Several detailed analyses of this prophetic work have
been published,[37] but one of the more unusual features of this
score is discussed in a lesser-known study by William L.
Ogdon.[38] Ogdon draws attention to the existence of a tone
reference comparable to the mese of the medieval modes.
His analysis reveals an intriguing fact, that the score
contains a twenty-three note gamut, comparable to the Greek
Greater Perfect System, in which the tone A serves as a
reference point. This reference tone is occasionally used
as a pivotal point for reversing the main direction of movement in Webern's variations. Ogdon's analytical procedure
was an application of an analytical method of linguistics.
Accordingly he noted the distribution relationships of all
pitch and rhythm symbols. The resultant gamut is interesting
in that the upper half is a mirror of the lower, but this

inverted symmetrical form is not a product of the original
twelve-tone ordering.  Separation of the pitches in construct-
ing the gamut did not equally distribute the twenty-three
tones in the various octave registers.  Further, only three
paired figures occur throughout the score, each constituting
the combination of a series note and its inverted complement.
The seven remaining chromatics always sound at a specific
pitch.  One of these was the central A, which the other six
surrounded symmetrically.  The three tone requirements
remaining at each end of the gamut were unspecified and
could be expressed by two or three different pitches.  This
symmetrical usage involved a tritone relationship to the
mese.

   Ogdon's analyses stimulate further examination of
Webern's scores for use of fourteenth- and fifteenth-century
techniques.  His study suggests that Webern's extension
of serial principles, through a unique combination of early
polyphony with Schoenberg's twentieth-century dodecaphonic
technique, created a stronger link between twentieth-century
music and the pre-tonal period than other present studies
would indicate.

   The relatively short span of twenty-eight years
(1908-1936) encompassing the piano compositions of Arnold
Schoenberg, Alban Berg, and Anton Webern, saw momentous
growth from somewhat nebulous ideas for a twelve-tone
discipline to the fruition of a highly organized new system.
In the piano works of Schoenberg the twelve-tone techniques
were gradually formulated.  The piano music of Berg and
Webern reveals the versatility of the Schoenberg technique
by its incorporation into two other highly individual styles.
Schoenberg was the innovator, whereas Berg and Webern
formed a bridge between the old and the new, although the
latter, by extending the concepts of serial composition,
provided also a springboard for the future.

Notes

1.   Roger Shattuck holds that the beginning of all modern
     artistic expression stems from the changing concepts
     of form between 1885 and World War I.  See Roger
     Shattuck, The Banquet Years: The Origins of the
     Avant-Garde in France 1885 to World War I (New
     York, Doubleday, 1961.)

2. Several contemporaries of Schoenberg also sought to
   devise a theoretical basis for a twelve-tone system.
   It is beyond the scope of this study to elaborate on
   other experiments with a twelve-tone chromatic which
   have passed into oblivion or developed along variant
   paths, or now lie dormant. Several entries in
   Chapter II provide information regarding the more
   interesting attempts to codify a twelve-tone practice.
   The method which most closely approached Schoenberg's concepts is described in the entry for Josef
   Hauer. Another very well-known and successful
   twelve-tone system, and one that differs considerably
   from Schoenberg's, has been that of Paul Hindemith.
   A useful summary of his theoretical writings and a
   bibliography can be found in the entry by Marion M.
   Scott, "Hindemith, Paul," Grove's Dictionary of
   Music and Musicians (5th ed.), IV, 286-291.

3. It is conceivable that circumstances could have led to
   such a theory much earlier. The chromaticism of
   the sixteenth century, introduced by Adrian Willaert
   (1480-1562), and developed by Cyprano de Rore
   (1516-1595), and others, approached a twelve-tone
   practice more closely than any other era, before
   being superseded by the establishment of tonality and
   its functional harmony. Cf. Edward E. Lowinsky,
   Secret Chromatic Art in the Netherlands Motet, trans.
   Carl Buchman (New York, Russell & Russell, 1946).

4. A collection of short writings from throughout the
   twentieth century that reveal the depth and scope these
   matters have acquired, has been selected by Susanne
   K. Langer, (ed.), Reflections on Art: A Source Book
   of Writings by Artists, Critics, and Philosophers
   (New York, Oxford Univ. Press, 1961).

5. Many aspects of the tangible relationship that has grown
   between art and psychology throughout this century
   are discussed by Rudolf Arnheim, Toward a Psychology of Art: Collected Essays (Berkeley, Univ. of Calif.
   Press, 1966).

6. The concept of motion in the history of both art and
   science has been traced by Gyorgy Kepes (ed.),
   The Nature and Art of Motion (New York, Braziller,
   1965).

7. Wagner's role in the rise and decline of tonality is
   submitted to an astute examination in the study of
   the path of music after Beethoven to mid-nineteenth
   century by Gerald Abraham, A Hundred Years of
   Music (3rd. ed.; Chicago, Aldine, 1964).

8. A provocative discussion of the primary musical
   significance for the twentieth century attributed to
   the line of development from Bruckner and Mahler
   to Schoenberg, is contained in an extensive study by
   Dika Newlin, Bruckner, Mahler, and Schoenberg
   (New York, Philosophical Library, 1949).

9. No single study of late romanticism fully discusses
   the relationship of chromatic harmony to the tonal
   harmony from which it evolved, and to the use of
   dissonant harmonies of atonalism. Most of the
   theoretical treatises in this field clarify some of
   the features that distinguish practices within the
   limits of functional harmony from those that surpass
   these limits. The most comprehensive in scope is
   by Ludmila Ulehla, Contemporary Harmony: Romanticism Through the Twelve-Tone Row (New York, The
   Free Press, 1966).

10. Schoenberg explains that the emancipation of the
    dissonance provided the comprehensibility that would
    permit the abolishment of a functional tonal center,
    in the essay, "Composition with Twelve Tones," in
    Arnold Schoenberg, Style and Idea (New York,
    Philosophical Library, 1950), pp. 104-105.

11. Simon Sechter (1788-1867) was a composer, teacher,
    and theorist, whose main pedagogical work was along
    the lines of Rameau's fundamental bass system.
    Simon Sechter, Die Grundsätze der Musikalischen
    Composition (3 vols.; Vienna, n.p., 1853-54).

12. Arnold Schoenberg, Harmonielehre (Vienna, Universal
    Edition, 1922).

13. Arnold Schoenberg, Structural Functions of Harmony
    (New York, Norton, 1954).

14. Schoenberg, op. cit., p. 103.

15. Brindle has chosen a dozen examples that dramatically illustrate the adaptability of serialism to different styles. Reginald Smith Brindle, Serial Composition (London, Oxford Univ. Press, 1966), pp. 139-53.

16. Schoenberg, op. cit., pp. 102-43.

17. Erwin Stein (ed.), Arnold Schoenberg Letters, trans. Eithne Wilkins and Ernst Kaiser (New York, St. Martin's, 1965).

18. Josef Rufer, Composition with Twelve Notes Related Only To One Another, trans. Humphrey Searle (London, Barrie and Rockliff, 1954).

19. Erwin Stein, Orpheus in New Guises (London, n.p., 1953).

20. The listing closely parallels that presented by Josef Rufer, op. cit., pp. 79-111.

21. Cf. Richard S. Hill, "Schönberg's Tone-Rows and the Tonal System of the Future," The Musical Quarterly, XXII (1936), 14-37.

22. Cf. George Perle, "Possible Chords in Twelve-Tone Music, The Score, IX (1954).

23. Cf. George Perle, Serial Composition and Atonality (2nd. ed. Berkeley, Univ. of Calif. Press, 1963), p. 89.

24. Perle discusses O. W. Neighbour's claim that this is true of Schoenberg's dodecaphonic harmony, which Neighbour describes simply as a further extension of Wagnerian harmony. Perle opposes Neighbour's judgement of Schoenberg, but considers it applicable to Berg. Ibid., pp. 90-92.

25. Cf. György Ligeti, "Metamorphoses of Musical Form," Die Reihe, VII, (1965), pp. 5-19.

26. Paul Brainard, "A Study of the Twelve-Tone Technique" (unpub. master's thesis, Eastman School of Music, Univ. of Rochester, 1951).

27. Considerable analysis of all the Schoenberg piano
    works is to be found in George Perle, Serial
    Composition and Atonality (2nd ed. Berkeley,
    Univ. of Calif. Press, 1968).

28. Schoenberg's own comments in Style and Idea provide
    further insight: "From the very beginning such
    compositions differed from all preceding music, not
    only harmonically but also melodically, thematically,
    and motivally. But the foremost characteristics
    of these pieces in statu nascendi were their extreme
    expressiveness and their extraordinary brevity. At
    this time, neither I nor my pupils were conscious
    of the reasons for these features. Later I dis-
    covered that our sense of form was right when it
    forced us to counterbalance extreme emotionality
    with extraordinary shortness. Thus, subconsciously,
    consequences were drawn from an innovation which,
    like every innovation, destroys while it produces.
    New colorful harmony was offered; but much was
    lost." Arnold Schoenberg, Style and Idea (New
    York, Philosophical Library, 1950), p. 105.

29. Nicolas Slonimsky, Music Since 1900 (3rd. ed. Boston,
    Coleman-Ross, 1949), pp. 680-81.

30. Throughout Style and Idea, op. cit., Schoenberg suggests
    that the future will establish an organization for
    asymmetry as significant as the traditional symmetry
    of form and rhythm. He explains that his own
    organization of phrase lengths, which tend to be
    symmetrical, is based on the idea that everything
    must serve some purpose relative to the basic
    material. He views the beginning of ordered irregu-
    larity, as incorporated into the musical language
    during late romanticism, particularly after Wagner,
    as both conscious and unconscious.

31. One such beginning, limited to scores of Schoenberg,
    Berg and Webern, has been made, based on Schoen-
    berg's statements in Structural Functions of Harmony
    and Perle's Serial Composition and Atonality, to
    prove that harmony is not a by-product of serial
    composition. Cf. Mary Emma Fiore, "The Formation
    and Structural Use of Vertical Constructs in Selected
    Serial Compositions" (Unpub. doctoral dissertation,
    Indiana Univ., 1963).

32. Joseph Machlis, Introduction to Contemporary Music
    (New York, Norton, 1961), pp. 366-70.

33. Webern's own lectures shed much light on these develop-
    ments. They have been published in a single volume:
    Willi Reich (ed.), Anton Webern; The Path to the
    New Music, trans. Leo Black (Bryn Mawr, Pa.,
    Theodore Presser, 1963).

34. Schoenberg's sentiment toward Webern fully expressed
    in a foreword to Webern's Six Bagatelles for String
    Quartet, Op. 9, reprinted in Friedrich Wildgans,
    Anton Webern, trans. Edith Temple Roberts and
    Humphrey Searle (London, Calder & Boyars, 1966),
    pp. 126-27.

35. One of the most complete discussions of this technique,
    which he translates as "melody of sound colours,"
    is to be found in Brindle, op. cit., pp. 125-128; 131.

36. René Leibowitz, Schoenberg and His School; The Con-
    temporary Stage of the Language of Music, trans.
    Dika Newlin (New York, Philosophical Library,
    1949), p. 238.

37. Cf. Armin Klammer, "Webern's Piano Variations, Op.
    27, 3rd Movement," Die Reihe, II (1958), 81-92;
    and Peter Westergaard, "Webern and 'Total Organ-
    ization': An Analysis of the Second Movement of the
    Piano Variations, Op. 27," Perspectives of New
    Music, I (1963), 107-120.

38. Wilbur Lee Ogdon, "Series and Structure: An Investiga-
    tion into the Purpose of the Twelve-Note Row in
    Selected Works of Schoenberg, Webern, Křenek, and
    Leibowitz" (unpub. doctoral dissertation, Indiana
    Univ., 1955).

Chapter II

Composers of Serial Piano Music

Since the Schoenberg School

AMY, GILBERT

(b. Paris, August 29, 1936)
Address: 28 rue Ducouédic, Paris 14? France

    Gilbert Amy received a musical training in Paris
under such teachers as Olivier Messiaen and Darius Milhaud.
In addition to chamber and orchestral music, Amy has composed several works for piano solo. Most of his scores
are based on serial principles, although occasionally some
aleatoric sections are present which have a specific function.
Amy inserts such passages to create a binary aspect to the
structure, without considering aleatory as an integral part
of the serial technique. For example, in Epigramme pour
Piano (1962) Amy uses chance on a limited basis so as to
open a single musical element at a time to oppose the
restriction of closed form. Amy's concept of serialism
considers the use of a basic row and its 47 transformations
as too confined. He views serialism and aleatory as two
diverse but compatible techniques. Amy seeks continually
to develop the musical possibilities that the juxtaposition of
these two techniques generate. His goal is to achieve what
he calls "champs sonores."[1] The piano works demonstrate
the application of his aesthetic to pitch, dynamics, rhythm,
and the opposition of silence and sound.

Piano Music

Sonate. Paris, Heugel & Cie, 1960.
Epigramme pour Piano. Paris, Heugel & Cie, 1962.
Cahiers d'Epigrammes pour Piano. Paris, Heugel & Cie,
    1966.

Bibliography

Austin, William. Music in the 20th Century: From Debussy
    through Stravinsky. New York, Norton, 1966.

"Amy, Gilbert," 1965 Supplement to Baker's Biographical Dictionary of Musicians (5th ed.), 3.

Charles, Daniel. "Entr'acte: 'Formal' or 'Informal' Music?" The Musical Quarterly, LI (January, 1965), 144-165.

Dibelius, Ulrich. Moderne Musik 1945-1965. Munich, R. Piper, 1966.

Goléa, Antoine. Vingt Ans de Musique Contemporaine: De Boulez à l'Inconnu. Paris, Seghers, 1962.

_____. "French Music Since 1945," The Musical Quarterly, LI (January, 1965), 22-37.

Hodeir, André. Since Debussy: A View of Contemporary Music. Trans. Noel Burch. New York, Grove, 1961.

Maegaard, Jan. Musikalsk Modernisme 1945-1962. Copenhagen, Stig Vendelkaers, 1964.

Salzman, Eric. Twentieth-Century Music: An Introduction Englewood Cliffs, N.J. Prentice-Hall, 1967.

APOSTEL, HANS ERICH

(b. Germany, January 22, 1901)
Address: Krongrasse 11; 1050 Vienna, Austria

The early compositions of Hans Erich Apostel were written in Germany, and reflect the influence of Wagner in their thick texture and extreme chromaticism. After contact with the music of Schoenberg, Apostel came to study with him in Vienna, where adoption of Schoenberg's compositional technique led Apostel to use a thinner texture that emphasizes linear elements and florid rhythmic patterns. Apostel's lyrical quality developed under subsequent study with Berg. Apostel remained in Vienna, and has continued to be a major exponent of twelve-tone writing in Austria. His interest in combining serial composition with traditional principles has led to an independent modification of the Schoenberg technique. The triad is predominant, later increasingly so, in his works, although his music is non-tonal. Elements of his earlier expressionism and neo-classicism remain in his later combinations of classical

forms with twelve-tone writing.  Since the mid-1940's
Apostel's style has gained much in clarity of expression.
The overly-thick romantic texture of the earlier works has
generally been abandoned.  The Suite, Op. 24 (1956), and
subsequent piano works, exemplify his modification of
Schoenberg's technique.  Apostel has become less interested
in synthesis of twelve-tone and traditional styles and more
concerned with exploiting the potential of the twelve-tone
concept.

Piano Music

Suite "Concise," Op. 24.  Vienna, Universal Edition, 1956.
Vier Kleine Klavierstücke, Op. 31a & Fantasie, Op. 31b.
    Munich, Doblinger, 1962.

Bibliography

Kaufmann, Harald.  Hans Erich Apostel.  Vienna, Csöngei,
    1964.

BABBITT, MILTON

(b.  Philadelphia, May 10, 1916)
Address:  Woolworth Center of Musical Studies; Princeton
University; Princeton, New Jersey.  08540

        Milton Babbitt received degrees in music and mathe-
matics at Princeton and New York University.  In addition
he studied privately with Roger Sessions and has been a
member of the faculty of Princeton University since 1954.
He is also head of the Columbia University Electronic
Institute.  He has lectured widely in both the United States
and Europe and has received numerous awards for his
compositions.

        Babbitt was one of the first composers to pursue
the course begun by Anton Webern.  He experimented with
extension of the twelve-tone concept to the serial ordering
of rhythm, and from there he pushed the concept to total
serialization.  On the basis of extensive theoretical study
and experience, stimulated by his initial use of the twelve-
tone method in 1945, Babbitt obtained success in serializing
a parameter other than pitch and supported his innovation
with theoretical writings.

Probably the earliest serialization of non-pitch elements occurs in Babbitt's Three Compositions for Piano (1947).[2] The pieces are clearly based on a computational system that is analogous to twelve-tone pitch ordering. Babbitt has followed the same basic procedures in subsequent serial works, except that the prime form for non-pitch elements does not necessarily have twelve components.[3]

Semi-Simple Variations is a unique treatment of rhythmic structure which Babbitt does not use elsewhere. It is a short piano piece prefaced with explanatory notes, created to teach the Schoenberg technique.

Babbitt has sought to extend the freedom of the twelve-tone system from within, by clarification of principles derived from known concepts of Arnold Schoenberg. He made the principle of set-association, or combinatoriality, the basis of his theories.[4] Babbitt views the twelve-tone set as the source of all development in a composition and asserts that all variation can and must be in strict adherence to the rule inherent in twelve-tone writing. He has stated emphatically, "The twelve-tone set must absolutely determine every aspect of the piece."[5]

In Partitions an extreme pointillistic style creates a sense of space, while the intricate rhythm creates a strong feeling of momentum. A concept of depth is emphasized by resourceful use of the sostenuto pedal. The serial procedures detectable in the score are not audible as such, but their contribution to the total design has been effectively planned.

Piano Music

Three Compositions for Piano (1947). New York, Boelke-
    Bomart, 1957.

Semi-Simple Variations (1956). Bryn Mawr, Pa., Theodore
    Presser, 1957.

"Partitions," New Music for the Piano. New York, Lawson-
    Gould, 1963.

"Duet," American Composers of Today, New York, Marks,
    1956.

Bibliography

Austin, William W. Music in the 20th Century: From Debussy through Stravinsky, New York, Norton, Inc., 1966.

"Babbitt, Milton," Baker's Biographical Dictionary of Musicians (5th ed.), 63.

Babbitt, Milton. "Edgard Varèse: A Few Observations of his Music," Perspectives of New Music, IV (Spring-Summer, 1966), 14-22.

_____. "An Introduction to the RCA Synthesizer," Journal of Music Theory, VIII (1964), 261-65.

_____. "Remarks on the Recent Stravinsky," Perspectives of New Music, II (Spring-Summer, 1964), 35-55.

_____. "Set Structure as a Compositional Determinant," Journal of Music Theory, V (1961), 72.

_____. "Some Aspects of Twelve-Tone Composition," The Score, 12 (June, 1955), 53-61.

_____. "Twelve-Tone Invariants as Compositional Determinants," The Musical Quarterly, XLVI (April, 1960), 246-59.

_____. "Twelve-Tone Rhythmic Structure and the Electronic Medium," Perspectives of New Music, I (Fall-Winter, 1962), 49-79.

_____. "Who Cares If You Listen?" High Fidelity, VIII (January, 1958), 38.

Bruno, A. "Two American 12-tone Composers: Babbitt & Weber...Opposing Views," Musical America, LXXI (February, 1951), 22; 170.

Burkhardt, Charles. Anthology for Musical Analysis. New York, Holt, Rinehart, & Winston, 1964.

Goldman, Richard Franko. "Current Chronicle: New York," The Musical Quarterly, XLVIII (January, 1962) 93-99.

Machlis, Joseph.  Introduction to Contemporary Music.
    New York, Norton, 1961.

Perle, George.  Serial Composition and Atonality.  2nd ed.
    Berkeley, Univ. of Calif. Press, 1968.

BARCE, RAMON

(b. Madrid, March 16, 1928)
Address:  Divino Vallés 27; Madrid 5, Spain

    Ramón Barce has largely taught himself composition.
His early atonal style gradually incorporated elements of
Schoenberg's twelve-tone technique.  Recently he has
devoted much time to theoretical writing, discussing the
concepts he is exploring in his own music: a harmonic
system associated with serial principles.  For example, he
is experimenting with a new type of tonal center, created by
carefully omitting a specific tone from the iterations of a
series until the ear demands its presentation.  The delayed
appearance of this note is usually followed by its frequent
repetition.  The alternation between saturated use of this
specific note and its prolonged absence maintains a unique
sense of a tone center. [6]  Barce is developing his ideas in
a set of ten serial studies for the piano now in progress.
Characteristic features in Estudio de Sonoridades, Op. 21,
No. 1 (1962), are glissandi, tremolos, dynamic contrasts,
pedal effects, and tone-clusters, utilized to create a variety
of timbres.  In this work Barce uses the contrast of
emphasizing either the use of all twelve notes or the absence
of a specific tone.  The latter he effects by use of consonant
and dissonant intervals in a thinner texture so as to direct
tension toward principal tones. [7] Another set of his piano
pieces, the Nueve Preludios (1965), is also based on this
new harmonic system.

Piano Music

Estudio de Sonoridades, Op. 21, No. 1 (1962), Facsim.
    reprod. n.d.

Estudio de Densidades, Op. 21, No. 2 (1965).  Facsim.
    reprod.  n.d.

Estudio de Dinámica, Op. 21, No. 3 (1966-68).  Facsim.
    reprod.  n.d.

Estudio de Valores, Op. 21, No. 4 (1967-68).   Facsim.
   reprod.   n.d.

Nueve Preludios (1965).   Facsim. reprod.   n.d.

Bibliography

Barce, Ramón.   "Control, Supercontrol, Infracontrol, "
   Atlántida, 15 (May-June, 1965), 303-15.

_____.   "Grafización, " Sonda, II (February, 1968).

_____.   "Las Cuatro Estaciónes, " Sonda, I (October,
   1967),   15-24.

_____.   "Música Abierta, Ventana al Infinito, "
   Atlántida, XXIX-XXX (September-December, 1967),
   515-26.

_____.   "Nuevo Sistema Atonal, " Atlántida, XXI (May-
   June, 1966), 329-43.

Custer, Arthur.   "Contemporary Music in Spain, " The
   Musical Quarterly, LI (January, 1965), 44-60.

Gillespie, John.   Five Centuries of Keyboard Music: An
   Historical Survey of Music for Harpsichord and Piano.
   Belmont, Calif., Wadsworth Pub. Co., 1965.

BARRAQUE, JEAN

(b. Paris, January 17, 1928.
Address:   2 Rue de l'Abbé Paturea; Paris 18,e France

      After studying with Jean Langlais and Olivier Messiaen,
Jean Barraqué developed an elaborate modification of the
serial system.   As did other French composers at mid-
century, Barraqué sought to move past the musical language
of Webern.   The tonal occurrences in his writing are not
considered a compromise, but a characteristic part of a
serial style in which he did not hesitate to synthesize selected elements of both traditional tonality and atonality.[8]

      The Sonate pour Piano (1950-52) contains a single
movement of massive proportions, in which Barraqué's

lyrical gifts and free style of serial composition are
apparent. The rhythmic structure is of great complexity,
with silence an integral part of its design.

Barraqué has suppressed the publication of much of
his music, as well as his writings on music which are
known to contain detailed analyses of other composers'
works (for instance Webern's Piano Variations, Op. 27
and a noteworthy discussion of Messiaen's analysis of
Stravinsky's Le Sacre du Printemps.)

Piano Music

Sonate pour Piano (1950-52). Florence, Bruzzichelli, n.d.

Bibliography

"Barraqué, Jean," 1965 Supplement to Baker's Biographical
    Dictionary of Musicians (5th ed.), 8.

Goléa, Antoine. "French Music Since 1945," trans. Lucile
    H. Brockway, The Musical Quarterly, LI (January, 1965),
    22-37.

Hodeir, André. Since Debussy: A View of Contemporary
    Music. Trans. Noel Burch. New York, Grove, 1961.

BAUR, JURG

(b. Düsseldorf, November 11, 1918)
Address: Direktor des Robert Schumann Konservatorium;
Fischerstrasse 110; 4 Düsseldorf; West Germany

Jürg Baur took his musical education at the Musik-
hochschule and Universität Köln, studying composition under
Philipp Jarnach, a strong advocate of the ideas of Ferruccio
Busoni. Baur has taught at the Robert Schumann Konservatorium in Düsseldorf since 1946, becoming director in
1965. The Capriccio for piano (1953) was one of his first
works clearly in a dodecaphonic style, which he has
employed since. He employs both free and a strict application of Schoenberg's techniques and uses mirror forms
extensively. Recently Baur has written two other piano
works using row techniques. A two-piano Sonata (1957)
employs a single tone row as the source for the melodic,

contrapuntal, and rhythmic aspects of the piece.[9]
Heptameron (1966), dedicated to Webern, is a set of seven
pieces using serial techniques throughout in which Baur
again features mirror structures to develop the relationships
of thematic, rhythmic, and contrapuntal elements.[10] The
structural inter-relationships reach a climactic point in the
middle sections of the set.

At present, there is no appreciable bibliography for
Baur.

Piano Music

Capriccio: Studie nach einer Zwölftonreithe (1953).
Wiesbaden, Breitkopf & Härtel, 1957.

Sonate für Zwei Klaviere. Wiesbaden, Breitkopf & Härtel,
1957.

Heptameron: Sieben Stücke (1964-65). Wiesbaden, Breitkopf
& Härtel, 1966.

BENNETT, RICHARD RODNEY

(b. Broadstairs, Kent, March 29, 1936)
Address: 4 Rheidol Terrace; London, N. 1., England

Richard Rodney Bennett studied composition with
Lennox Berkeley and Howard Ferguson, and with Pierre
Boulez from 1957 to 1959. The association with Boulez
is reflected in the greater rhythmic complexity of Bennett's
later works; this can be observed by comparing the Sonata
for Piano (1956) with later piano scores, Fantasy (1962) and
Five Studies (1965). All three scores employ serial techniques.

Bennett's works tend toward total serialization, but
with a flavor more reminiscent of Schoenberg than of Webern.
Other styles are integrated into Bennett's dodecaphonic writing on occasion, such as elements of jazz, and the influence
of Bartok is particularly noticeable in the Sonata for Piano.

Piano Music

Sonata for Piano. London, Universal Edition, 1956.

Fantasy for Piano (1962).   London,  Mills Music,  1963.

5 Studies for Piano.   London,  Universal Edition,  1965.

Bibliography

"Bennett,  Richard Rodney, " 1965 Supplement to Baker's
    Biographical Dictionary of Musicians (5th ed. ),  11.

Maw,  Nicholas.   "Richard Rodney Bennett, " The Musical
    Times,  No. 1428 (February,  1962).  95-97.

Porter,  Andrew.  "Some New British Composers, " The
    Musical Quarterly,  LI (January,  1965),  12-21.


BERIO,  ANGELO LUCIANO


(b.  Oneglia,  Italy,  October 24,  1925)
Address: Via Moscati 7; Milan,  Italy.

        Luciano Berio began the study of composition under
his father,  and continued with G. C.   Paribeni and Giorio
Ghedini at the Conservatory of Milan,  and Luigi Dallapicolla
at Tanglewood.   Berio belongs to an Italian generation of
composers who have greatly increased their country's involvement with serial composition.   In Berio's case,  he has incorporated serial principles extensively in the composition
of electronic music,  which he considers the practical means
for utilizing the potential of sound phenomena.   Berio joined
the staff of Italian Radio and,  in close association with Bruno
Maderna,  established the Studio di Fonologia Musicale at
Milan in 1953 in order to carry on experimental work on
acoustics.   These two composers also established the
Incontri Musicali concert series and Berio founded and
edited the progressive magazine of the same title.   Berio
was a composer in residence at Tanglewood in 1960 and
1966 and has taught composition at Juilliard intermittently
for the last three years.

        In the Cinque Variazioni per Pianoforte,  Berio's
treatment of the variation form in a twelve-tone work is
relatively conventional.   (First completed in 1953,  a revised
edition is forthcoming. )  Berio considers the row and its
transformations as meaningless in themselves.   There is
not a rigidly systematized permutation system in his work,

but as Berio states, the derivation procedures are similar
to those employed by Berg in his opera Lulu.[11]

Berio was one of the first Italians who felt a need
to suppress his native over-emotionalism, yet he sought to
retain personal expression within a framework of total
control. He applied a permutation system to the original
row that would permit strict control of a thematic line. Durations, pauses, intensity, timbre, and other elements are
determined through permutations of the basic series. The
system is an interpretation of the perpetual variation idea,
inherent in the original Schoenberg system, and results in
an open form.

Berio's concept of open form as derived from the
perpetual variation technique has developed into a dominant
force in his compositions. Compared to the 1953 version
of the Cinque Variazioni, in which remnants of the traditional, closed, repetitive, variation form serve as reinforcement to the theme, a more recent work, Sequenza IV
(1967), demonstrates the perpetual variation principle as
maintaining unity by emphasizing aspects of the original row
in a process of disintegration.

Many of Berio's works experiment with an innovative
notational system designed to keep pace with the needs of
electronic music, which has accelerated in development in
the last two decades.

Piano Music

Cinque Variazioni per Pianoforte. Milan, Suvini Zerboni,
    1954.

Rounds for Harpsichord. London, Universal Edition, 1966.

Sequenza IV. London, Universal Edition, 1967.

Bibliography

Beckwith, John and Udo Kasemets (eds.), The Modern
    Composer and His World. Toronto, University of
    Toronto Press, 1961.

Berio, Luciano. "Musik und Dichtung," aus dem Italienischen

übersetzt von. K. -H Metzger, Darmstädter Beiträge zur Neuen Musik, II (1959), 36.

_____ . "Poesie e Musica, " Incontri Musicali, III.

_____ . "Remarks to the Kind Lady of Baltimore, " Electronic Music Review, I (January, 1967), 58-9.

"Berio, Luciano, " 1965 Supplement to Baker's Biographical Dictionary of Musicians (5th ed. ), 12.

Bertolotto, Mario. "The New Music in Italy, " The Musical Quarterly, LI (January, 1965), 63-64.

Goldman, Richard Franko. "Current Chronicle: United States, " The Musical Quarterly, XLVII (April, 1961), 238-239.

_____ . "Reviews of Records, " The Musical Quarterly, XLVIII (July, 1962), 409.

Prieberg, Fred K. "Imaginäres Gespräch mit Luciano Berio, " Melos, XXXII (1965), 156.

Santi, Piero. "Luciano Berio, " trans. Leo Black, Die Reihe, IV (1960), 98-102.

Vlad, Roman. Storia della Dodecafonia. Milan, Suvini Zerboni, 1958.

Zillig, Winfried. Variationen über Neue Musik. Munich, Nymphenburger, 1959.

## BLACHER, BORIS

(b. Newchang, China, January 3, 1903)
Address: Direktor der Stattl. Hochschule für Musik; Fasanenstrasse 1; 1 Berlin-Charlottenburg 2; West Germany

     Boris Blacher was born in China, but when he was nineteen his family returned to their homeland and settled in Berlin. His early interest in architecture was forsaken for the study of musicology at Berlin University. In 1948 he became a professor at the Hochschule für Musik in West Berlin, and in 1953, the head of this school. Teaching positions at Tanglewood and Dartmouth College summer sessions have widened his international influence.

Blacher began to use the Schoenberg technique in
1928, but has not employed it continuously; frequently he
uses a definite tonal center in dodecaphonic works. At
other times, either a free atonal counterpoint or elements
of neo-classicism appear in his style.

The influence of jazz sounds, as well as of jazz
rhythms, is also an effective force in such works as the
second of the Trois Pièces pour Piano, Op. 18 (1943).

The early set of piano sonatinas (Op. 14) is a
relatively simple score in which the main interest lies in
the catchy asymmetrical rhythms. Although influenced by
Schoenberg, Blacher was equally influenced by the rhythmic
innovations of Stravinsky. It is not surprising, in view of
his interest in rhythm, that the use of twelve-tone rows
became secondary to Blacher's invention and development
of a system of variable meters. The meter changes at
each bar correlate with the mathematical series selected
to establish a rhythmic row equivalent to a pitch series.
On occasion, chromatic patterns which are not legitimate
rows are juggled to accommodate his rhythmic design.
Blacher's system can certainly be considered as a serial
technique, but differs considerably from the path of rhythmic
serialization chosen by Messiaen, and that developed by
Boulez and Stockhausen, although both directions were
primarily inspired by Stravinsky. [12]

Blacher's first well-developed usage of his variable
meter system appears in a piano work, Ornamente, Op. 37
(1950). There is no serialization of the pitch although the
melodic material is highly chromatic and each of the seven
pieces is completely organized on tone-row principles.
Much the same can be said for the Sonate, Op. 39 (1951).
This is a clear example among Blacher's piano works of
the manner in which he will work with an ostinato, much
in the style of Stravinsky, to set up a rhythmic field.

Blacher's variable meter technique remained essentially the same during the 1950's, but recently he has begun
to experiment with its possible projections.

Piano Music

Zwei Sonatinen, Op. 14.    Berlin, Bote & Bock, 1955.

Trois Pièces pour Piano, Op. 18.    Vienna,    Universal
    Edition, 1946.

_____.    Ornamente,    Op. 37.    (1950).    Berlin, Bote &
    Bock, 1951.

_____.    Sonate für Klavier, Op. 39.    Berlin, Bote &
    Bock, 1951.

Bibliography

Austin, William W.    Music in the 20th Century: From
    Debussy through Stravinsky.    New York, Norton, 1966.

"Blacher,  Boris, " Baker's Biographical Dictionary of
    Musicians  (5th ed.),  158-59.

Burt, Francis.    "The Teaching and Ideas of Boris Blacher, "
    The Score, (September, 1954), 12.

Dibelius, Ulrich.    Moderne Musik 1945-1965.    Munich, R.
    Piper, 1966.

Elston, Arnold.    "Some Rhythmic Practices in Contemporary
    Music, " The Musical Quarterly, XLII (July,  1956),
    318-29.

Hansen,  Peter S.    An Introduction to Twentieth Century
    Music.    Boston,  Allyn and Bacon,  1961.

Hartog,  Howard (ed.).    European Music in the Twentieth
    Century.    New York,  Praeger,  1957.

Kosuzek,  G.  F.  "Boris Blacher, " The Score, August, 1949.

Lindlar,  H.  (ed.).    Die Stimme der Komponisten.    Roden-
    kirchen,  Germany,  n. p.,  1958.

Machlis,  Joseph.    Introduction to Contemporary Music.
    New York,  Norton,  1961.

Muller-Marein,  J.,  and H.  Reinhardt,  (eds.).    Das Musik-
    alische Selbstportrait.    Hamburg,  n. p.,  1963.

Murray, Bain. "Current Chronicle: Cleveland," The
　　Musical Quarterly. XLIV (April, 1958), 231-35.

Rufer, Josef. Composition with Twelve Notes... Trans.
　　Humphrey Searle. London, Barrie and Rockliff, 1954.

　　　　　　　. "Boris Blacher and his Metri Variabili," Il
　　Diapason, (September, 1951).

Rutz, Hans. "Blacher, Boris," Grove's Dictionary of
　　Music and Musicians (5th ed.), I, 746-47.

Stuckenschmidt, Hans Heinz. Boris Blacher. Berlin, n.p.,
　　1964.

　　　　　　　. "Synthesis and New Experiments: Four
　　Contemporary German Composers, trans. Abram Loft,
　　The Musical Quarterly, XXXVIII (July, 1952), 353-68.

Vlad, Roman. Storia della Dodecafonia. Milan, Suvini
　　Zerboni, 1958.

Von Lewinski, Wolf-Eberhard. "The Variety of Trends in
　　Modern German Music," trans. Donald Mintz, The
　　Musical Quarterly, LI (January, 1965), 174-79.

　　　　　　　. "Current Chronicle: Germany," The Musical
　　Quarterly, LII (July, 1966), 376-79.

Wörner, Karl H. Neue Musik in der Entscheidung. Mainz,
　　n.p., 1954.

## BOULEZ, PIERRE

(b. Montbrison, France, March 26, 1925)
Address:　24 Weidestrasse; Baden-Baden; West Germany

　　　　Pierre Boulez's growing interest in music led him to
abandon his plans for a career in mathematics and to under-
take the study of musical composition with Olivier Messiaen
and René Leibowitz at the Paris Conservatory. Leibowitz's
teaching upheld a strict usage of Schoenberg's twelve-tone
technique, and herein Boulez found an ideal means for
utilizing to their utmost the rhythmic concepts expounded by
Messiaen. [13] Boulez proceeded to apply the principles of
the Schoenberg technique to effect a serial ordering of rhyth-

mic design and then extended the application to all elements
of musical expression.  Messiaen's classes on rhythm had
attracted students from many countries.  Boulez's ideas
were enthusiastically received among many from this group,
in particular by Karlheinz Stockhausen, and were quickly
incorporated into the post-Webern movement that saw re-
surgence of interest in serial composition following World
War II.

In the early 1940's the ideas of Schoenberg and
Webern were diverging considerably . In post war France
this split developed as a conservative approach, advocating
a strict Schoenberg technique, in opposition to the viewpoint which sought extension of serial composition along the
path indicated by Webern.  Following this latter branch,
Boulez became a key-figure in the European exploitation of
the concept of total serialization.  Not only his musical
compositions, but his writings on contemporary music, his
teaching (principally at Darmstadt) and his other activities
in conjunction with the promotion of avant-garde music
have been a major stimulus to twentieth-century music.  In
recent years he has received considerable acclaim as a
conductor.

Boulez emerged as the international leader in extending the basic concepts of serial composition by his total
organization of musical elements.  He incorporated new
techniques into his serial style, such as improvisational
and chance elements, and has also experimented with a new
notational system.

The piano works of Boulez are among the most
frequently performed contemporary scores.  His twelve-tone
composition began in 1946 and included the Première Sonate
(1946), in which the influence of Messiaen is particularly
evident in the rhythmic design.[14]  His later piano works are
considerably more complex.  Norman Demuth marks the
Deuxième Sonate (1948) as a peak of French twelve-tone
writing.[15] In the last of his three sonatas, Boulez creates
another landmark in the application of total serialization
by the incorporation of chance under the control of the total
structure.[16]

Boulez's piano works include two sets of Structures
for two pianos (1952; 1961)[17]  György Ligeti, in his extensive

and detailed study of the first movement of the earlier set, explains this phase of Boulez's composition as a culmination of an extension of Webern's search for form, in that Boulez had reached a concept of structure based on the relationships of musical materials in time. [18]

## Piano Music

Première Sonate (1946).   Paris, Amphion Editions Musicales, 1951.

Deuxième Sonate (1948).   Paris, Heugel & Cie, 1950.

Troisième Sonate pour Piano (1957).   London, Universal Edition, 1961.

Structures (1952; 1961).   2 vols.   London, Universal Edition, 1955, 1962.

## Bibliography

Austin, William W.   Music in the 20th Century: From Debussy through Stravinsky.   New York, Norton, 1966.

Barrault, Jean Louis, et al.   La Musique et ses Problèmes Contemporains.   Paris, Juilliard, 1954.

Boulez, Pierre.   "Alea," trans.   David Noakes and Paul Jacobs, Perspectives of New Music, III (Fall-Winter, 1964), 42-53.

_____.   "At the End of Fruitful Land...," Die Reihe, I (1958), 19-29.

_____.   "Debussy: 'Jeux'," Gravesaner Blätter, II (1956), 5.

_____.   "Discipline et Communication," Darmstädter Beiträge zur Neuen Musik, IV (1961), 25-37.

_____.   "Eventuellement," La Revue Musicale, (April, 1952).

_____.   "Expériences, Autruches et Musique," Nouvelle Revue Française III (1955), 1174.

_____ ₒ "Gespräch 'Unter Zwei Augen²,'' Melos, XXX (1963), 185.

_____ • "Interview with Barrie Hall,'' Music and Musicians, XIV (September, 1965), 18.

_____ ₒ "Musikdenken Heute 1,'' Darmstädter Beiträge zur Neuen Musik, V (1963), 7-123.

_____ ₒ "Necessité d'une Orientation Esthétique,'' Mercure de France, CCL (1964), 624; CCLI (1964), 110.

_____ • Penser La Musique Aujourd'hui. Switzerland, Gonthier, 1963.

_____ ₒ "Poésie--Centre et Absence--Musique,'' Melos, XXX (1963), 185.

_____ • "Probabilités Critiques du Compositeur,'' Domaine Musical, No. 1 (1954).

_____ ₒ Relevés d'Apprenti. Paris, Seuil, 1966.

_____ • "Sonate, Que Me Veux-tu?'' trans. David Noakes and Paul Jacobs, Perspectives of New Music, I (Spring, 1963), 32-44.

_____ ₒ "Tendances de la Musique Récente,'' La Revue Musicale, No. 236 (1957), 28.

_____ ₒ "The Threshold,'' Die Reihe, II (1958), 40-41.

_____ • "Wie Arbeitet die Avant-garde?'' Melos, XXVIII (1961), 301.

_____ • "Wo ist Echte Tradition?'' Melos, XXVII (1960) 289.

"Boulez, Pierre,'' Baker's Biographical Dictionary of Musicians. Fifth Edition with 1965 Supplement, 191; 17.

Bourdet, Denise. Visages d'Aujourd'hui. Paris, n. p., 1960.

Bradshaw, Susan, and Richard Rodney Bennett, "In Search of

Boulez," Music and Musicians, XI (January, 1963), 10;
XI (August, 1963), 14.

Cadieu, Martine, "Duo avec Pierre Boulez," Nouvelles
Littéraires, Aug. 16, 1962, 11.

Carter, Elliott, "Current Chronicle: Italy," The Musical
Quarterly, XLV (October, 1959), 530-41.

Collaer, Paul. A History of Modern Music. Trans. Sally
Abeles. New York, World, 1961.

Cowell, Henry, "Current Chronicle: New York," The Musical Quarterly, XXXVIII (January, 1965), 123-36.

Craft, Robert, "Boulez and Stockhausen," The Score, XXIV
(November, 1958), 54-62.

Crocker, Richard L. A History of Musical Style. New
York, McGraw-Hill, 1966.

Dallin, Leon. Techniques of Twentieth Century Composition.
2nd ed. Dubuque, Iowa, Wm. C. Brown, 1964.

Demuth, Norman. French Piano Music: A Survey with Notes
on its Performance. London, Museum Press, 1959.

Dibelius, Ulrich. Moderne Musik 1945-1965. Munich, R.
Piper, 1966.

Galli, Hans. Moderne Musik-leicht Verständlich. Munich,
Francke, 1964.

Gillespie, John. Five Centuries of Keyboard Music: An
Historical Survey of Music for Harpsichord and Piano.
Belmont, Calif., Wadsworth Pub. Co., 1965.

Goehr, Alexander. "Is There Only One Way?" The Score,
XXVI (1960), 63.

Goldbeck, Frederick E. "Boulez, Pierre," Grove's Dictionary of Music and Musicians (5th ed.), I, 844.

_____. "Current Chronicle: France," The Musical
Quarterly, XXXVI (April, 1950), 291-95.

Goldman, Richard Franko. "Current Chronicle: United
States, The Musical Quarterly, XLVII (April, 1961),
233-39.

Goléa, Antoine. Esthétique de la Musique Contemporaine.
Paris, Presses Universitaires de France, 1954.

_____. "French Music Since 1945," trans. Lucile H.
Brockway, The Musical Quarterly, LI (January, 1965),
22-37.

_____. Rencontres avec Pierre Boulez. Paris,
Juilliard, 1958.

_____. Vingt Ans de Musique Contemporaine: de
Messaiaen à Boulez. Paris, Seghers, 1962.

Hansen, Peter S. An Introduction to Twentieth Century
Music. Boston, Allyn and Bacon, 1961.

Hartog, Howard (ed.). European Music in the Twentieth
Century. New York, Praeger, 1957.

Helm, Everett. "Current Chronicle: Germany," The Musical Quarterly, XLV (January, 1959), 100-104.

Hodeir, André. Since Debussy: A View of Contemporary
Music. Trans. Noel Burch. New York, Grove, 1961.

Karkoschka, Erhard. Das Schriftbild der Neuen Musik.
Celle, Germany, Hermann Moeck, 1966.

Kohn, Karl. "Current Chronicle; Los Angeles," The Musical Quarterly, XLIX (July, 1963), 360-69.

Křenek, Ernst. "Is the Twelve-Tone Technique on the
Decline?" The Musical Quarterly, XXIX (October, 1953),
513-27.

Lesure, Francois. "Profili di Musicisti Contemporanei,"
Musica d'Oggi, (January, 1958), 19-21.

Ligeti, György. "Some Remarks on Boulez' 3rd Piano
Sonata," Die Reihe, V (1961), 56-58.

_____. "Pierre Boulez," Die Reihe, IV (1960), 36-62.

Machlis, Joseph. Introduction to Contemporary Music. New York, Norton, 1961.

Maegaard, Jan. Musikalsk Modernisme 1945-1962. Copenhagen, Stig Vendelkaers, 1964.

McLeod, Jenny. "Boulez at Basle," Composer, No. 17 (October, 1965), 13-14.

Mitchell, Donald. The Language of Modern Music. New York, St. Martin's, 1966.

Nono, Luigi. "Die Entwicklung der Reihentechnik," Darm-städter Beiträge zur Neuen Musik, I (1958), 25-37.

Philippot, Michel P. "Pierre Boulez Aujourd'hui, Entre Hier et Demain," Critique, XX (1964), 943.

Prieberg, Fred K. Lexikon der Neuen Musik. Freiburg, Karl Alber, 1958.

Reti, Rudolph. Tonality in Modern Music. New York, Collier, 1962.

Roy, Jean. Présences Contemporaines: Musique Française. Paris, DeBresse, 1962.

Salzman, Eric. Twentieth-Century Music: An Introduction. Englewood Cliffs, N.J., Prentice-Hall, 1967.

Searle, Humphrey. "New Kind of Music (Boulez's methods of composition," Twentieth Century, 161 (May, 1957), 480-83.

Vlad, Roman. Storia della Dodecafonia. Milan, Suvini Zerboni, 1958.

Wilkinson, Mark. "Pierre Boulez' 'Structure la': Some Thoughts on Twelve-Tone Method," Gravesaner Blätter, X (1958), 23-29.

Wörner, Karl H. "Current Chronicle: Germany," The Musi-cal Quarterly, XLV (January, 1959), 237-41.

Boulez, Pierre                                              57

          。 "Current Chronicle: Germany," The Musical
    Quarterly, XLVI (April, 1960), 270-75.

Zillig, Winfried。 Variationen über Neue Musik. Munich,
    Nymphenburger, 1959.


BROWN, EARLE

(b. Lunenburg, Massachusetts, December 26, 1926)
Address:  28 Greenwich Avenue, New York, New York 10011

       Earle Brown studied mathematics and engineering
at Northeastern University, but turned eventually toward the
study of counterpoint and composition with Roslyn Henning
(1947-50)。 He also studied the Schillinger method with
Kenneth McKillop and later taught it. In his own later
composition he has tended to loosen the ideas of Schillinger[19]
Brown has been closely associated with John Cage and
David Tudor on Project for Music for Magnetic Tape。
Brown was an editor and a recording engineer for Capitol
Records from 1955 through 1960 and is currently an artistic
director for the Contemporary Sound Series of Time Records.

       Brown's association with twelve-tone writing is most
obvious in the Three Pieces for Piano (1951). Slight liberties are taken in the ordering, as the counterpoint receives
precedence, but the use of two rows in double counterpoint
can be readily followed. Perspectives (1952) takes greater
liberties, and comes close to being totally chromatic, rather
than in a free twelve-tone style.

       Brown's association with John Cage encouraged him
to go even further in his theorizing. His wide interest in
musical philosophy also developed in large part from his
interest in art and aesthetics. He explains this influence
as coming most specifically from the work of Alexander
Calder, Jackson Pollock, and Max Ernst.[20] Concepts which
Brown developed materialized in such piano works as Folio
and Four Systems (1952-54). This composition fully illustrates Brown's musical credo. It contains the first concepts
of open form and the first use of graphic scoring using
Brown's time notation. [21] On the theory that a performer
can utilize an intuitive sense of time and time relationships,
Brown has experimented with the development of a time
notation to indicate proportionally pitch, dynamics, and

duration. Gilbert Chase has published Brown's explanation
of his notation system.[22]

The application of indeterminacy and aleatory principles was developed by John Cage, Morton Feldman, and
Earle Brown, between 1951-54. The European adoption
of these ideas was stimulated largely by David Tudor's
performances of the piano works of this group at Darmstadt in the mid-1950's.[23]

Although since 1952 Brown's works do not permit
categorization as completely serial or twelve-tone styles,
a relationship clearly exists. The aleatory principles, and
the concern for space, time, and sound, and the consequent
changes in his formal concepts, have since become inter-
woven with twelve-tone, serial, atonal, and electronic music.

Piano Music

Three Pieces for Piano (1951).   London, Schott, 1959.

Perspectives for Piano (1952).   Mainz, Ars Viva, 1959.

Folio and Four Systems (1952-54).   New York, Assoc.
    Music Pub. 1961.

Corroboree For Two or Three Pianos (1964).   Unpub. ms.

Nine Rarebits for One or Two Harpsichords (1965).   Unpub.
    ms.

Bibliography

Brown, Earle.   Jacket notes, Earle Brown and Morton
    Feldman, Time recording 58007.

_____ .   "Form in New Music, " Source, I (1967), 48-51.

_____ .   "Notation und Ausführung Neuer Musik, "
    Darmstädter Beiträge zur Neuen Musik, IX (1965),
    64-86.

"Brown, Earle, " 1965 Supplement to Baker's Biographical
    Dictionary of Musicians (5th ed.), 19.

Cage, John. Silence. Cambridge, Mass., M.I.T. Press, 1966.

Chase, Gilbert. American Composers on American Music. Baton Rouge, Louisiana State Univ. Press, 1966.

_____. America's Music: From the Pilgrims to the Present. Rev. 2nd. ed. New York, McGraw-Hill, 1966.

Kostelanetz, Richard (ed.). New American Arts. New York, Horizon, 1965.

Mellers, Wilfred. Music in a Newfoundland: Themes and Developments in the History of American Music. New York, Knopf, 1965.

Yates, Peter. Twentieth Century Music: Its Evolution from the End of the Harmonic Era into the Present Era of Sound. New York, Pantheon, 1967.

BUSSOTTI, SYLVANO

(b. Florence, Italy, October 1, 1931)
Address: Via del Portico d'Ottavia 9; Rome, Italy


Sylvano Bussotti studied with Max Deutsch in Paris, and with Luigi Dallapiccola at the Conservatory of Florence. He has also studied painting in Paris and has experimented extensively with attempts to combine graphic art and musical notation. This system is employed in the piano works, most impressively in Five Piano Pieces for David Tudor (1959). A relationship to John Cage's pieces for Tudor is evident in the type of sounds and the aleatory technique.

Pour Clavier (1961) also features aleatory ideas resembling Cage's usage. The material is derived from Bussotti's earlier chamber work, Pièces de Choir II (1960).

A two-piano work, Tableau Vivants (1964) is to be part of a yet incomplete gigantic cantata entitled Passion Selon Sade.

Piano Music

Five Piano Pieces for David Tudor (1959).  London, Universal Edition, 1959.

"Per Tre sul Piano." Sette Fogli (1959).  London, Universal Edition, n. d.

Pour Clavier (1961).  Celle, Germany, Hermann Moeck, 1962.

Tableaux Vivants für Zwei Klaviere zu Vier Händen (1964).  Milan, Ricordi, n. d.

Bibliography

Austin, William W.  Music in the 20th Century: From Debussy through Stravinsky, New York, Norton, 1966.

Bortolotto, Mario.  "The New Music in Italy," trans. William C. Holmes, The Musical Quarterly, LI (January, 1965), 61-77.

"Bussotti, Sylvano," 1965 Supplement to Baker's Biographical Dictionary of Musicians (5th ed.), 21.

Goldman, Richard Franko.  "Reviews of Records," The Musical Quarterly, XLVIII (July, 1962), 409-410.

CASTIGLIONI, NICCOLO

(b. Milan, July 17, 1932)
Address:  Via Nazario Sauro 6; Milan, Italy

Niccolò Castiglioni, a noted concert pianist, studied composition with Boris Blacher and Giorgio Ghedini.

The constant symmetrical permutation that is typical of his serial style is exemplified in the piano score Cangianti (1959).  The significance of the title, which means changes, is easily grasped.  Three rows are announced simultaneously.  The second is derived from the original by interchange of the hexachords, and the third, by numerical re-ordering of the series.  The derivation procedures are perpetuated in like manner.

Piano Music

Four Canti per Pianoforte (1954).    Milan,  Suvini Zerboni,
    n. d.

Inizio di Movimento per Pianoforte.    Milan,  Suvini Zerboni,
    1958.

Cangianti per Pianoforte.    Milan,  Suvini Zerboni,  1959.

Bibliography

Castiglioni, Niccolò.  Il Linguaggio Musicale dal Rina-
    scimento a Oggi.    Milan,  n. p.,  1959.

"Castiglioni,  Niccolò, "  1965 Supplement to Baker's Biograph-
    ical Dictionary of Musicians (5th ed. ),  23.

CLEMENTI, ALDO

(b.   Catania,  Italy,  May 25,  1925)
Address:  c/o Edizioni Suvini Zerboni; Galleria del Corso 4;
Milan, Italy

        Aldo Clementi was a student of Goffredo Petrassi
and Bruno Maderna and has attended Darmstadt courses.
The early work of Clementi shows a strong influence from
Stravinsky.   His later style is based both on a primary
concern for intervallic logic akin to that of Webern and on
the concept that the inner time of experience is to be
ignored.   His utilization of relationships among intervals,
sounds,  and space in order to achieve a spatial construction
is completely devoid of any traditional connotations.

        Intavolatura per Clavicembalo (1963),  is built on
three rows,  presented simultaneously.   The title means
system of notation and the work represents Clementi's
contribution to the need for a new notation to express
modern music.   The basic material of Composizione No. 1
per Pianoforte (1957) is embodied in an eighteen-note
pattern,  reduced to seventeen on subsequent recurrence,
then sixteen,  and so on.   This is a unique treatment of the
row principle.   Clementi is among those Italian composers
who have carried serialism towards a free style by adding
innovations.   Their experiments do not suggest an abandon-

ment of serialism but rather herald a new stage of development in which serial techniques are camouflaged.

Piano Music

Composizione No. 1 per Pianoforte (1957). Milan, Suvini
    Zerboni, 1958.

Intavolatura per Clavicembalo (1963).    Milan, Suvini Zerboni,
    1964.

Bibliography

Bortolotto, Mario.  "The New Music in Italy, " trans.
    William C. Holmes, The Musical Quarterly, LI
    (January, 1965), 61-77.

"Clementi, Aldo, " 1965 Supplement to Baker's Biographical
    Dictionary of Musicians (5th ed.), 26.

Kohn, Karl.  "Current Chronicle: Los Angeles, " The Musi-
    cal Quarterly, L (July, 1964), 370-79.

COPLAND, AARON

(b.  Brooklyn, November 14, 1900)
Address:  Rock Hill, R. F. D.  1, Peekskill, New York  10566

    Although Aaron Copland was to become an important
American serialist from among the older generation, as well as
one of the most influential, his early works provide only a
hint of his future significance in the serial field.  The influence
of Rubin Goldmark and Nadia Boulanger, with whom he studied,
and Stravinsky did not contribute to Copland's adoption of dodecaphonic principles.  He first attempted twelve-tone writing in a
vocal work of 1927.  The Piano Variations (1930)[24] represents
only a tentative serial style.  The Piano Sonata (1939-41)[25] is a
work of great importance, marking Copland's maturity, but
bears little relationship to serial composition. [26]  However, the
Piano Fantasy (1957) is impressive for Copland's use of a free
serial technique. [27]  The initial melodic material constitutes a
powerful ten-note theme.  The remaining tones of the chromatic
scale are utilized to create cadential points. [28]

    Many American composers have in common a concern for
the harmonic or vertical aspect of twelve-tone writing, whereas

the Italian preoccupation is for linear design, and the French, for rhythmic structure. Copland was a leader in the use of chord spacing; Arthur Berger attributes this directly to the influence of Stravinsky. [29] Berger foresees that Copland's treatment of chord spacing may be one of the great musical contributions of the last two decades.

Piano Music

Piano Variations (1930). New York, Boosey & Hawkes, 1956.

Piano Sonata (1939-41). New York, Boosey & Hawkes, 1942.

Piano Fantasy (1955-57). New York, Boosey & Hawkes, 1957.

Bibliography

Austin, William W. Music in the 20th Century: From Debussy through Stravinsky. New York, Norton, 1966.

Bauer, Marion. "Aaron Copland," The Book of Modern Composers New York, Putnam, 1942.

Berger, Arthur. Aaron Copland. New York, Oxford Univ. Press, 1953.

_____. "Aaron Copland's 'Piano Fantasy'," Juilliard Review, V (1957), 13.

_____. "The Music of Aaron Copland," The Musical Quarterly, XXXI (October, 1945), 420-47.

Cole, Hugo. "Aaron Copland," Tempo, LXXVI (Spring, 1966), 2-6; LXXVII (Summer, 1966), 9-15.

Copland, Aaron. "The Composer Speaks. A Tape Recorded Interview," Audio & Record Review III (July, 1964), 19.

_____. Copland on Music. New York, Norton, 1963.

_____. Music and Imagination. New York, New Amer. Lib. of World Lit., 1952.

_____. The New Music. Rev. ed. New York, Norton, 1968.

_____. What to Listen for in Music. Rev. ed. New York, McGraw-Hill, 1957.

"Copland, Aaron," Baker's Biographical Dictionary of Musicians. Fifth Edition with 1965 Supplement, 317-18; 28.

Dobrin, Arnold. Aaron Copland. New York, Crowell, 1967.

Eschmann, Karl. Changing Forms in Modern Music. Boston, Schirmer, 1945.

Evans, Peter. "Compromises with Serialism," Proceedings of the Royal Music Association, (1961-62), 1-16.

_____. "Copland on the Serial Road: An Analysis of 'Connotations'," Perspectives of New Music, II (1964), 141-49.

_____. "The Thematic Techniques of Copland's Recent Works," Tempo, 51 (1959), 2-13.

Garvie, Peter. "Aaron Copland," Canadian Music Journal, VI (1962), 3.

Goldman, Richard Franko. "Aaron Copland," The Musical Quarterly, XLVII (January, 1961), 1-3.

Kirkpatrick, John. "Aaron Copland's Piano Sonata," Modern Music, XIX (1942), 246.

Mellers, Wilfrid M. "Copland, Aaron," Grove's Dictionary of Music and Musicians (5th ed.), II, 428-29.

_____. Music and Society: England and the European Tradition. 2nd ed. London, Dennis Dobson, 1950.

_____. Music in a Newfoundland: Themes and Developments in the History of American Music. New York, Knopf, 1965.

Overton, Hall. "Copland's Jazz Roots," Jazz Today, I (November, 1956), 40.

Reis, Claire R. Composers in America: Biographical Sketches of Contemporary Composers with a Record of their Works. Rev. and enl. ed. New York, Macmillan, 1947.

Robertson, Alec (ed.). Chamber Music. London, Penguin, 1957.

Salazar, Adolfo. Music in our Time: Trends in Music Since the Romantic Era. Trans. Isabel Pope. New York, W. W. Norton, 1946.

Salzman, Eric, and Paul Des Marais. "Aaron Copland's 'Nonet': Two Views," Perspectives of New Music, I (Fall 1962), 172-79.

Smith, Julia. Aaron Copland. New York, Dutton, 1955.

Sternfield, Fredrick W. "Copland as a Film Composer," The Musical Quarterly, XXXVII (April, 1951), 161-75.

Wilson, Edmund. "The Jazz Problem," The New Republic, XLV (1926), 217.

Wörner, Karl H. "Copland, Aaron," Die Musik in Geschichte und Gegenwart, II, 1661-3.

DALLAPICCOLA, LUIGI

(b.  Pisino, Istria, Italy, (now Pazin, Yugoslavia)
February 3, 1904)
Address:  Via Romana 34; Florence, Italy

Luigi Dallapiccola received musical training in Italy, principally at the Cherubini Conservatory in Florence, where he became a faculty member in 1934. Dallapiccola has also taught at Tanglewood and at Queens College in New York.

Italian experimentation with twelve-tone techniques emerged slowly because prominent teachers and composers, for example Alfred Casella,[30] frowned upon its use and stifled its development. Furthermore, the Italian love for a lyrical vocal line required that dodecaphonic writing should enhance and not inhibit this characteristic of their music. Dallapiccola and Camillo Togni wrote the only significant twelve-tone works in the 1940's. By mid-century Dallapiccola had become a leader in the Italian development of dodecaphony and his influence became apparent in new Italian scores at such important international centers as Darmstadt and Tanglewood.

Dallapiccola's set of eleven piano pieces, Quaderno Musicale di Annalibera (1952),[31] is based on the following row: A# B E♭ G♭ A♭ D G D♭ F A C E. The intervallic structure creates a series that is lyrical, lends itself to either a strict or free contrapuntal treatment, and permits subtle tonal suggestions in vertical ordering. These qualities are essential for creating a serial style compatible with the Italian musical aesthetic. Dallapiccola has used this series similarly in other works: Variazione per Orchestra and Canti di Liberazione. Italian serial composition rapidly became characterized by complex textures, incorporating advanced serial techniques and forms in which permutation of the row forms became both a dominant feature and the source of continuous variation. The influence of Dallapiccola's twelve-tone composition has continued to indicate that a lyrical quality can be acquired by careful consideration of the intervallic structure in planning the ordering of the basic series and that specific types of design facilitates the extensive use of permutational techniques by which this lyricism can be maintained.

Piano Music

Quaderno Musicale Di Annalibera. Milan, Suvini Zerboni, 1953.

Bibliography

Austin, William W. Music in the 20th Century: From Debussy through Stravinsky. New York, Norton, 1966.

Ballo, Ferdinando. "Le Musiche Chorali di Dallapiccola," Rassegna Musicale, X (April, 1937), 136-41.

Basart, Ann P. "The Twelve-Tone Compositions of Luigi Dallapiccola." Unpub. master's thesis, Univ. of Calif. 1960.

Brindle, Reginald Smith. "Current Chronicle: Italy," The Musical Quarterly, XLI (October, 1955), 524-26.

_____. "Current Chronicle: Italy," The Musical Quarterly, XLIII (April, 1957), 240-45.

Cadieu, Martine. "Duo avec Luigi Dallapiccola," Nouvelles Littéraires, (March 1, 1962), 9.

Collaer, Paul.  A History of Modern Music.  Trans. Sally
Abeles.  New York, World, 1961.

Dallapiccola, Luigi.  "The Genesis of the Canti di Prigionia
and Il Prigioniero:  An Autobiographical Fragment, "
trans. Jonathan Schiller, The Musical Quarterly, XXXIX
(July,  1953),  355-72.

_____.  "On the Twelve-Note Road, " Musical Survey, IV
(October,  1951),  318-32.

"Dallapiccola,  Luigi, " Baker's Biographical Dictionary of
Musicians.  Fifth Edition with 1965 Supplement,  342; 30.

D'Amico,  Fedele.  "Recensioni: Luigi Dallapiccola, "
Rassegna Musicale, XVII (April,  1947),  165-70.

_____.  "Luigi Dallapiccola, " Melos,  XX  (March,  1953),
69-74.

Dibelius,  Ulrich.  Moderne Musik 1945-1965.  Munich,  R.
Piper,  1966.

Gatti,  Guido M.  "Casella, Alfredo, " Grove's Dictionary of
Music and Musicians (5th ed.),  II,  106-108.

_____.  "Current Chronicle: Italy, " The Musical Quarter-
ly, XXV (January,  1949),  136-39.

_____.  "Dallapiccola, Luigi, " Grove's Dictionary of
Music and Musicians (5th ed.),  II,  582-83.

_____.  "L'Opera di Luigi Dallapiccola, " Rassegna
Musicale,  II (1965),  7-156.

Gavazzeni,  Gianandrea.  Musicisti d'Europa:  Studi sui
Contemporanei.  Milan,  Suvini Zerboni,  1954.

Gillespie,  John.  Five Centuries of Keyboard Music:  An
Historical Survey of Music for Harpsichord and Piano.
Belmont,  Calif.,  Wadsworth Pub. Co., 1965.

Goldman,  Richard Franko.  "Current Chronicle: New York, "
The Musical Quarterly,  XXXVII (July,  1951),  405-10.

Goléa, Antoine. Esthétique de la Musique Contemporaine.
    Paris, Presses Universitaires de France, 1954.

_____. Vingt Ans de Musique Contemporaine: de
    Messiaen à Boulez. Paris, Seghers, 1962.

Hartog, Howard (ed.). European Music in the Twentieth
    Century. New York, Praeger, 1957.

Herz, Gerhard. "Current Chronicle: Louisville, Kentucky,"
    The Musical Quarterly, XLI (January, 1955), 79-85.

Hines, Robert Stephan (ed.). The Composer's Point of
    View: Essays on Twentieth-Century Choral Music By
    Those Who Wrote It. Norman, Univ. of Oklahoma
    Press, 1963.

Hodeir, André. Since Debussy: A View of Contemporary
    Music. Trans. Noel Burch. New York, Grove, 1961.

Hutcheson, Ernest. The Literature of the Piano: A Guide
    for Amateur and Student. 3rd ed., rev. Rudolf Ganz.
    New York, Knopf, 1964.

Keller, Hans. "The Half-year's New Music," The Music
    Review, XV (August, 1954), 214-15.

Kirby, F. E. A Short History of Keyboard Music. New
    York, The Free Press, 1966.

Machlis, Joseph. Introduction to Contemporary Music.
    New York, Norton, 1961.

Mila, Massimo. "Dallapiccola, Luigi," Die Musik in Ges-
    chichte und Gegenwart, II, 1873-76.

_____. " 'Il Prigioniero' di Luigi Dallapiccola,"
    Rassegna Musicale, XX (October, 1950), 303-11.

_____. "L'Incontro Heine-Dallapiccola," Rassegna
    Musicale, XXVII (December, 1957), 301-08.

Nathan, Hans. "The Twelve-tone Compositions of Luigi
    Dallapiccola," The Musical Quarterly, XLIV (July, 1958),
    289-310.

Perkins, John Macivor. "Dallapiccola's Art of Canon, " Perspectives of New Music, I (Spring, 1963), 95-106.

Prieberg, Fred K. Lexikon der Neuen Musik. Freiburg, Karl Alber, 1958.

Reti, Rudolph. Tonality in Modern Music. New York, Collier, 1962.

Rufer, Josef. Composition with Twelve Notes. Trans. Humphrey Searle. London, Barrie & Rockliff, 1954.

Salzman, Eric. Twentieth-Century Music: An Introduction. Englewood Cliffs, N.J., Prentice-Hall, 1967.

Searle, Humphrey. "Luigi Dallapiccola, " The Listener, XL (November 18, 1948).

Stuckenschmidt, Hans Heinz. Schöpfer der Neuen Musik: Portraits und Studien. Frankfurt, Suhrkamp, 1958.

Vlad, Roman. "Dallapiccola, 1948-55, " The Score, XV (March, 1956), 39-62.

_____. "Luigi Dallapiccola, " trans. Toni del Renzio, Horizon, XX (December, 1949-January, 1950), 379-391.

_____. Luigi Dallapiccola. Trans. Cynthia Jolly. Milan, Suvini Zerboni, 1957.

_____. Modernità e Tradizione nella Musica Contemporanea. Milan, Einaudi, 1955.

_____. Storia della Dodecafonia. Milan, Suvini Zerboni, 1958.

Wildberger, Jacques. "Dallapiccolas 'Cinque Canti', " Melos, XXVI (January, 1959), 7-10.

Wörner, Karl H. "Dallapiccolas Job, " Melos, XXI (July-August, 1954), 208-10.

Zillig, Winfried. Variationen über Neue Musik. Munich, Nymphenburger, 1959.

DECAUX, ABEL

(b.  1869; d.  1941)

Abel Decaux, an organist-composer who taught organ in Rochester, New York, for a brief period, as well as in his native France, wrote a number of piano works. Norman Demuth has described four pieces entitled Clair de Lune (1901-1907) as the earliest examples of serial writing.[32] The works are out-of-print but Demuth includes a few excerpts to illustrate what he aptly describes as "serial impressionism." The vision of Decaux is obvious even in these short examples, particularly in the striking sonorities. The thematic and harmonic treatment, original at their time, suggest similarity to the serial style about to be established by Schoenberg. Decaux's work was unique but his isolation and obscurity was almost complete and apparently none of his immediate successors in the field of serial composition were acquainted with his ideas.

Bibliography

Austin, William W.  Music in the 20th Century: From Debussy through Stravinsky.  New York, Norton, 1966.

Brelet, Gisèle. "Un ³Schoenberg Français²: Abel Decaux," Schweizerische Musikzeitung, CI (1961), 33.

Demuth, Norman.  French Piano Music.  London, Museum Press, 1959.

DE KRUYF, TON

(b. Leerdam, The Netherlands, October 3, 1937)
Address:  Burmanstraat 11; Amsterdam, The Netherlands.

Ton de Kruyf is largely self-taught in the use of serial techniques, which he has employed since 1958.

Sgrafitti per Pianoforte (1960) gets its title from an Italian word meaning to steal, or pilfer, apropos of the manner in which the serial ordering of the notes is constantly juggled. Also, de Kruyf may either delete or supplement the tones of the thematic sequence, so that more or less than twelve tones occur.

Piano Music

Sgrafitti per Pianoforte (1960).    Amsterdam, Donemus,
    1963.

Bibliography

"Kruyf, Ton de, " 1965 Supplement to Baker's Biographical
    Dictionary of Musicians (5th ed.), 73.

DE LEEUW, TON

(b.  Rotterdam, November 16, 1926)
Address:  Costeruslaan 4; Hilversum, The Netherlands

        Ton de Leeuw studied mainly with Henk Badings,
Olivier Messiaen, and Thomas de Hartmann.   Although his
compositions are few, they display a variety of contemporary
techniques.

        The rhythmic element is the dominant feature in his
style, as he employs ever-changing permutations of the initial rhythmic ideas.   Men Go Their Ways (1963-64), for
piano solo, reflects his interest in oriental music, being
five interpretations of a Japanese haiku.   Musical expression
of a series of geometric structures constitutes one layer of
the texture.   A second layer incorporates the element of
chance. [33] The score provides both traditional and a proportional notation, indicating relative time-values.

Piano Music

Men Go Their Ways.   Amsterdam, Donemus, 1964.

Bibliography

"Leeuw, Ton de, " 1965 Supplement to Baker's Biographical
    Dictionary of Musicians (5th ed.), 76.

Leeuw, Ton de.   "Mensen en Muziek in India: Reisdagboekbla-
    den, " Mens en Melodie, XVIII (1963), 213, 219.

_____ . "Music of the 20th Century," Sonorum Speculum,
XX (1964), 1.

_____ . Muziek van de Twintigste Eeuw: een Onderzoek
naar haar Elementen & Structur. Utrecht, Oosthoek,
1964.

McDermott, Vincent. "Current Chronicle: The Netherlands," The Musical Quarterly, LII (October, 1966),
511-20.

Paap, Wouter. "De Componist Ton de Leeuw," Mens en
Melodie, XVIII (1963), 134.

Wouters, Jos. "Dutch Music in the 20th Century," The
Musical Quarterly, LI (Jan., 1965), pp. 97-110.

_____ . "Ton de Leeuw," Sonorum Speculum, XIX
(1964), 1-28.


DE PABLO, LUIS

(b. Bilbao, Spain, January 28, 1930)
Address: Velásquez 17; Madrid 1, Spain


        Luis de Pablo received his musical training in
Madrid.  He was attracted to the use of serial techniques
from his earliest composition, although tonality is sometimes incorporated into a predominantly serial idiom, in
his works.  The Sonata para Piano, Op. 3 (1953),[34] is
considered the first serial work written in Spain.[35]  It
demonstrates a use of serialism at an advanced level that
has an affinity with the late Webern style, as evidenced by
the striking use of silence, the thin texture of the canonic
writing, and the types of dissonant sounds.  The originality
stems from the treatment of the rhythmic element.  The key
to the over-all structure lies in the continuous variation and
transformation of the non-retrogradable rhythmic patterns, a
hallmark of de Pablo's compositions.

        By 1957 de Pablo's mastery of serialism led him
to renounce or revise his previous scores.  The Libro
para el Pianista, Op. 11 (1960), is only partially serial, in
that it employs the chance principle.  (The composer intends
to add to the three sections presently constituting the work.)

Piano Music

Sonata para Piano, Op. 3 (1953).   Madrid, Union Musical
    Espanola, 1960.

Movil I fur Zwei Klaviere (1958).   Darmstadt, Tonos, n.d.

Libro para el Pianista (1961-62).   Darmstadt, Tonos, 1964.

Movil II pour un Piano et Deux Pianistes (1959-67).   Paris,
    Salabert, n.d.

Bibliography

Custer, Arthur.   "Contemporary Music in Spain," The
    Musical Quarterly, LI (1965),  44-60.

"De Pablo, Luis," 1965 Supplement to Baker's Biographical
    Dictionary of Musicians (5th ed.),  32-33.

Haines, Edmund.   "Current Chronicle: Spain," The Musical
    Quarterly, LII (1966),  380-83.


DICKINSON, PETER


(b.   Lytham St. Annes, Lancashire, November 15, 1934)
Address:   11 Tregunter Road; London S. W. 10, England

       Peter Dickinson received an M.A. degree in music
from the University of Cambridge.   He then lived in New
York from 1958 until 1960, studying with Bernard Wagenaar
at Juilliard.   Interest in the styles of Schoenberg and Ives
and in indeterminacy developed from his contacts with such
American composers as Henry Cowell and John Cage.

       The Five Essays for Piano (1956) is among the early
twelve-tone works written in a strict style during Dickinson's
student days.   The pieces are united by a logical design,
according to which the O form of the series is the basis
for the first; the O and I; R; and R and R and I forms,
respectively, the material for the next three, and finally,
the last is a fugue employing all four of the basic forms.
Tonal elements occur frequently in the form of major or
minor triads derived from the row.

Dickinson's twelve-tone writing has developed rather freely so that the components of a row are frequently other than twelve tones.   The Variations for Piano (1957) contains short tone rows combined with rhythmic series.   This work has been transformed into an orchestral ballet entitled Vitalities.

Dickinson has begun to combine his twelve-tone techniques with electronic composition.   He also writes much music in a simple vein, generally tonal in nature, to satisfy his desire to provide easy music for educational purposes or church usage.   Five Diversions and Five Forgeries (both dated 1963) are light piano works intended for young students.

Piano Music

Five Essays for Piano (1956).   Facsim.   reprod.

Variations for Piano (1957).   Facsim.   reprod.

Bibliography

"Dickinson, Peter, " 1965 Supplement to Baker's Biographical
    Dictionary of Musicians (5th ed.),  34.

Lowens, Irving.   "Current Chronicle: Washington, " The
    Musical Quarterly, LIII (1967),  400-402.

Norrington, Roger.   "Peter Dickinson, " The Musical Times,
    (1965),  109-110.

DONATONI, FRANCO

(b. Verona, June 9, 1927)
Address:   Via Carpi 20; Milan, Italy

Franco Donatoni received a diploma in music from Bologna University in 1951.   He later studied with Ildebrando Pizzetti in Rome and is now on the faculty of the Milan Conservatory.   His compositions include several chamber and orchestral works in an experimental style seeking to combine serial and aleatory methods.

Donatoni's first use of the Schoenberg technique is found in Cinque Pezzi per Due Pianoforte (1954) for two

pianos. The Composizione in Quattro Moviment (1955) is
a fairly straightforward twelve-tone work, employing the
basic row in all four of its movements, with minor re-
ordering of the pitch series. The row is used both melodically and harmonically, with the harmonic structures
frequently constituting the main musical events. The work
being devoid of strong or weak beats, rhythmic movement
is a by-product of the efforts to create a time-space relationship by the contrast between chordal structures, which
are repeated two or more times in close succession, and
short melodic figures containing  wide leaps (usually notated
as triplets). Wide intervals and pointillism, balanced by
the frequent interpolation of chords, and distinctive features
in much of Donatoni's writing.

The inspiration of Boulez's Second Piano Sonata, and
Donatoni's increasing interest in pure sound, led to the
piano score, Tre Espressione (1957).[36] In this work, the
emphasis is shifted gradually from series of sounds to
improvisational, totally chromatic sections.

Doubles (1961) has a more complex style, moving
beyond the Webern influence. Donatoni's system of notation
is highly developed. Intricate asymmetrical rhythms,
derived from the basic series, are bracketed in terms of
the basic unit. The original tone-row does not recur although the nature of the original row is somewhat maintained
by the close correspondence to its counterpart in the antecedent row that specific tones enjoy in each new form of
the series. To this is added one further device for the
maintenance of unity:  the relationship between the rows,
as well as of each derived row to the original is to be re-
inforced by the constant recurrence of three-note segments
of identical pitches.

Babai per Clavicembalo (1964) is a set of pieces
depicted in Donatoni's graphic notation. He has extended to
a highly sophisticated level his use of integral variation as
the basis of continual transformation of a basic series. The
work is a revision of Doubles. Performance of it requires
the use of a contraption constructed of wooden prongs at-
tached to the piano.

Piano Music

Cinque Pezzi per Due Pianoforte (1954). Padua, Zanibon, n.d.

Composizione in Quattro Movimenti (1955).   London,  Schott,
    1957.

Tre Improvisazioni per Pianoforte (1957).   London,  Schott,
    1958.

Doubles: Esercizi per Clavicembalo.   Milan,  Suvini Zerboni,
    1961.

Babai per Clavicembalo (1964).   Milan,  Suvini Zerboni,  1965.

Bibliography

Bortolotto,  Mario.   "The New Music in Italy, " trans.
    William C. Holmes, The Musical Quarterly,  LI
    (January,  1965),  61-77.

Brindle,  Reginald Smith.   "The Lunatic Fringe: III,  Compu-
    tational Composition, " The Musical Times,  No. 97,
    (July,  1956),  354-56.

"Donatoni,  Franco, " Baker's Biographical Dictionary of
    Musicians.   Fifth Edition with 1965 Supplement,  35.

Maegaard,  Jan.   Musikalsk Modernisme 1945-1962.
    Copenhagen,  Stig Vendelkaers,  1964.

FORTNER,  WOLFGANG

(b.   Leipzig,  October 12,  1907)
Address: Mühltalstrasse 122; 69 Heidelberg,  West Germany

        Wolfgang Fortner studied philosophy and received his
musical training at the Leipzig Conservatory in the years
1927 to 1931.   In addition to composing,  he has become a
famed composition teacher,  a conductor,  and an active
organizer of contemporary concerts.   As a teacher,  Fortner
advocates studying the styles of major composers as the
surest way to develop originality.

        Two piano works,  the Sonatina (1936) and the
Kammer-musik (1944) precede his dodecaphonic style.   The
Sieben Elegien für Klavier (1950) employs a strict twelve-
tone technique.   All of the seven pieces are based on a single
row,  developed in each,  so as to produce a sense of striking

contrast within the work as a whole. Almost all the
standard transpositions and retrograde forms occur in this
work.

Epigramme für Klavier (1964) is the only piano solo
work Fortner has written since the Elegien. Comparison
of these two works reveals a considerable change of style.
In Epigramme, the rhythmic design breaks away from the
symmetry of neo-classic writing and assumes a very free
movement. The score exemplifies Fortner's mature serial
style, a forceful combination of a rhythmic design closely
allied with that of Schoenberg and Webern, and the use of
contrapuntal techniques associated more closely with Bach
and Max Reger.

Piano Music

Sieben Elegien für Klavier (1950). London, Schott, 1951.

Epigramme für Klavier (1964). Mainz, Schott, 1965.

Bibliography

Austin, William W. Music in the 20th Century: From
    Debussy through Stravinsky. New York, Norton, 1966.

Bartlett, K. W. "Fortner, Wolfgang," Grove's Dictionary
    of Music and Musicians (5th ed.), III, 451-52.

Dangel, Arthur. "Wolfgang Fortner (Impromptus)," Melos,
    XXVII (March, 1960), 79-84; (April, 1960), 107-112.

Driesch, Kurt. "Wolfgang Fortner: Zum Funfzigsten Geburt-
    stag des Deutschen Komponisten," Geist und Zeit, VI
    (1957), 119-124.

Engelmann, Hans Ulrich. "Fortners Phantasie über B-A-C-H,"
    Melos, XXI (May, 1954), 131-135.

"Fortner, Wolfgang," Baker's Biographical Dictionary of
    Music and Musicians. Fifth Edition with 1965 Musical
    Supplement, 498; 43.

Fortner, Wolfgang. "Bluthochzeit, nach Federico Garcia
    Lorca," Melos, XXIV (March, 1957), 71-73.

_____. "Geistliche Musik Heute. Vortrag beim X. Schütz-Fest, Düsseldorf 1956," Die Stimme der Komponisten, H. Lindlar, ed. Rodenkirchen, Germany, n.p., 1958.

_____. "Komposition als Unterricht," Archiv für Musikwissenschaft, XVI (1954), 100.

_____. "Subtile Verständigung, Akzente, IV (1957), 121.

_____. "Die Weltsprache der Neuen Musik," Das Musikalische Selbstportrait, J. Müller-Marein and H. Reinhardt, eds. Hamburg, n.p., 1963.

Friedländer, Walther. "Moderner Kompositionsunterricht bei Wolfgang Fortner an der Nordwestdeutschen Musikakademie," Neue Zeitschrift für Musik, CXVI (November, 1955), 113-114.

Helm, Everett. "Current Chronicle: Germany," The Musical Quarterly, XXXVII (April, 1951), 267-269.

_____. "Current Chronicle: Germany," The Musical Quarterly, XXXVII (October, 1952), 606-610.

_____. "Six Modern German Composers," American-German Review, XXIII (December, 1956-January, 1957), 12-15.

Laaff, Ernst. "Fortner, Wolfgang," Die Musik in Geschichte und Gegenwart, IV, 580-83.

_____. "Wolfgang Fortner," Melos, XXI (November, 1954), 307-310.

Laux, Karl. "Wolfgang Fortner," Musik und Musiker der Gegenwart, 97-104.

Lindlar, H., ed. Wolfgang Fortner: eine Monographie: Werkanalysen, Aufsätze, Reden. Rodenkirchen, Germany, Tonger, 1960.

Prieberg, Fred K. Lexikon der Neuen Musik. Freiburg, Karl Alber, 1958.

Rufer, Josef.  Composition with Twelve Notes Related Only
    to one Another.  Trans.  Humphrey Searle.  London,
    Barrie and Rockliff, 1954.

Stephan, Rudolf.  "Gegenwärtiges Komponieren; Ein Uber-
    blick: Fortner, Pepping, Orff, Egk, Hartmann,"
    Deutsche Universitätszeitung, VI (Sept. 28, 1951), 12-13.

Stuckenschmidt, Hans Heinz.  "Synthesis and New Exper-
    iments: Four Contemporary German Composers," trans.
    Abram Loft.  The Musical Quarterly, XXXVIII (July,
    1952), 353-368.

Unger, Udo.  Die Klavierfuge im Zwanzigsten Jahrhundert.
    Regemsburg, Germany, Gustav Bosse, 1956.

Vlad, Roman.  Storia della Dodecafonia.  Milan, Suvini
    Zerboni, 1958.

Wörner, Karl H.  Neue Musik in der Entscheidung.  Mainz,
    Schott, 1954.

_____.  "Wolfgang Fortner in Seinen Werken Seit
    1945," Schweizerische Musikzeitung, XCIII (June, 1953),
    260-263.

Zillig, Winfried.  Variationen über Neue Musik.  Munich,
    Nymphenburger, 1959.


FRICKER, PETER RACINE

(b.  London, September 5, 1920)
Address:  G 155 Verdura Avenue; Goleta, Santa Barbara,
California, 93106

     Peter Racine Fricker studied at the Royal College
of Music in London, where R. O. Morris was his principal
composition teacher.  Following the war he studied with
Mátyás Seiber for about two years and broadened his musical scope to admit both Schoenberg's concept and jazz style.

     Two of his piano works are written in twelve-tone
style, "Four Sonnets for Piano" (1955) and Variations for
Piano Op. 31, (1958).  Each of the short sonnets is derived
from one of the four basic forms of the row.  Although

Fricker employs considerable flexibility in ordering the row,
he remains within the strict dodecaphonic style as re-ordering usually occurs within a four note segment. This type
of freedom is also found in the Variations, based on a row
that is never stated in its complete form.[37] This elaborate
work contains many sections of a rhapsodic nature. In such
passages tonal implications are particularly evident, in
spite of the twelve-tone basis of the work. This tonal
quality can be attributed to rhythmic patterns and chordal
qualities highly reminiscent of Chopin or Liszt. The Twelve
Studies for Piano, Op. 38 (1961), move into the category of
free serialism, as does most of Fricker's work of the last
few years.[38] The preponderance of thick vertical structures
is reduced to an exploitation of one or more specific intervals in each study. The strong influence of virtuoso styles
of the romantic era is retained. Fricker's twelve-tone
and serial techniques tend to be camouflaged by the more
traditional forces he includes.

   Fricker was the Director of  Music at Morley
College in London for several years before assuming a
position on the faculty of the University of California at
Santa Barbara in 1964.

## Piano Music

"Four Sonnets for Piano," (1950) Contemporary British
   Piano Music. London, Schott, 1956.

Variations for Piano, Op. 31 (1958). London, Schott, 1959.

Twelve Studies for Piano, Op. 38 (1961). London, Schott,
   1962.

## Bibliography

Cooke, Deryck. "Fricker, Peter Racine," Die Musik in Geschichte und Gegenwart, IV, 936-37.

Mason, Colin. "Fricker, Peter Racine," Grove's Dictionary
   of Music and Musicians (5th ed.), III, 498-500.

"Fricker, Peter Racine," Baker's Biographical Dictionary of
   Musicians. Fifth Edition with 1965 Supplement, 512; 44.

Schafer, Murray. British Composers in Interview. London,
    Faber & Faber, 1963.


GOEHR, ALEXANDER

(b. Berlin, August 10, 1932)
Address: 3 Meredyth Road; Barnes; London S. W. 1,
England

    Alexander Goehr is the son of the former conductor,
Walter Goehr, who had been a student of Schoenberg. The
younger Goehr studied at the Paris Conservatory, where he
was a student of Olivier Messiaen from 1955 to 1956.

    Goehr's music is characterized by much dissonance
which can be interpreted harmonically with the same ease as
traditional harmonies. His rhythmic expression is rather
complex and partly derives from the ideas of Messiaen.
His early works can generally be described as polyphonic
atonality, but Goehr gradually progressed toward a more
dodecaphonic style and is now ranked as a serial composer.

    Goehr's Sonata for Piano, Op. 2 (1952), was intended
as a tribute to Serge Prokofieff and the opening theme of
Prokofieff's Seventh Symphony is incorporated in the con-
clusion. The score is dominated by a complex rhythmic
movement controlling all the other musical elements.

    In the Capriccio for Piano, Op. 6 (1957), the row is
so constructed that permutation of the hexachords in the
prime forms is guaranteed. Goehr then extended his permutation techniques to the derived forms.

    In 1954 Goehr participated, with several progressive
English composers, in the founding of the New Manhattan
Group. For the most part, however, Goehr is considered
a serial composer belonging to no school.

Piano Music

Sonata for Piano, Op. 2 (1952). London, Schott, 1955.

Capriccio for Piano, Op. 6 (1958). London, Schott, 1959.

Three Pieces for Piano, Op. 18 (1965).   London, Schott,
    n. d.

Bibliography

"Goehr, Alexander, " 1965 Supplement to Baker's Biographic-
    al Dictionary of Musicians (5th ed. ),  48.

Goehr, Alexander.  "Is There Only One War?" The Score,
    XXVI (1960),  63.

Porter, Andrew.  "Some New British Composers, " The
    Musical Quarterly, LI (January,  1965),  12-21.

Schafer, Murray.  British Composers in Interview.   London,
    Faber & Faber,  1963.

HALFFTER, CRISTOBAL

(b.   Madrid, March 24,  1930)
Address:   Calle de la Bola 2; Madrid, Spain

        Cristobal Halffter, a nephew of the composers
Ernesto and Rudolfo Halffter, studied under Conrado del
Campo and Alexandre Tansman.   His earlier compositions
are in an atonal style, marked by the influence of Bartók
and Stravinsky.   He has employed serial techniques since
the mid-1950's.

        Whereas a piano sonata he composed in 1951 is neo-
classic, the Introducción, Fuga y Final, Op.  15 (1957), is
one of Haffter's first twelve-tone works.[39]   Halffter tends
to maintain wide separation of the registers between the two
hands and to contrast thin textures with passages in which
the texture is thickened by considerable octave doubling.

        The Formantes por Dos Pianos, Op.  26 (1961),
employs both serial and aleatory principles.[40]

Piano Music

Formantes por Dos Pianos, Op.  26 (1961).   o. p.

Introducción, Fuga y Final, Op.  15 (1957).   Madrid, Union
    Musical Espanola,  1959.

Bibliography

Chase, Gilbert. The Music of Spain. 2nd rev. ed.
    New York, Dover, 1959.

Custer, Arthur. "Contemporary Music in Spain," The
    Musical Quarterly, LI (January, 1965), 44-60.

Gillespie, John. Five Centuries of Keyboard Music: An
    Historical Survey of Music for Harpsichord and Piano.
    Belmont, Calif., Wadsworth Pub. Co., 1965.

Haines, Edmund. "Current Chronicle: Spain," The Musical
    Quarterly, LII (July, 1966), 380-83.

"Halffter, Cristobal," 1965 Supplement to Baker's Biographi-
    cal Dictionary of Musicians (5th ed.), 52.

## HAMILTON, IAIN ELLIS

(b. Glasgow, June 6, 1922)
Address: 40 Park Avenue, New York, New York

Iain Hamilton abandoned his engineering profession at
the age of twenty-four and turned to music. He studied
composition with William Alwyn and piano with Harold Crax-
ton at the Royal Academy of Music in London and completed
his B. Mus. degree at London University.

The Piano Sonata, Op. 13 (1951), is representative
of his early composition. The most striking feature of
the early works is the rhythm which is reminiscent of the
rhythm of Béla Bartók. The beginning of his serial usage is
evident in the Three Pieces for Piano, Op. 30 (1955).
While considerable evidence of tonality is apparent, these
pieces fall within the classic twelve-tone technique of Schoenberg.

Even though Hamilton has employed serial techniques
increasingly, he has not abandoned tonality. Rather, he
shows a masterful control over varied stylistic features
in which he effectively imposes a serial form as in
Nocturnes with Cadenzas (1963). He has been able to avoid
suggestions of an overtly synthetical style.

Hamilton lectures widely in both Europe and the United States, and has been very active in organizations promoting contemporary music. In 1962 he joined the faculty at Duke University in North Carolina.

## Piano Music

"Three Pieces for Piano, Op. 30." Contemporary British Piano Music. London, Schott, 1956.

Nocturnes with Cadenzas (1963). London, Schott, 1968.

## Bibliography

Beckwith, John and Udo Kasemets, eds. The Modern Composer and His World. Toronto, Univ. of Toronto Press, 1961.

Farmer, Henry George. "Hamilton, Iain," Die Musik in Geschichte und Gegenwart, V, 1419-21.

Hamilton, Iain. "Reflections of a British Composer in America," Perspectives of New Music, V (1966), 134-38.

"Hamilton, Iain," Baker's Biographical Dictionary of Music. Fifth Edition with 1965 Supplement, 646; 53.

Mason, Colin. "Hamilton, Iain," Grove's Dictionary of Music and Musicians (5th ed.), IV, 32-33.

Schafer, Murray. British Composers in Interview. London, Faber & Faber, 1963.

## HAUER, JOSEF MATTHIAS

(b. Wiener-Neustadt, Austria, March 19, 1883; d. Vienna, September 22, 1959)

Joseph Hauer originated a system of composition analagous to Wolfgang von Goethe's basic concepts in his Farbenlehre.[41] Hauer's basic premise was that the interval provided the composer with a source for all rhythmic and melodic development. Hauer disregarded both the distinction between consonance and dissonance and the principle of diatonic tendencies of scale tones. The twelve scale degrees

were calculated as having a potential of 479,001,600 rows.
(This is the maximum number of rows in any twelve-tone
system.) Hauer demonstrated that this potential could be
reduced to 44 tropes in which patterned arrangements of the
two hexachords constitute a row.  Only two chords derived
from each segment were to be employed for harmonic
purposes.  The inner notes of each trope could be freely
rearranged for thematic purposes but this freedom did not
apply to the chords.  A composition could be extended by
permutation, inversion, or transposition of a trope, but as
no specific order is employed within a set,  retrograde
motion is not a basic technique.[42]

Hauer compared his principles to those of gravitation
and tension in the science of mechanics.  He considered
gravity to be produced by the overtones of a sound, and
tension  by the twelve chromatic tones of each independent
row.  However, if certain tones are emphasized,  the balance
is such that tonal music actually results, although Hauer's
aim was to avoid emphasis on any specific tones and thereby
maintain an equal balance and an atonal quality.

There is a close parallel between the time periods
during which Hauer and Schoenberg devised their similar
systems.  Hauer began the classification of his tropes about
1908, and completed his method about 1918.  Schoenberg's
semi-retirement, during which he clarified his concepts,
was from 1915 to 1923.[43]

Many of Hauer's theoretical ideas are obviously
similar to Schoenberg's.  However, the similarities in
theory between the systems of Hauer and Schoenberg are
not always apparent in practice.  The intended freedom of
dissonance in Hauer's musical style is not audibly effective.
Predetermination of the chords which may accompany each
segment places a limitation on the harmonic material.  The
linear potential is also restricted by the inflexibility of a
twelve-tone row divided, essentially, into two six-tone rows
within which the hexachordal relationships are confined.
The result is a harmonic texture that sounds tonal in the
traditional sense and which projects a monotonous quality
through the excessive repetitions.

Hauer's system fell into oblivion for two main
reasons.  His compositions tend to be repetitious in style,
and so reminiscent of such romantic composers as Scriabin,

Satie, and Chopin, that his innovations were ignored. He
also invented a system of notation that was not accepted.[44]
Consequently, his compositions are largely unpublished although a number of his books are still in circulation.

Piano Music

Zwölftonspiel. Eigentum und Verlag von J. M. Hauer für
    alle Länder, 1946.

Zwölftonspiel (1955). Vienna, Fortissimo, 1963.

Zwölftonspiel (zu Vier Händen). Wiesbaden, Doblinger, 1956.

Bibliography

Austin, William W.  Music in the 20th Century: From
    Debussy through Stravinsky.  New York, Norton, 1966.

Bauer, Marion.  Twentieth Century Music.  New York,
    Putnum, 1947.

Brindle, Reginald Smith.  Serial Composition.  London,
    Oxford Univ. Press, 1966.

Dibelius, Ulrich.  Moderne Musik 1945-1964.  Munich, R.
    Piper, 1966.

Eimert, Herbert.  "Hauer, Josef Matthias," Die Musik in
    Geschichte und Gegenwart, V, 1823-24.

Eisenmann, Will.  "Zur Sache Hauer," Schweizerische
    Musikzeitung, LXXXVIII (September, 1948), 353-354.

Eschmann, Karl.  Changing Forms in Modern Music.
    Boston, Schirmer, 1945.

Galli, Hans.  Moderne Musik-leicht Verständlich.  Munich,
    Francke, 1964.

Goethe, Johann Wolfgang von.  Farbenlehre.  Leipzig,
    Insel, 1926.

Glover, Robert F.  "The Theories and Music of Josef
    Matthias Hauer."  Unpub. doctoral dissertation, Columbia
    Univ. N.Y., n.d.

"Hauer, Josef Matthias," Baker's Biographical Dictionary of
    Music and Musicians. Fifth Edition with 1965 Supplement
    671; 54.

Hauer, Josef Matthias. "Atonale Musik," Die Musik, XVI
    (November, 1923), 103-106.

_____. "Melos und Rhythmus," Melos, III (1922), 186.

_____. Sphärenmusik," Melos, III (1922), 132.

_____. Von Melos zur Pauke: eine Einführung in die
    Zwölftonmusik. Vienna, Universal Edition, 1925.

_____. Zwölftontechnik, Die Lehre von den Tropen.
    Vienna, Universal Edition, 1926.

_____. Vom Wesen des Musikalischen: ein Lehrbuch
    der Atonalen Musik. Berlin, Schlesinger, 1923.

Lichtenfeld, Monika. Untersuchungen zur Theorie der
    Zwölftontechnik bei Josef Matthias Hauer. Regensburg,
    Germany, Gustav Bosse, 1964.

_____. "Schönberg und Hauer," Melos, XXXII (1965),
    118.

Machabey, Armand. "La Singulière Figure de Jean-Mathias
    Hauer, Musicien Autrichien," Revue Musicale, XII
    (March, 1931), 221-233.

Melichar, Alois. Musik in der Zwangsjacke: Die Deutsche
    Musik Zwischen Orff und Schönberg. Vienna, Wancura,
    1958.

Mila, Massimo. "Lettera da Venezia," Rassegna Musicale,
    XXIV (October, December, 1954), 352.

Mitchell, Donald. The Language of Modern Music. New
    York, St. Martin's, 1966.

Perle, George. "The Harmonic Problem in Twelve-Tone
    Music," The Music Review, XV (November, 1954),
    257-267.

Pfrogner, Hermann. Die Zwölfordnung der Töne. Zürich,
    Amalthea, 1953.

Picht, Hermann. Joseph Hauer: Ein Vorkaempfer Geistiger Musikauffassung. Stuttgart, n.p., 1934.

Pöstinger, Oswald. "Das Josef-Matthias-Hauer-Studio: eine Pflegestätte Echter Geistigkeit," Musik-Erziehung, XVIII (1965), 168.

Prieberg, Fred K. Lexikon der Neuen Musik. Freiburg, Karl Alber, 1958.

Redlich, Hans Ferdinand. "Hauer, Josef (Matthias)," Grove's Dictionary of Music and Musicians (5th ed.), IV, 135-137.

Reich, Willi. "Joseph Matthias Hauer," Die Musik, XXIII (May, 1931), 477-581.

_____. "Versuch einer Geschichte der Zwölftonmusik," Alte und Neue Musik; das Basler Kammerorchester . . . 1926-1501. Zürich, Atlantis, 1952.

Reti, Rudolph. Tonality in Modern Music. New York, Collier, 1962.

Rochberg, George. "The Harmonic Tendency of the Hexachord," Journal of Music Theory, III (November, 1959), 208-230.

Salazar, Adolfo. Music in Our Time: Trends in Music Since the Romantic Era. Trans. Isabel Pope. New York, Norton, 1946.

Schlee, Alfred. "Vienna Since the Anschluss," Modern Music, XXIII (Spring, 1946), 95-99.

Schmale, Erich. "Die Zwölftonmusik von Josef Matthias Hauer," Schweizerische Musikzeitung, LXXXVIII (July, 1948), 305-306.

Schwieger, Johannes. "Josef Matthias Hauer," Osterreichische Musik Zeitschrift, XII (March, 1957), 108-109.

Searle, Humphrey. "Twelve-note Music," Grove's Dictionary of Music and Musicians (5th ed.), VIII, 617-23.

Simbriger, Heinrich. "Die Situation der Zwölftonmusik, "
   Musik und Kirche, XXVI (September-October, 1956),
   209-223.

Smolyan, Walter, Josef Matthias Hauer. Vienna, Oster-
   reichischer Bundesverlag, 1965.

Stein, Erwin. Arnold Schoenberg Letters. Trans. Eithne
   Wilkins and Ernst Kaiser. New York, St. Martin's,
   1965.

Stephan, Rudolph. "Uber Josef Matthias Hauer, " Archiv
   für Musikwissenschaft, XVIII (1961), 265.

Stuckenschmidt, Hans Heinz. "Josef Matthias Hauer, "
   Musikblätter des Anbruch, X (August-September, 1928),
   245-249.

Vlad, Roman. Storia della Dodecafonia. Milan, Suvini
   Zerboni, 1958.

Wildgans, Friedrich. "Josef Matthias Hauer zum 75.
   Geburtstag, " Osterreichische Musik Zeitschrift, XIII
   (March, 1958), 108-110.


HENZE, HANS WERNER

(b. Gütersloh, Germany, July 1, 1926)
Address: Castel Gandolfo di Roma; Via dei Caghi 8; Rome,
Italy


Hans Werner Henze began his musical career as a
pianist and percussionist. Following World War II, he
studied composition with Wolfgang Fortner. Recently Henze
has concentrated upon the writing of operas but his list of
works includes a wide variety of other styles and forms.

Henze's first twelve-tone work was a Violin Concerto
(1947). Interest in serial techniques led him to study with
René Leibowitz in 1948. The Variationen für Klavier (1950)
date from a period in which he was experimenting with the
synthesis of old and new forms. These variations are
written in a fairly strict dodecaphonic style derived from
Schoenberg's technique. It is interesting to note that Henze's

use of twelve-tone ideas is usually followed by one or more
works in a more atonal vein.   For example, the Sonata per
Pianoforte (1959) and Six Absences (1961) revert to atonalism
according to this pattern.   Motivic treatment similar to
Schoenberg's is often featured in Henze's atonal style.   On
occasion, a pointillistic style similar to that of Webern becomes a dominant feature, as in the Sonata. Henze thereby
reveals both characteristics in his atonal works which in
the early stages of twelve-tone writing differentiated the
styles of Schoenberg and Webern.

Piano Music

Variationen für Klavier, Op. 13.   London, Schott, 1950.

Sonata per Pianoforte (1959).   Mainz, Schott, 1960.

Six Absences (1961).   Mainz, Schott, 1964.

Bibliography

Austin, William W.   Music in the 20th Century: From
    Debussy through Stravinsky.   New York, Norton, 1966.

Bartlett, K. W. "Henze, Hans Werner," Grove's Dictionary
    of Music and Musicians (5th ed.), IV, 244-245.

Cadieu, Martine.   "Hans Werner Henze," Nouvelles Littér-
    aires (October   11,  1962), 9.

Dibelius, Ulrich.   Moderne Musik 1945-1965.   Munich, R.
    Piper, 1966.

Helm, Everett.   "Current Chronicle: Germany," The
    Musical Quarterly, XLV (April, 1959), 241-248.

_____ .  "Six Modern German Composers," American-
    German Review, XXII (December-January, 1957), 12-15.

_____ .  "Current Chronicle: Germany," The Musical
    Quarterly, LII (January, 1966), 101-106.

_____ .  "Current Chronicle: Germany," The Musical
    Quarterly, LIII (July, 1965), 408-15.

"Henze, Hans Werner," Baker's Biographical Dictionary
   of Music and Musicians. Fifth Edition with 1965 Supplement, 696-697; 56.

Henze, Hans Werner. "Das Neue 'Marienleben'," Melos,
   XVI (1949), 75.

_____. Essays. Mainz & Dondon, n.p., 1964.

_____. "Gefahren in der Neuen Musik," Die Stimme
   der Komponisten, H. Lindlar, ed. Rodenkirchen, Germany, n.p., 1958.

_____. "In einem Einzigen Satz," Melos, XXXII (1965),
   74.

Kay, Norman. "Henze, Present-Day Romantic," Music and
   Musicians, XIII (January, 1965), 201.

LaMotte, Diether de. Hans Werner Henze: Der Prinz von
   Homburg: eine Versuch über die Komposition und den
   Komponisten. Mainz, n.p., 1960.

Mitchell, Donald. The Language of Modern Music. New
   York, St. Martin's, 1966.

Pauli, Hansjörg. "Hans Werner Henze," Musica, XIII
   (1959), 26.

_____. "Hans Werner Henze's Italian Music," The
   Score (1959), 26-37.

Prieberg, Fred K. Lexikon der Neuen Musik. Freiburg,
   Karl Alber, 1958.

Rostand, Claude. "König Hirsch de H. Werner Henze,"
   La Table Ronde, CIX (January, 1957), 157-158.

Rufer, Josef. Composition with Twelve Notes Related Only
   to One Another. Trans. Humphrey Searle. London,
   Barrie and Rockliff, 1954.

Stephan, Rudolf. "Hans Werner Henze," Die Reihe, IV
   (1960), 29-35.

Stuckenschmidt, Hans Heinz. "Hans Werner Henze:
  Porträt eines Komponisten," Neue Zeitschrift für Musik,
  CXVIII (September, 1957), 491-492.

_____. "Henze, Hans Werner," Die Musik in Geschichte
  und Gegenwart, VI, 176-79.

_____. " ⁸Konig Hirsch⁸ (Re Cervo) di Hans Werner
  Henze," Rassegna Musicale, XXVII (June, 1957), 153-155.

_____. "Synthesis and New Experiments: Four Contempo-
  rary German Composers," trans. Abram Loft, The
  Musical Quarterly, XXXVIII (July, 1952), 353-68.

Vlad, Roman. Storia della Dodecafonia. Milan, Suvini
  Zerboni, 1958.

Zillig, Winfried. Variationen über Neue Musik. Munich,
  Nymphenburger, 1959.


JELINEK, HANNS

(b. Vienna, December 5, 1901)
Address: Schellein-Gasse 46; 1040 Vienna, Austria

     Hanns Jelinek is considered the main proponent of
strict adherence to the Schoenberg technique in Austria today.   He studied with both Schoenberg and Berg and adopted the twelve-tone method in the 1930⁸s.   Since Opus 13,
his second string quartet, all his works which bear opus
numbers are in the twelve-tone idiom.

     Jelinek is famous primarily as a leading theoretician
on the subject of strict dodecaphony, his most important
text being Anleitung zur Zwölfton-komposition.   The piano
works of Op. 15 and 21 are designed to supply musical
examples to this theoretical text.   He classifies dodecaphony
into three types: (1) vertical (tones of the row mingle with
different voices), (2) horizontal (complete rows are iterated
melodically), and (3) broken (segments derived from the row
appear simultaneously in different voices).

     The first volume deals exclusively with type one.
In the latter chapters of this volume, he dealt with trans-

position, referring to each of the four basic forms as a
modus. In the second volume he makes further classifications
of twelve-tone schemes into four species and three genera.
The species are: (1) use of a row without modification, (2)
repetitions of individual tones within the row, (3) repetitions
of groups of notes within the row, and (4) division of a
melodic line to simulate polyphony within a single statement
of the row.

The three genera denote respectively themes qualified
by proximity to the concept of a basic twelve-tone row,
partial themes of more or less than twelve notes, and finally
complex themes in which some of the notes are omitted from
the theme itself and relegated to subordinate voices.

The second volume is particularly interesting for the
discussion of what Jelinek considers as abuses in the development of the system (he refers in particular to certain
aspects of total serialization) and for the clarification of
much of the terminology which has become associated with
twelve-tone writing.

Jelinek advocates that the young composer use the
twelve-tone technique conservatively rather than attempt to
exploit all its potential. Jelinek's viewpoint is that developing composition skill by acquiring a basic discipline
in the handling of a single row is a pre-requisite to the
control of more adventuresome experiments.

Piano Music

Four Two-part Inventions, Op. 15, No. 1. Vienna, Universal
    Edition, 1949.

Six Short Character-Sketches, Op. 15, No. 2. Vienna,
    Universal Edition, 1951.

Three Dances, Op. 15, No. 3. Vienna, Universal Edition,
    1951.

Four Toccatas, Op. 15, No. 4. Vienna, Universal Edition,
    1951.

Suite in E/Mi, Op. 15, No. 5. Vienna, Universal Edition,
    1951.

Vier Strukturen für Klavier, Op. 20. Wolfenbüttel, Germany, K. H. Möseler, 1953.

Zwölftonfibel für Klavier, Op. 21. 12 vols. bound in 6 vols. Wolfenbüttel, Germany, K. H. Möseler, 1953, 1954, 1955.

Bibliography

Blaukopf, Kurt. "Current Chronicle: Austria," The Musical Quarterly, XXXVII (July, 1951), 413-416.

Fiechtner, Helmut A. "Hanns Jelinek," Melos, XX (September, 1953), 242-245.

"Jelinek, Hanns," Baker's Biographical Dictionary of Musicians (5th ed.), 779.

Jelinek, Hanns. Anleitung zur Zwölftonkomposition Nebst Allerlei Paralipomena: Appendix zu "Zwölftonwerk," Op. 15. 1er Teil: Allgemeines und Vertikale Dodekaphonik. Vienna, Universal Edition, 1952; 2er Teil: Horizontale Dodekaphonik, Kombinationen und Ableitungen. 1958.

_____. Anhang zu Hanns Jelinek Anleitung zur Zwölftonkomposition: Tabellen und Kompositionsbeispiele von Schoenberg, Webern und Jelinek. 2 vols. Vienna, Universal Edition, n. d.

_____. "Die Krebsgleichen Allintervallreihen," Archiv für Musikwissenschaft, XVIII (1961), 115.

_____. "Versuch über der Sinn der Verwendung von Zwölftonreihen," Melos, XVIII (September, 1961), 252-255.

Klein, Rudolf. "Contemporary Music in Austria," trans. Helen Lange, The Musical Quarterly, LI (January, 1965), 180-190.

Křenek, Ernst. "Reviews of Books," The Musical Quarterly, XL (April, 1954), 250-256.

Prieberg, Fred K. Lexikon der Neuen Musik. Freiburg, Karl Alber, 1958.

Redlich, Hans F.  "Hanns Jelinek," Music Review, XXI
    (February, 1960), 66-72.

Rufer, Josef.  Composition with Twelve Notes Related Only
    to One Another.  Trans.  Humphrey Searle.  London,
    Barrie and Rockliff.  1954.

Tenschert, Roland.  "Hanns Jelinek; zu Seinem 'Zwölfton-
    werk, Op. 15'," Schweizerische Musikzeitung, 91
    (November, 1951), 452-454.

Wildgans, Friedrich.  "Jelinek, Hanns," Die Musik in
    Geschichte und Gegenwart, VI, 1847-50.

Wörner, Karl H.  Neue Musik in der Entscheidung.  Mainz,
    Schott, 1954.


JOLIVET, ANDRE

(b.  Paris, August 8, 1905)
Address: 6 rue Meissouier; Paris 17e, France

As a youth André Jolivet was intrigued by contemporary ideas for expression in art and literature.  He experimented with both painting and writing but his success
in composing a musical setting to some of his own poetry
spurred him to choose a career in musical composition.
He studied with Edgard Varèse who stimulated Jolivet's
interest in new uses of sound.  An intense pre-occupation
with sound which then developed led Jolivet to considerable
activity in the area of electronic music and in 1936 he became one of the earliest users of the ondes martenot.[45]

Jolivet accepts a primitive credo which includes a
belief that life-giving forces exist in both animate and in-
animate things.  His Mana Suite (1935) is a set of six
piano pieces dedicated to Louise Varèse.  The music is
described in a lengthy introduction to the score by Olivier
Messiaen as an effort to express musically the force which
exists in some small articles of wire, straw, or copper
given to Jolivet by Varèse.  Jolivet exploits the keyboard
fully to create a continuum of changing sonorities, employs
another continuum of rhythmic events, and utilizes serial
techniques to maintain control.

Jolivet's efforts to capture musically a psychic state of mind, by coupling mysticism and magic with experiments in sound, has resulted in a variety of styles. At times the effect is atonal but this atonality may be mixed with either strict or free dodecaphony, or possibly some modality, or may even be quite traditional in some respects. While the vertical and horizontal pitch organization of his atonal and serial writing is quite characteristic of the early Austrian dodecaphony, Jolivet's imagination is most fertile in the areas of rhythm and dynamics. He has borrowed from Varése, Bartók, Stravinsky, and French contemporary composers to develop his own ideas about using rhythmic and dynamic effects to bind complex textural relationships into large designs.

The two piano sonatas of 1945 and 1957 are similar in their contrapuntal texture but the earlier is an atonal work whereas the second is serial. The tone-row is frequently treated as two hexachords. The first segment is usually presented in strict iteration whereas the second may be freely re-ordered or may be converted into vertical structures. The initial tone of the original row (G) is often inserted between a statement of the two hexachords. The row also appears in incomplete forms.

Piano Music

Mana: Six Pièces pour Piano (1935). Paris, Costallat, 1946.

Cinq Danses Rituelles. Paris, Durand, 1939.

Première Sonate. London, Universal Edition, 1945.

Deuxième Sonate (1957). Paris, Heugel & Cie, 1959.

Bibliography

Austin, William W. Music in the 20th Century: From Debussy through Stravinsky. New York, Norton, 1966.

Beaufils, Marcel. "Le Concerto pour Piano d'André Jolivet," La Musique Contemporaine, II-III (1952).

Bourdet, Denise. Visages d'Aujourd'hui. Paris, Plon, 1960.

Cohn, Arthur.  Twentieth-century Music in Western
Europe, the Compositions and the Recordings.  Philadelphia, Lippincott, 1965.

Collaer, Paul.  A History of Modern Music.  Trans. Sally
Abeles.  New York, World, 1961.

Delapierre, Guy Bernard.  "Les Danses Rituelles d'André
Jolivet, " Confluences, (December, 1945).

Demarquez, Suzanne.  André Jolivet.  Paris, Ventadour,
1958.

Gillespie, John.  Five Centuries of Keyboard Music: An
Historical Survey of Music for Harpsichord and Piano.
Belmont, Calif., Wadsworth Pub. Co., 1965.

Goldbeck, Frederick.  "The Strange Case of A. Jolivet, "
The Musical Quarterly, XXXV (July, 1949), 479-81.

Goléa, Antoine.  Esthétique de la Musique Contemporaine.
Paris, Presses Universitaires de France, 1954.

_____.  "French Music Since 1945, " trans. Lucile H.
Brockway, The Musical Quarterly, LI (January, 1965),
22-37.

_____.  "Rencontres avec André Jolivet, " In prepa-
ration.

Hartog, Howard (ed.).  European Music in the Twentieth
Century.  New York, Praeger, 1957.

Jolivet, André.  "A Propos du Premier Concerto pour
Ondes, " Revue Internationale de Musique, X (1951).

_____.  "Musique et Exotisme, " L'Exotisme dans
l'Art et la Pensée, R. Bezombes, ed.  Paris, n.p., 1953.
p. 159.

_____.  "Paradoxes de la Creation Musicale, " L'Age
Nouveau, XCII (May, 1955), 89.

_____.  "Réponse à une Enquête, " Contrepoints, L
(January, 1946).

"Jolivet," Zodiaque, XXXIII (April, 1957).

"Jolivet, André," Baker's Biographical Dictionary of
    Musicians.  Fifth Edition with 1965 Supplement,  787; 62.

Kirby, F. E.  A Short History of Keyboard Music, New
    York, The Free Press, 1966.

Lowens, Irving.  "Current Chronicle:  Washington, D.C.,"
    The Musical Quarterly, XLV (July, 1959), 385-88.

Machlis, Joseph.  Introduction to Contemporary Music.  New
    York, Norton, 1961.

Michel, Gérard.  "André Jolivet, Essai sur un Système
    Esthètique Musical," La Revue Musicale, CCIV (January,
    1947).

Moreux, Serge.  "Un Musicien d'Aujourd'hui," Polyphonie,
    (1949).

_____.  "Un Nouveau Béla Bartók," La Revue
    Française, XXXVI.

_____.  "Psyché d'André Jolivet," Psyché, VIII
    (June, 1947).

Myers, Rollo H.  "Jolivet, André," Grove's Dictionary of
    Music and Musicians (5th ed.), IV, 651.

Reti, Rudoph.  Tonality in Modern Music.  New York,
    Collier, 1962.

Roy, Jean.  Présences Contemporaines:  Musique Française.
    Paris, DeBresse, 1962.

KETTING, OTTO

(b.  Amsterdam, September 3, 1935)
Address:  Erasmusplein 1; The Hague, The Netherlands

    Otto Ketting, son of composer Piet Ketting, supple-
mented a musical education at The Hague Conservatory with
further study in Munich.

The Komposition mit zwölf Tönen (1956) is a set of seven short piano pieces in a twelve-tone style reminiscent of Schoenberg's expressionism.  A clearly iterated row is developed in a predominantly contrapuntal texture.  Repetitions of vertical and horizontal groupings establish a relatively traditional design.  The pieces contain a repetitious rhythmic pattern and constitute an experiment in the application of serial techniques to parameters other than pitch.  Ketting was a pioneer of this extension of serial technique in The Netherlands in the late 1950's.  The sixth piece contains the most adventuresome exploitation of this feature.

After 1957, Ketting abandoned much of the traditional tendencies in his composition and developed a style having a closer affinity with Webern.

Piano Music

Komposition mit zwölf Tönen (1956).   Amsterdam, Donemus, 1957.

Bibliography

"Ketting, Otto, " 1965 Supplement to Baker's Biographical Dictionary of Musicians (5th ed.), 67.

Ketting, Otto.  "Arnold Schönberg in Amerika, " Mens en Melodie, XIII (March, 1958), 79-81.

Wouters, Jos.  "Dutch Music in the 20th Century, " The Musical Quarterly, LI (January, 1965), 97-110.

KLEBE, GISELHER

(b.  Mannheim, June 28, 1925)
Address: 4935 Hiddesen bei; Bentweg 5a; Detmold, West Germany

Giselher Klebe received his musical training at the Berlin Conservatory where Josef Rufer and Boris Blacher were among his teachers.  Klebe's compositions include a wide variety of forms and styles.  In his early works the influences of Mahler, Stravinsky, Hindemith, and jazz are rather obvious, as in the Sonate für zwei Klaviere, Op. 4

Use of the Schoenberg twelve-tone technique became a
basic part of Klebe's style in the 1950's and the development
of it can be traced in his piano works composed since 1951.
Wiegenlieder für Christinchen, Op. 13, is dedicated to
Blacher and features the use of Blacher's variable meter
system. Twelve-tone rows are also employed. But whereas Op. 13 employs twelve-tone techniques in a perfunctory
manner, a drastic change of style is apparent in the Vier
Inventionen, Op. 25 (1957), and the Drei Romanzen, Op. 43
(1963). In both scores Klebe has incorporated selected
style features from Schoenberg, Berg, and Webern into his
own progressive style. The result is a composite texture
revealing a mastery of free serial techniques.

Piano Music

Wiegenlieder für Christinchen: Neun Stücke für Klavier, Op.
13. Berlin, Bote & Bock, 1953.

Vier Inventionen, Op. 27. Berlin, Bote & Bock, 1957.

Drei Romanzen für Klavier, Op. 43. Berlin, Bote & Bock,
1964.

Bibliography

Dibelius, Ulrich. Moderne Musik 1945-1965. Munich,
R. Piper, 1966.

Goléa, Antoine. Vingt Ans de Musique Contemporaine: de
Boulez à l'Inconnu. Paris, Seghers, 1962.

Hartog, Howard (ed.). European Music in the Twentieth
Century. New York, Praeger, 1957.

Helm, Everett. "Operas by Egk, Klebe, and Fortner, "
Musical Review, XVIII (August, 1957), 226-28.

Klebe, Giselher. "First Practical Work, " Die Reihe, I
(1958), 17-18.

_____. "Uber meine Oper 'Die Raüber', " Melos, XXIV
(March, 1957), 73-76.

"Klebe, Giselher, " Baker's Biographical Dictionary of

Musicians. Fifth Edition with 1965 Supplement, 836; 68.

Machlis, Joseph. Introduction to Contemporary Music. New York, Norton, 1961.

Maegaard, Jan. Musikalsk Modernisme 1945-1962. Copenhagen, Stig Vendelkaers, 1964.

Mann, Robert W. "Vita Musicale: Stoccolma," Rassegna Musicale, XXVI (April, 1956), 141-42.

McCredie, Andrew D. "Giselher Klebe," Music Review, XXVI (1965), 220-35.

Prieberg, Fred K. Lexikon der Neuen Musik. Freiburg, Karl Alber, 1958.

Stuckenschmidt, Hans Heinz. "Synthesis and New Experiments: Four Contemporary German Composers," trans. Abram Loft, The Musical Quarterly, XXXVIII (July, 1952), 353-68.

Von Lewinski, Wolf-Eberhard. "Current Chronicle: Germany," The Musical Quarterly, LII (July, 1966), 376-79.

_____. "Giselher Klebe," trans. Leo Black, Die Reihe, IV (1960), 89-97.

_____. "The Variety of Trends in Modern German Music," trans. Donald Mintz, The Musical Quarterly, LI (January, 1965), 166-79.

Wörner, Karl H. "Current Chronicle: Germany," The Musical Quarterly, XLVI (January, 1960), 80-83.

_____. "Klebe, Giselher," Die Musik in Geschichte und Gegenwart, VII, 1194-95.

Zillig, Winfried. Variationen über Neue Musik. Munich, Nymphenburger, 1959.

KOECHLIN, CHARLES

(b.  Paris, November 27, 1867; d.  Var Department,
France, January 1, 1951)

    Charles Koechlin was an astute student of the Schoen-
berg technique, as well as an experimenter with most of
the new ideas at the fore in the early twentieth century.
René Leibowitz, the Polish emigré, is the composer-theorist
usually credited with being the most effective influence in
transmitting the twelve-tone method to France.  But Koechlin was also a prolific composer, writer, and well-known
teacher who fostered progressive ideas in France.  Inas-
much as he has no associations with a major group or
school his influence faded rapidly.

    Koechlin studied with Gabriel Fauré, whose effect
upon him is obvious in some works, but Koechlin's self-
study was the most formative element on both his composition
and teaching.  He was a self-appointed protector of French
musical culture, but not merely to preserve tradition.  He
constantly sought for means with which old and new ideas
could be exploited so as to retain a style identifiable as
French.  Koechlin endeavored to combine with various
contemporary styles those rhythmic principles based on
mathematical proportions used in classical Greece, in the
Middle Ages, and during the Renaissance, as well as
Oriental rhythmic practices.  The results of his work were
revealed in compositions, teaching, theoretical works,
numerous articles, and intermittent lecture tours in Europe
and the United States from 1918 to 1937.  Koechlin thus
contributed significantly to the serialization of rhythm by
maintaining the interest in rhythmic complexities begun by
French composers in previous centuries.

Piano Music

Paysages et Marines, Op. 63. 2 vols. Paris, Mathot, 1918.

Bibliography

Austin, William W.  Music in the 20th Century:  From
    Debussy through Stravinsky.  New York, Norton, 1966.

Calvocoressi, Michel-Dmitri. "Charles Koechlin's Instrumen
    tal Works, "  Music and Letters, V (1924), 357.

_____ . Charles Koechlin. Paris, Sénart, 1920.

Collaer, Paul. A History of Modern Music. Trans. Sally
    Abeles. New York, World, 1961.

Cooper, Martin. French Music: From the Death of
    Berlioz to the Death of Fauré. London, Oxford Univ.
    Press, 1961.

Demuth, Norman. French Piano Music: A Survey with
    Notes on its Performance. London, Museum Press,
    1959.

Gillespie, John. Five Centuries of Keyboard Music: An
    Historical Survey of Music for Harpsichord and Piano.
    Belmont, Calif., Wadsworth Pub. Co., 1965.

Hartog, Howard (ed.). European Music in the Twentieth
    Century. New York, Praeger, 1957.

Herscher-Clément, Jeanne. "L'Oeuvre de Charles Koech-
    lin," La Revue Musicale, XVII (1936), 315.

Jourdan-Morhange, Hélène. Mes Amis Musiciens. Paris,
    Les Editeurs Français Reunis, 1953.

"Koechlin, Charles," Baker's Biographical Dictionary of
    Musicians. Fifth Edition with 1965 Supplement, 849;
    69.

Koechlin, Charles. "Art, Liberté, Tour d'Ivoire, "
    Contrepoints, VI (1950), 104.

_____ . "Eclipse de la Mélancolie: Quelques Pages sur
    l'Art d'Aujourd'hui, " Contrepoints, I (1946), 8.

_____ . "Le Retour à Bach, " La Revue Musicale, VIII
    (1926), 1.

_____ . "Les Tendances de la Musique Moderne
    Française, " Encyclopédie de la Musique du Conservatoire
    de Paris, 2nd. Part, I. Paris, n.d., 1925.

_____ . "Musique et Mathématique, La Revue Musicale,
    XII (1931), 424.

_____. Traité de l'Harmonie. 3 vols. Paris, M.
Eschig, 1925-30.

Mellers, Wilfred. "A Plea for Charles Koechlin," Music
Review, III (1942), 190.

_____. Studies in Contemporary Music. London,
Dobson, 1947.

Myers, Rollo H. "Koechlin, Charles," Grove's Dictionary
of Music and Musicians (5th ed.), IV, 805-12.

_____. "Charles Koechlin--Some Recollections,"
Music and Letters, XLVI (1965), 217.

Renaudin, Pierre, "Koechlin, Charles," Die Musik in
Geschichte und Gegenwart, VII, 1316-21.

_____. Charles Koechlin, Notice-Bio-Bibliographique.
Paris, n.p., 1952.

Roy, Jean. Présences Contemporaines: Musique Française.
Paris, DeBresse, 1962.

Salazar, Adolfo. Music in Our Time: Trends in Music
Since the Romantic Era. Trans. Isabel Pope. New
York, Norton, 1946.


KOELLREUTTER, HANS JOACHIM

(b. Freiburg, September 2, 1915)
Address: German-Indian Institute; New Delhi, India

        Hans Joachim Koellreutter left Germany in 1938. He
moved to Brazil and taught composition there for many years
at the Brazil Conservatory, and later became instructor at
the Musical Institute in São Paulo. He is considered the father
of Brazilian atonalism. Musica 1941 consists of three piano
pieces in a twelve-tone vein, indicating his adoption of the
Schoenberg technique by at least that date. Recently, however,
Koellreutter has abandoned twelve-tone writing. He now
serves as director of the German-Indian Institute in New
Delhi.

## Piano Music

Musica 1941. Montevideo, Editorial Cooperativa
    Interamericana de Compositores, 1942.

## Bibliography

Fraser, Norman. "Koellreutter, Hans Joachim," Grove's
    Dictionary of Music and Musicians (5th ed.), IV, 812.

Friskin, James and Irwin Freundlich. Music for the Piano.
    New York, Rinehart, 1954.

"Koellreutter, Hans Joachim," Baker's Biographical Diction-
    ary of Musicians (5th ed.), 849.


## KOFFLER, JOSEF

(b.  Stryj, Poland, November 28, 1896; d. Warsaw, 1943)

        Josef Koffler received a Ph.D. in musicology from
the University of Vienna in 1923 and acquired a position
on the faculty of Lvov Conservatory in the following year.

        Koffler's early compositions were mainly neo-
classical but during the 1920's he undertook a thorough
study of the Schoenberg principles.  It is controversial
as to whether or not he studied with Schoenberg personally.
Koffler subsequently destroyed most of his earlier scores,
although he retained some of the neo-classic as well as
impressionistic flavors in his style.  Thenceforth, though
not always a strict twelve-tone composer, he could not be
considered either a tonal composer.  The highly chromatic
and rather dissonant Sonatine, Op. 12, can be described as
neither tonal nor twelve-tone.  Reminiscent of Shostakovich
and to a lesser degree of Berg, it is not typical of his
later works.

        Koffler was the only Polish composer to adopt twelve-
tone writing before World War II.  His attempts to interest
other Poles in it, through his capacities as a teacher and
music editor, were unsuccessful.  Koffler's demise during
the Nazi persecution stifled the adoption of serial composition
in Poland for almost a decade.

Piano Music

Sonatine, Op. 12.   Vienna,  Universal Edition,  1931.

Bibliography

Halski, Czeslaw R.   "Koffler, Jozef," Grove's Dictionary
   of Music and Musicians (5th ed.),  IV,  813-14.

"Koffler,  Josef," Baker's Biographical Dictionary of
   Musicians (5th ed.),  850.

Swolkien,  Henryk.   "Schönberg's First Polish Disciple,"
   Osterreichische Gesellschaft für Musik, July/August/
   September (1965),  5-6.

KOHS,  ELLIS BONOFF

(b.   Chicago,  May 12,  1916)
Address: 8025 Highland Trail;  Los Angeles,  California

       Ellis Kohs received his musical training at the
San Francisco Conservatory, Juilliard, Harvard, and
Chicago University.   His main composition teachers were
Carl Bricken,  Bernard Wagenaar,  and Walter Piston and
his musicological studies were conducted principally with
Willi Apel and Hugo Leichentritt.   Kohs has held his current
teaching post at the University of Southern California since
1950.

       Kohs envisages the resources of musical composition
as constituting a unified field theory.   Accordingly his
compositions embrace both traditional functional harmony and
dodecaphonic writing.   In his work, tonality and atonality
are combined in a compatible manner.

       Kohs is noted for his exploitation of the twelve-tone
technique within the traditional variation form.   In the
Piano Variations (1946), he achieves this by the free interchange of single pitches or segments of the row.   Idiomatic
figures with traditional connotations, such as arpeggios, are
associated with specific segments to reinforce the tonal
character of the work.   Similar tonal features predominate
in the piano Toccata (1946-47).

Kohs, Ellis Bonoff

The Piano Sonata No. 2 (1962) is the third of the
four part Studies in Variation. (A quartet, quintet, and
an unaccompanied violin sonata constitute the balance of
the set.) The sonata exemplifies Kohs' unique ability to
amalgamate numerous ideas from the past and present into
a unified structure. His material incorporates ideas stemming as far back as organum, with such contemporary ideas
as twelve-tone writing, tone-clusters, impressionistic chords,
and rhythmic patterns reminiscent of Bartók or Stravinsky.
Octave doublings are a prominent feature in all his works.

The comparative absence of the transposed forms of
a row is a typical feature of Kohs' composition. He has
partially explained their omission by historical precedence,
as in the association of certain Wagnerian motives with
specific pitch levels.[46] Such recurring pitch levels reinforce
the auditory memory and function as a point of reference
when a basic row is subjected to free re-ordering.

Piano Music

Piano Variations (1946). New York, Merrymount Music
  Press, 1950.

Toccata (1946-47). New York, Merrymount Music Press,
  1949.

Piano Sonata No. 2 (1962). Los Angeles, Cameo Music, n.d.

Bibliography

Glanville-Hicks, Peggy. "Kohs, Ellis B.," Grove's Dictionary of Music and Musicians (5th ed.), IV, 815.

Kohs, Ellis B. "Thoughts from the Workbench," American
  Composers' Alliance Bulletin, Autumn, 1956.

"Kohs, Ellis B.," Baker's Biographical Dictionary of Musicians. Fifth Edition with 1965 Supplement, 851-52; 69.

Machlis, Joseph. Introduction to Contemporary Music. New
  York, Norton, 1961.

KRENEK, ERNST

(b.  Vienna, August 23, 1900)
Address: Tujunga, California

        Ernst Křenek was raised in Austria and it was here
that his principal musical studies were carried out with
Franz Schreker.  In the 1920's Křenek had contacts with
Ferruccio Busoni, Hermann Scherchen, and Arthur Schnabel.
Křenek began composing about 1917 in a late romantic vein
and moved quickly to an atonal style (Op. 6-17) in the years
1921 to 1923.  From about 1923 until 1930 (i.e., Op. 17-
66), Křenek was involved with a period of experimentation
using jazz and other ideas such as those of Béla Bartók
and Paul Hindemith.  After 1930 Schoenberg's twelve-tone
technique was used increasingly.  The opera Charles V
(1933) represented his first major twelve-tone work.  The
first twelve-tone piano composition was the Zwölf Variation-
en (Op. 79, 1937, later revised), written in the year Křenek
first visited America.  Since his arrival in this country,
where he has had considerable influence as an author and
as a teacher in widely scattered schools and universities,
his music has been almost exclusively twelve-tone.

        In 1938 Křenek took up permanent residence in the
United States, becoming a citizen in 1954.  He provided a
needed stimulus to the spread of the Schoenberg technique
in America and his subsequent career was largely shaped
by his involvement in popularizing the twelve-tone technique.
At the time of Křenek's arrival in America the development
of contemporary music was lagging.  Interest in the music
and ideas of Bartók, Hindemith, Stravinsky, Milhaud, and
others, as well as Schoenberg, had been dulled by a conservative attitude.  True, Aaron Copland, Roger Sessions, and
Adolph Weiss, to mention a few, had organized concerts
dedicated to contemporary music, beginning in the late 1920's.
Also, the League of Composers had begun publication of
Modern Music, containing not only articles but complete
scores.  But in the immediate pre-war years the opponents
of contemporary music undermined these efforts and the
progressive climate began to disintegrate.  After teaching
for some years at Malkin Conservatory in Boston, Křenek
accepted an invitation from Vassar in 1939 to teach theory
and composition.  Here the environment stimulated him to

write three major works to revive interest in Schoenberg's
technique.  A collection of essays, Music Here and Now,
clarifying many principles of contemporary music, was
directed to the general public.  A second book, Studies in
Counterpoint, was the first published attempt to create a
manual of instruction based on elementary principles of
twelve-tone writing.  Křenek was not concerned with publish-
ing a detailed study of the Schoenberg method but he felt
a need for presenting a succinct guide enabling a composition
student to grasp the essentials of twelve-tone writing.  The
third part of the project to increase the general public's
familiarity with and interest in twelve-tone music was the
set of Twelve Short Piano Pieces, Op. 83.  These are
written in the twelve-tone technique and are intended express-
ly as teaching pieces requiring of the pianist only moderate
technical ability.  Křenek supplied sufficient explanations to
enable the interested person to follow the use of the four
basic forms of the row and to comprehend how the rows
were manipulated to provide both melodic and harmonic
material.  Streamliner, No. 7, for example, illustrates
exceptions to the rule generally forbidding repetitions of
tones within the statement of a series, by employing bat-
teries of major or minor thirds as characteristic motives.
Křenek sought with such rule-breaking to obliterate the
prejudice that strict twelve-tone writing inhibited individual
creativity.  His Op. 83 has served as a stimulus to other
composers to write pedagogical works, demonstrating that
twelve-tone writing can be musically interesting in the
simplest expression, particularly if the method is employed
as Schoenberg intended--as a means to musical expression
and not a strict method to be followed slavishly.

        Although Křenek's efforts to popularize the Schoen-
berg twelve-tone technique in America have been widely
recognized for their effectiveness, his personal interpretation of the twelve-tone concepts has increasingly demonstrated modification or extension of Schoenberg's method.
Whereas Křenek's early twelve-tone works of the late
1930's were conceived along the lines of the classical
methods, his theories already anticipated future development.
In Studies in Counterpoint[47] he stated his belief that atonal
music would find the use of a strict twelve-tone technique
unnecessary as the essence of the technique became second
nature to the composer.  In the 1940's Křenek became one
of the first composers to make significant modifications   of

the Schoenberg practice through a conscious re-organization
and not merely a free approach.  Both the third and fourth
piano sonatas are based on what Křenek calls the principle
of serial rotation of the series, an experiment crucial to
the development of total serialization.  In the Sonata No. 3,
Op. 92, No. 4 ( 1943, later revised), segmental treatment
of groups of two or four tones from the basic row is
characteristic.  Glenn Gould feels an $A^b$ major tonality
permeates the sonata as a direct result of the unique type
of segmentation which Křenek employs.[48]  Harmonic material in this sonata is expressed primarily as fourth chords
and a pointillistic style is interspersed with increasing
frequency as the music progresses.

In the Sonata No. 4 (1948) the segmentation principle
is even more extensively used.  The basic twelve-tone row
($E^b$ F B G C $D^b$ A E D $B^b$ $G^b$ $A^b$ ) rarely appears, but is
continuously broken into groups which lend themselves to
transposition, inversion, and rotation within themselves.
The row is the common source for all regroupings and
changing relationships; thus unity is maintained throughout.

Twenty Miniatures (1954) for piano reverts to strict
twelve-tone writing, but in the several other piano works
Křenek has continued to develop a free serial style.

Basler Massarbeit für Zwei Klaviere (1958) contains
six rows, five being derived from a basic row by application
of the rotation principle.  The numerical values of the
interval patterns of the rows, as stated in ascending form,
are the basis both for serializing the rhythmic movement
and for determining the number of notes in each phase of
time.  Křenek provides extensive comments to explain the
structure and to facilitate performance.

Seldom has a composer revealed within his own work
so many facets of musical evolution.  Křenek's compositions
exemplify all major trends of the twentieth-century, recently
including electronic music.  A desire to transmit his broad
experience to others has fostered extensive writing on music.
His essays reveal a vital interest in the aesthetic and
psychological aspects of music as well as its theory.
Křenek's theoretical discussions of twelve-tone composition
place considerable emphasis on vertical structuring.  One
of the most controversial ideas that Křenek has put forth
is a suggested classification of the harmonies inherent in the

row according to relative degrees of dissonance perception.[49]

Piano Music

Zwölf Variationen, in Drei Sätzen, Op. 79 (1937; rev. 1940
    and 1957). Frankfurt, H. Assman, 1962.

12 Short Piano Pieces Written in the Twelve-Tone Tech-
    nique, Op. 83 (1938). New York, Schirmer, 1939.

Sonata No. 3, Op. 92, No. 4 (1943; rev. 1960). New York,
    Assoc. Music Pub., 1945.

Eight Piano Pieces (1946). New York, Mercury Music Corp.,
    1946.

Piano Sonata No. 4 (1948). Long Island City, Queens N.Y.,
    Bomart Music Publications, 1950.

Piano Sonata No. 5 (1950). Unpub. ms.

Piano Sonata No. 6 (1951). Unpub. ms.

Twenty Miniatures (1954). Copenhagen, W. Hansen, 1957.

Sechs Vermessene (1958). Kassel, Germany, Bärenreiter,
    1960.

Basler Massarbeit für Zwei Klaviere (1958). Kassel,
    Germany, Bärenreiter, 1961.

Bibliography

Appleton, Jon. "Current Chronicle: Rochester, Michigan,"
    The Musical Quarterly, LIV (January, 1965), 92-96.

Austin, William W. Music in the 20th Century: From
    Debussy through Stravinsky. New York, Norton, 1966.

Bach, David Joseph. "New Music by Berg, Webern, Křenek,"
    Modern Music, XII (November-December, 1934), 31-38.

Beckwith, John and Udo Kasemets (eds.). The Modern
    Composer and His World. Toronto, Univ. of Toronto
    Press, 1961.

Burkhard, Willy. "Versuch einer Kritischen Auseinandersetzung mit der Zwölftontechnik," Schweizerische Musikzeitung, XCIV (March, 1954), 85-93.

Carner, Mosco. A Study of Twentieth-Century Harmony: Volume Two Contemporary Harmony. 4th ed. London, Williams, 1942.

Colucci, Matthew Joseph. "A Comparative Study of Contemporary Musical Theories in Selected Writings of Piston, Křenek, and Hindemith." Unpub. doctoral dissertation, Univ. of Penn., 1957.

Collaer, Paul. A History of Modern Music. Trans. Sally Abeles. New York, World, 1961.

Dallin, Leon. Techniques of Twentieth Century Composition. 2nd ed. Dubuque, Iowa, Wm. C. Brown, 1964.

Dibelius, Ulrich. Moderne Musik 1945-1965. Munich, R. Piper, 1966.

Erickson, Robert. "Křenek's Amerikanische Texte," Schweizerische Musikzeitung, XCIII (March, 1953), 104-108.

_____. "Křenek's Later Music (1930-1947)," Music Review, IX (February, 1948), 29-44.

Eschmann, Karl. Changing Forms in Modern Music. Boston, Schirmer, 1945.

Fiechtner, Helmut A. "Ernst Křenek," Musica, VII (January, 1953), 7-10.

Friskin, James, and Irwin Freundlich. Music for the Piano. New York, Rinehart, 1954.

Galli, Hans. Moderne Musik-leicht Verständlich. Munich, Francke, 1964.

Gillespie, John. Five Centuries of Keyboard Music: An Historical Survey of Music for Harpsichord and Piano. Belmont, Calif., Wadsworth Pub. Co., 1965.

Gould, Glenn. Jacket notes, Berg, Schoenberg, Křenek. Columbia recording ML 5336.

Hodeir, André. Since Debussy: A View of Contemporary Music. Trans. Noel Burch. New York, Grove, 1961.

Hutcheson, Ernest. The Literature of the Piano: A Guide for Amateur and Student. 3rd ed. rev. Rudolf Ganz. New York, Knopf, 1964.

Joachim, Heinz. "Current Chronicle: Germany," The Musical Quarterly, XLII (January, 1956), 92-98.

_____. "Ernst Křenek," Schweizerische Musikzeitung, 95 (January, 1955), 1-5.

Kirby, F. E. A Short History of Keyboard Music. New York, The Free Press, 1966.

Křenek, Ernst. "A Glance Over the Shoulders of the Young," Die Reihe, I (1958), 14-16.

_____. "Amerikas Einfluss auf Eingewanderte Komponisten," Musica, XIII (1959), 757.

_____. "Bericht über Versuche in Total Determinierter Musik," Darmstädter Beiträge zur Neuen Musik, I (1958), 17.

_____. "A Composer's Influences," Perspectives of New Music, III (Fall-Winter, 1964), 36-41.

_____. Exploring Music. Trans. Margaret Shenfield & Geoffrey Skelton. London, Calder and Boyars, 1966.

_____. "Extents and Limits of Serial Techniques," The Musical Quarterly, XLVI (April, 1960), 210-32.

_____. Gedanken Unterwegs: Dokumente einer Reise. Munich, n.p., 1959.

_____. "Is the Twelve-tone Technique On the Decline?" The Musical Quarterly, XXXIX (October, 1953) 513-27.

_____. "Kurzer Rechenschaftsbericht," Schweizerische Musikzeitung, 90 (June, 1950), 299-301.

_____ . Music Here and Now. Trans. B. Fles.
New York, n. p., 1939.

_____ . "New Developments of the Twelve-tone Technique, " Music Review, IV (1943), 81.

_____ . Selbstdarstellung. Zürich, Atlantis, 1948.

_____ . "Self-analysis, " New Mexico Quarterly, XXIII
(Spring, 1953), 5-57.

_____ . "Sestina, " Melos, VII-VIII (July-August, 1958),
235-38.

_____ . "Some Current Terms, " Perspectives of New
Music. IV (Spring-Summer, 1966), 81-84.

_____ . Studies in Counterpoint. New York, Schirmer,
1940.

_____ . "Versuch einer Selbstanalyse: 'Jonny' zur
Zwölftonmusik," Melos, XVI (February, 1949), 33-38.

_____ . "Zu meinem Kammermusikwerken 1936-1950, "
Schweizerische Musikzeitung, XCIII (March, 1953),
104-108.

_____ . Zur Sprache Gebracht: Essays über Musik.
Munich, n. p., 1959.

"Křenek, Ernst, " Baker's Biographical Dictionary of Musicians. Fifth Edition with 1965 Supplement, 871-2; 72.

Leibowitz, René. Schoenberg and His School. Trans.
Dika Newlin. New York, Philosophical Library, 1949.

Machlis, Joseph. Introduction to Contemporary Music. New
York, Norton, 1961.

Morgenstern, Sam (ed. ). Composers on Music: An Anthology of Composers' Writings from Palestrina to Copland.
New York, Bonanza, 1966.

Ogdon, Wilbur Lee. "Series and Structure: An Investigation Into the Purpose of the Twelve-note Row in Selected

Works of Schoenberg, Webern, Křenek and Leibowitz, "
Unpub. doctoral dissertation, Indiana Univ., Bloomington,
1955.

Redlich, Hans Ferdinand. "Křenek, Ernst, " Grove²s Dictionary of Music and Musicians (5th ed.), IV, 844-48.

Reich, Willi. "Ernst Křeneks Arbeit in der Zwölftontechnik, " Schweizerische Musikzeitung, LXXXIX
(February, 1949), 49-53.

_____. "Ernst Křenek als Musikschriftsteller, " Schwei-
zerische Musikzeitung, XCIII (March, 1953), 113-14.

Reis, Claire R. Composers in America: Biographical
Sketches of Contemporary Composers with a Record of
Their Works. Rev. and enl. ed. New York, MacMillan,
1947.

Rufer, Josef. Composition with Twelve Notes Related Only
to One Another. Trans. Humphrey Searle. London,
Barrie and Rockliff, 1954.

Saathen, Friedrich. "Ernst Křeneks Botschaft im Wort, "
Schweizerische Musikzeitung, XCIX (February, 1959),
45-50.

Salzman, Eric. Twentieth-Century Music: An Introduction.
Englewood Cliffs, N.J., Prentice-Hall, 1967.

Norman, Gertrude, and Miriam Lubell Shrifte (eds.).
Letters of Composers. New York, Grosset & Dunlap,
1946.

Schuh, Willi. "Zu Ernst Křenek Invention, " Schweizerische
Musikzeitung, XCIII (March, 1953), 115.

Vellekoop, Gerrit. "De ²Lamentatio Jeremiae Prophetae²
van Ernst Krsjenek, " Mens en melodie, XIII (November,
1958), 326-29.

Vlad, Roman. Storia della Dodecafonia. Milan, Suvini
Zerboni, 1958.

Weissmann, Adolph. "Ernst Křenek, " Modern Music, VI
(November-December, 1928), 17-23.

Worner, Karl H. "Křenek, Ernst," Die Musik in Geschichte und Gegenwart, VII, 1759-63.

_____. Neue Musik in der Entscheidung. Mainz, Schott,
    1954.

Zillig, Winfried. Variationen über neue Musik. Munich,
    Nymphenburger, 1959.


LEIBOWITZ, RENE

(b. Warsaw, February 17, 1913)
Address: 14 rue Saint Guillaume; Paris 7ᵉ, France

        René Leibowitz was born and lived his early years in
Warsaw, but Paris has been his residence since 1926. In
1931 and 1932 he studied in Vienna with Anton Webern,
then for a few months in Berlin he was with Schoenberg,
and finally studied with Maurice Ravel and Pierre Monteux
in Paris. Leibowitz developed a style of composition that
reflects his dedication to the twelve-tone technique as
formulated by Schoenberg, and he became an active pro-
ponent. On occasion the influence of Berg or Webern is
quite apparent in his composition[50] and in fact, Leibowitz
has been a participant in the spread of Webern's ideas.

        Although he has gained fame as a conductor,
Leibowitz concentrated his efforts in the areas of musicology and theory and wrote several books on contemporary
music. The most famous are Schoenberg and His School
(1946), which was the first extensive theoretical discussion
of this group, and the Introduction à la Musique de Douze
Sons. His writings, beginning in the year of Webern's
death, include analyses of many works of the Second Viennese School and were a major stimulus to the spread of
dodecaphonic composition in France. His contacts with
French composers, through his writings and as a teacher
at the Paris Conservatory, led to the first twelve-tone
composition using the Schoenberg technique among the
French. Although Leibowitz has maintained a conservative
approach toward serial composition, it was nevertheless his
enthusiasm for dodecaphonic writing at an opportune moment
which stimulated in large measure the innovations of the
group around Messiaen, and particularly the work of Pierre
Boulez and Karlheinz Stockhausen. It was Leibowitz who

acquainted Boulez with the Schoenberg technique and thereby brought twelve-tone composition into impact with the new rhythmic concepts emerging in the classes of Messiaen.[51] For some years Leibowitz was temporarily associated with the radical group surrounding Messiaen and Boulez, but his strict dedication to the classical method sparked an important split in the French attitude toward serial composition. Many of Leibowitz's sentiments, appearing at length in the still unpublished (though completed) Traité de la Composition avec Douze Sons, did not hold complete accord even among other advocates of a strict dodecaphonic style. Leibowitz asserted that the twelve-tone system having evolved from Western traditions of the 19th century necessarily maintains an association with those traditions. Furthermore, Leibowitz was not particularly interested in seeking extensions of the original method, but only in perfecting the use of its initial formulation. This conservatism aroused strong opposition among his French contemporaries, many of whom viewed the original method as a starting point for adventures in serial expansion and considered the use of traditionalism or synthesism as bordering on decadence. Thus it was in France that two trends of twelve-tone composition, conservative and radical, met in their most rigorous clash to date, thereby stimulating a whole new wave of ideas related to serial composition, as well as leading to even more divergent paths.

An early Piano Sonata, Op. 1 (1939), remains unpublished. The only other piano work is the Quatre Pièces, Op. 8 (1947). Considering the date of composition, the set is remarkable as a predecessor of compositional styles not yet developed, as well as for the full exploitation of the classical twelve-tone technique. The rhythmic complexity of it is indicative of Leibowitz's participation in the efforts to free rhythm from tradition during the 1940's. There are many lyrical sections in which the combinations of leaps and rhythmic movement recall the Sprechstimme of Schoenberg. Also in this Op. 8 there is continual use of the full keyboard range in a manner suggesting affinity with Webern's pointillism but the texture is usually thicker and the fuller harmonies convey a more romantic flavor typical of Schoenberg and Berg.

Piano Music

Quatre Pièces Pour Piano, Op. 8. Vienna, Universal

Edition, 1947.

Bibliography

Austin, William W. Music in the 20th Century: From Debussy through Stravinsky. New York, Norton, 1966.

Babbitt, Milton. "Schoenberg et Son Ecole, and Qu'est-çe Que la Musique de Douze Sons?" Journal of the American Musicological Society, III (1950), 60.

Galli, Hans. Moderne Musik-leicht Verständlich. Munich, Francke, 1964.

Goléa, Antoine. Vingt Ans de Musique Contemporaine: de Boulez à l'Inconnu. Paris, Seghers, 1962.

Hodeir, André. Since Debussy: A View of Contemporary Music. Trans. Noel Burch. New York, Grove, 1961.

Leibowitz, René, and Konrad Wolff. Erich Itor Kahn, un Grand Representant de la Musique Contemporaine. Paris.

Leibowitz, René. Histoire de l'Opera. Paris, Correa, 1957.

_____. Introduction à la Musique de Douze Sons. Paris, L'Arche, 1949.

_____. L'Artiste et Sa Conscience. Paris, L'Arche, 1950.

_____. L'Evolution de la Musique, de Bach à Schoenberg. Paris, Correa, 1951.

_____. Qu'est-çe Que la Musique de Douze Sons? Liège, Dynamo, 1948.

_____. Schoenberg and His School. Trans. Dika Newlin. New York, Philosophical Library, 1949.

_____. Un Traité Connu de la Technique de la Variation 14me. Liège, Dynamo, 1950.

"Leibowitz, René." Baker's Biographical Dictionary of Musicians. Fifth Edition with 1965 Supplement, 931-33;77.

Morel, Jean-Marie. "Leibowitz, René," Die Musik in
    Geschichte und Gegenwart, VIII, 504-505.

Ogdon, Wilbur Lee. "Series and Structure: An Invest-
    igation Into the Purpose of the Twelve-note Row in
    Selected Works of Schoenberg, Webern, Křenek and
    Leibowitz," Unpub. doctoral dissertation, Indiana Univ.,
    Bloomington, 1955.

Rufer, Josef. Composition with Twelve Notes Related Only
    to One Another. Trans. Humphrey Searle. London,
    Barrie and Rockliff, 1954.

Searle, Humphrey. "Leibowitz, René," Grove's Dictionary
    of Music and Musicians (5th ed.), V, 117.

## LUTYENS, ELISABETH

(b.  London,  July 9,  1906)
Address: 76a Belsize Park Gardens; London, N.W. 3,
England

  Elisabeth Lutyens received her musical training at
the Royal College of Music in London.  She and Humphrey
Searle introduced twelve-tone concepts into Great Britain
about 1939.  In that year, her first serial work appeared,
the Concerto for Nine Instruments (1939).

  Whereas Searle's dodecaphony was, for him, a
drastic style change, largely inspired by external influences,
Lutyens' twelve-tone writing evolved quite naturally.  She
retains the romantic flavor of her early work through an
expressionistic phase and into the increasingly atonal and
chromatic writing of the 1930's.  The first emergence of
a twelve-tone style in her work is not particularly obvious
as it was rather loosely employed.  Since 1939 all her
works can be described as serial and are always based on
a single row.  She has destroyed all her work composed
before 1935.

  All the piano works are formulated on a small scale
and are characteristic of her development of thematic material with extreme economy of means.  The Five Intermezzi,
Op. 9 (1942), begins with a twelve-tone idiom that gradually

becomes less rigorous. The Three Improvisations (1948) is similarly a rather free dodecaphonic treatment of an uncomplicated and romantic expression. Five Bagatelles, Op. 48 (1963), marks a movement of Lutyens' serial style toward that of Webern.

Piano Music

Five Intermezzi, Op. 9 (1942). London, Alfred Lengnick, 1947.

Three Improvisations. London, Alfred Lengnick, 1948.

Piano e Forte. Mills Music, n. d.

Five Bagatelles for Piano (1963). London, Schott, 1965.

Bibliography

Hartog, Howard (ed.). European Music in the Twentieth Century. New York, Praeger, 1957.

Henderson, Robert. "Elisabeth Lutyens," The Musical Times, CIV (1963), 551.

"Lutyens, Elisabeth," Baker's Biographical Dictionary of Musicians (5th ed.), 995.

Mason, Colin. "Lutyens, Elisabeth," Grove's Dictionary of Music and Musicians (5th ed.), V, 448-49.

Schafer, Murray. British Composers in Interview. London, Faber & Faber, 1963.

Weissman, John S. "Lutyens, Elisabeth," Die Musik in Geschichte und Gegenwart, VIII, 1349-51.

LYBBERT, DONALD

(b. Cresco, Iowa, February 19, 1923)
Address: 61 Jane Street, New York, New York 10014

Donald Lybbert received a B. Mus. degree from the University of Iowa in 1946 and an M. A. from Columbia University in 1950, where Elliott Carter and Otto Luening

were among his teachers.  In 1961 he studied with Nadia
Boulanger and presently is Chairman of the Department of
Music of Hunter College, New York.

Lybbert views Schoenberg's twelve-tone technique
as an ingenious system for eliminating the problem of pitch
redundancy in the chromatic music that evolved from functional harmony.[52]  Lybbert's work is serially oriented, in
that a basic set serves as a frame of reference.  The freedom of his ordering defies description as a specific permutational system.  This continuous set alteration has striking
similarities with Italian  work in the last decade.

In the Sonata Brevis (1962) the linear movement is
frequently diverted into short sections concerned only with
sound changes between vertical structures.  There is constant fluctuation between  duple  and triple rhythmic patterns.
These chordal and rhythmic features often convey a sense
of traditional orientation that stabilizes an otherwise open
form.   The construction methods of the Movement for Piano
(four-hands) are similar.

Piano Music

Sonata Brevis (1962).   New York, C. F. Peters, 1963.

Movement for Piano (four-hands).   New York, C.F. Peters,
    n.d.

Bibliography

"Lybbert, Donald, " 1965 Supplement to Baker's Biographical
    Dictionary of Musicians (5th ed.),  81.

MARTIN, FRANK

(b.  Geneva, September 15, 1890)
Address: Bollelaan 11; Naarden N.H., The Netherlands

Frank Martin studied piano and composition with
Joseph Lauber at the Geneva Conservatory.  His early music
was along conventional lines with French impressionism the
most obvious influence.   Martin became attracted to Arnold
Schoenberg's music in the 1930's.  His study of the twelve-
tone technique led him to become one of the first of those

writing in a predominantly French style to adopt features
of dodecaphony.  Twelve-tone rows are only employed
melodically in his work and the traditional tonal function
of accompaniment chords are retained, in spite of liberal
chromaticism.  On occasion  Martin even employs the row
as a fundamental bass and juxtaposes groups of triads above
to create his own flavor of harmonic progressions and to
organize structural sections.  Contrapuntal texture, as such,
is therefore infrequent in his work.  In a lengthy credo,
Martin has stated that he considers rules as a means of renewal,  to be imposed upon one's self only as necessary.[53]

   Within his large output the piano work which most
fully exemplifies a use of twelve-tone features is his unpublished concerto of 1934.  The Preludes (1948) contain a
free total chromatic style, with the melodic line providing
a semblance of serial ordering, contrasted with tonal harmonic progressions.  Martin has also experimented with
rhythmic ideas from ancient and oriental cultures and from
jazz.  The rhythmic style demonstrated in these pieces has
become influential among his contemporaries.  The rhythmic
variation is as significant as the melodic alterations.  The
set of eight preludes as a whole exemplifies Martin's success
in synthesizing French clarity of line and form and German
harmony within selected elements of a twelve-tone style.[54]
In like manner Martin's mature work reveals the manner in
which he by-passed the strict use of the Schoenberg technique, without ever wholly abandoning basic precepts of
traditional tonality.

Piano Music

Martin, Frank.  8 Préludes pour le Piano (1948).  Vienna,
   Universal Edition,  1949.

Bibliography

Ansermet, Ernest.  "Der Weg Frank Martins," Osterreichische Musikzeitschrift, XI (1956),  172.

Austin, William W.  Music in the 20th Century: From
   Debussy through Stravinsky.  New York, Norton, 1966.

Bernheimer, Martin.  "Current Chronicle: Munich," The
   Musical Quarterly, XLVIII (October, 1962), 525-28.

Hartog, Howard (ed.). European Music in the Twentieth
Century. New York, Praeger, 1957.

Hines, Robert Stephan (ed.). The Composer's Point of
View: Essays on Twentieth-Century Choral Music by
Those Who Wrote It. Norman, Okla., Univ. of
Oklahoma Press, 1963.

Koelliker, Andre. Frank Martin. Lausanne, n.p., 1963.

Machlis, Joseph. Introduction to Contemporary Music. New
York, Norton, 1961.

"Martin, Frank," Baker's Biographical Dictionary of Musicians. Fifth Edition with 1965 Supplement, 1035-36; 84.

Martin, Frank. "A Propos du Language Musical
Contemporain," Schweizerische Musikzeitung, LXXVII
(1937), 501.

_____. "A Propos de Mon Concerto de Violon," La
Revue Musicale, CCXII (1952), 111.

_____. "Généralisation de la Sensibilité," L'Age
Nouveau, XCII (May, 1955), 66.

_____. "Le Compositeur Moderne et les Textes Sacres,"
Schweizerische Musikzeitung, LXXXVI (1946), 261.

_____. "Les Sources du Rhythme Musical," Revue
Musicale de la Suisse Romande, XVIII (September, 1965),
3.

_____. "Literatur und Musik," Osterreichische
Musikzeitschrift, XIV (1959), 403.

_____. "Moderne Musik and Publikum," Osterreichische
Musikzeitschrift, XV (1960), 412.

_____. "Notes Biographiques," Polyphonie, II (1948),
81.

_____. Notwendigkeit einer Gegenwartskunst: Gedanken
zum "Vin Herbe." Amriswil, Switzerland, n.p., 1957.

_____ .  "Responsabilité du Compositeur, "  Polyphonie,
    II (1948).

_____ .  "Schoenberg et Nous, "  Polyphonie,  IV  (1949),
    68.

Mohr,  Ernst.   "Martin,  Frank, "  Die  Musik  in  Geschichte
    und  Gegenwart,  VIII,  1705-09.

Mooser,  R₀  Aloys.   Regards  Sur  la  Musique  Contemporaine
    1921-46₀   Lausanne,  Griffon,  1947.

Reich,  Willi.   "On  Swiss  Musical  Composition  of  the
    Present, "  The  Musical  Quarterly,  LI  (January,  1965),
    78-91₀

Saathen,  Friedrich.   "Current  Chronicle:  Austria, "  The
    Musical  Quarterly,  XLII  (October,  1956),  533-535.

Tupper,  Janet  Eloise.   "Stylistic  Analysis  of  Selected
    Works  by  Frank  Martin. "   Unpub₀  doctoral  dissertation,
    Indiana  Univ₀,  Bloomington,  1964.

Vlad,  Roman.   Modernità  e  Tradizione  nella  Musica
    Contemporanea.   Turin,  n₀ p.,  1955₀

Von  Fischer,  Kurt₀   "Martin,  Frank, "  Grove's  Dictionary
    of  Music  and  Musicians  (5th  ed₀),  V,  592-94.

Von  Klein,  Rudolf.   Frank  Martin:  Sein  Leben  und  Werk₀
    Vienna,  Verlag  Osterreichische  Musikzeitschrift,  1960₀

MARTINO, DONALD

(b.   Plainfield,  New  Jersey,  May  16,  1931)
Address: 96 Elaine Road; Milford, Connecticut

       Donald  Martino  received  a  music  degree  from
Princeton  University  and  supplemented  this  study  with  a
Fulbright  award  spent  in  Florence.   He  is  currently  a
member  of  the  music  faculty  at  Yale₀

       Martino's  serial  writing  features  the  use  of  sets
derived  from  the  available  forms  of  a  single,  stated  row₀
This  practice  is  in  contrast  to  the  technique  of  employing

several rows as a source set. Martino frequently reiterates the prime row, a device he considers desirable, but does not follow the practice of other composers who employ continuous permutation without an original series or even a closely related form appearing. In applying the serial principle to other parameters, Martino maintains consideration for the motivic patterns already in existence in the pitchrow so as to create a design that lends itself to partitioning. This also facilitates the continual process of derivation of sets, as well as reinforcement of the musical structure.[55]

In the Piano Fantasy (1958) the first derived set is a combination of the original series and its inversion. Each new prime is successively combined with its inversion or retrograde inversion.

In an article describing his use of the derivation technique, Martino has acknowledged his indebtedness to Milton Babbitt for ideas regarding the use of derived sets.[56]

Piano Music

Piano Fantasy (1958). New York, Composers Facsim. Ed.,
    1962.

Bibliography

Burrows, David. "Current Chronicle: New Haven," The
    Musical Quarterly, LII (July, 1966), 368-73.

_____ . "Notation in General--Articulation in Part-
    icular," Perspectives of New Music, IV (Spring-Summer,
    1966), 47-58.

_____ . "The Source Set and its Aggregate Formations,"
    Journal of Music Theory, V (November, 1961), 224-74.

"Martino, Donald," 1965 Supplement to Baker's Biographical
    Dictionary of Musicians (5th ed.), 84.

MERKU, PAVLE

(b. Trieste, July 12, 1927)
Address: Via Rossetti, 113; Trieste 415, Italy

Pavle Merku undertook the study of composition of
1944, mainly with Vito Levi in Trieste.  His interest in
contemporary styles, in particular that of Alban Berg,  led
Merku to an intensive study of the compositions of the
Schoenberg School.  His first use of a twelve-tone series
occurs in the Concertino (1957) for small orchestra.  Merku
has not consistently used serial methods, although he feels
them to be a great source of musical expression.  He considers his adoption of the twelve-tone technique to have been
a natural development, since his music had become so highly chromatic.[57]

Phyllobolia (1963) consists of a set of short piano
pieces,  of which the first, third, and last, are serial.  The
last is a canon developed from the four basic forms of the
row.

There is no significant bibliography for Merku.

Piano Music

Phyllobolia (1963).  Milan, Suvini Zerboni, n. d.

MESSIAEN, OLIVIER EUGENE PROSPER CHARLES

(b.  Avignon, December 10, 1908)
Address: 13 Villa du Danube; Paris 19[e], France

Olivier Messiaen supplemented his musical training
at the Paris Conservatory with extensive self-study of
plainsong, Hindu music, bird-songs, and micro-tonal music.
In 1936 he was a co-founder of Jeunesses Musicales, an
important organization for the international promotion of
contemporary music.

Messiaen's teachings and writings have solidified his position as one of the great theoreticians on rhythm.  In the mid-
1940's Messiaen organized a private class in analysis, aesthetics, and rhythmic techniques.  Two of the attractions in these
classes were his discussions and analyses of Debussy's Pelléas
et Mélisande and Stravinsky's Le Sacre du Printemps.  In 1947
Messiaen accepted an invitation to teach at the Paris Conservatory, where his ideas stimulated Boulez to convert Messiaen's
concept of athematic rhythm into the principle of irrational

rhythm.[58] Thus a workable way to serialize rhythm was
devised which in turn encouraged further extensions of
serial principles.[59] The interchange of ideas between Messia-
en and his students has continued to influence contemporary
musicians, particularly those writing serial and electronic
music.

In Technique of My Musical Language Messiaen describes his modal system in detail, and also states his
own evaluation as to the main influences on his composition,
such as Debussy, Satie, Scriabin, and Stravinsky.

Melodically, Messiaen's system of modes of limited
transposition has some parallel with the Schoenberg dodecaphony, of which it may be seen as only a variant form.
Messiaen regards the melodic element as supreme.   He
judges rhythm and harmony as latent in melody, an idea
compatible with Schoenberg's belief that basic shape of the
original row contains the essence of the resultant form.
Although his rhythmic formulations were not well-defined,
Schoenberg had always stressed the importance of the pitch
row as the source for the intervallic and chordal structures.
The motivic principle as a basis for development or variation of a row was of fundamental importance to Schoenberg
who held that the basic shape of a piece of music is derived
from the combination of small units within it.   The modal
concept implies the pre-existence within a musical work of
a sort of scaffolding, which supports the linear structure.
Contemporary composers have sought a single modal basis,
as well as a multiple modality, such as Messiaen's system.
One of the major stimuli for modality in contemporary music
evolved from Debussy's modal studies, which incorporated
some ideas from the Russians; Messiaen's starting-point was
based on Debussy's findings.

The Quatre Etudes de Rhythme (1949) are a practical
application of Messiaen's rhythmic innovations which receive
their theoretical explication in Traité du Rythme.   Messiaen
uses the twelve tones in an unorthodox fashion, as only the
basic pattern and various re-arrangements are employed
without recourse to the basic 48 forms.   A pitch series
appears in similar forms in three registers that are cor-
related with series of twenty-four durations, twelve attacks,
and seven intensities.   There is some motivic development,
which, if it were not inconsistent, would in conjunction with
Messiaen's concept of reiterated modal patterns, make the

Messiaen style resemble the early isorhythmic technique.

As with the Schoenberg twelve-tone technique, the use of Messiaen's rhythmic modes can be controlled so as to place emphasis on either a tonal or non-tonal quality.

Piano Music

Mode de Valeurs et d'Intensités (1949).  Paris, Durand & Cie, 1950.

Neumes Rhythmiques (1950).  Paris, Durand & Cie, 1950.

Ile de Feu 1.  Paris, Durand & Cie, 1950.

Ile de Feu 2.  Paris, Durand & Cie, 1950.

Bibliography

Aprahamian, Felix.  "Messiaen, Olivier, " Grove's Dictionary of Music and Musicians (5th ed.), V, 722-25.

Austin, William W.  Music in the 20th Century: From Debussy through Stravinsky.  New York, Norton, 1966.

Boulez, Pierre, et al.  "Hommage à Messiaen, " Melos, XXV (1958), 386.

Brennecke, Wilfried, and Jean Claude Henry.  "Messiaen, Olivier, " Die Musik in Geschichte und Gegenwart, IX, 218-21.

Collaer, Paul.  A History of Modern Music.  Trans.  Sally Abeles.  New York, World, 1961.

Dallin, Leon.  Techniques of Twentieth Century Composition. 2nd ed.  Dubuque, Iowa, Wm. C. Brown, 1964.

Dibelius, Ulrich.  Moderne Musik 1945-1965.  Munich, R. Piper, 1966.

Drew, David.  "Messiaen, a Provisional Study, " The Score, XIII (1955), 59; XIV (1955), 41.

Elston, Arnold.  "Some Rhythmic Practices in Contemporary Music, " The Musical Quarterly, XLII (July, 1956), 318-29.

Friskin, James, and Irwin Freundlich. Music for the Piano.
New York, Rinehart, 1954.

Gavoty, B. Musique et Mystique: le 'Cas' Messiaen. Paris,
n. p., 1945.

Gillespie, John. Five Centuries of Keyboard Music: An
Historical Survey of Music for Harpsichord and Piano.
Belmont, Calif., Wadsworth Pub. Co., 1965.

Goléa, Antoine. "French Music Since 1945," trans. Lucile
H. Brockway, The Musical Quarterly, LI (January, 1965),
22-37.

_____. Vingt Ans de Musique Contemporaine: de
Messiaen à Boulez. Paris, Seghers, 1962.

Hansen, Peter S. An Introduction to Twentieth Century Music.
Boston, Allyn and Bacon, 1961.

Hartog, Howard (ed.). European Music in the Twentieth
Century. New York, Praeger, 1957.

Hodeir, André. Since Debussy: A View of Contemporary
Music. Trans. Noel Burch. New York, Grove, 1961.

Hutcheson, Ernest. The Literature of the Piano: A Guide
for Amateur and Student. 3rd ed., rev. Rudolph Ganz.
New York, Knopf, 1964.

Karkoschka, Erhard. Das Schriftbild der Neuen Musik.
Celle, Germany, Hermann Moeck, 1966.

Kirby, F. E. A Short History of Keyboard Music. New
York, The Free Press, 1966.

Machlis, Joseph. Introduction to Contemporary Music. New
York, Norton, 1961.

Maegaard, Jan. Musikalsk Modernisme 1945-1962. Copenhagen, Stig Vendelkaers, 1964.

Messiaen, Olivier. The Technique of My Musical Language.
Trans. John Satterfield. 2 vols. Paris, Alphonse Leduc,
1956.

_____. Traité du Rythme. Paris, n. p., 1954.

"Messiaen, Olivier, " Baker's Biographical Dictionary of
   Musicians. Fifth Edition with 1965 Supplement. 1078-
   79; 88.

Messiaen, Pierre. Images. Paris, n. p., 1944.

Mitchell, Donald. The Language of Modern Music. New
   York, St. Martin's, 1966.

Quenetain, Tanneguy de. "Messiaen, Poet of Nature, "
   Music and Musicians, XI (May, 1963), 8.

Rostand, Claude. La Musique Française Contemporaine.
   Paris, n. p., 1952.

_____. Olivier Messiaen. Paris, n. p., 1958.

Roy, Jean. Présences Contemporaines: Musique Française.
   Paris, DeBresse, 1962.

Salzman, Eric. Twentieth-Century Music: An Introduction.
   Englewood Cliffs, N. J., Prentice-Hall, 1967.

Yates, Peter. Twentieth Century Music: Its Evolution from
   the End of the Harmonic Era into the Present Era of
   Sound. New York, Pantheon, 1967.

Zinke-Bianchini, Virginia. Olivier Messiaen. Paris, n. p.,
   1949.

NIGG, SERGE

(b. Paris, June 6, 1924)
Address: 135 Avenue de Versailles, Paris 16$^e$, France


    Serge Nigg was a student at the Paris Conservatory
in the early 1940's. Following study with Olivier Messiaen,
Nigg's work became increasingly chromatic. The atonal
nature of the Piano Sonata No. 1 (1943) reflects this trend.
Contacts with René Leibowitz in 1945 exposed Nigg to the
Schoenberg technique. Extensive study with Leibowitz[60]
crystallized in 1946 in Nigg's Variations for Piano and Ten

Instruments, one of the first dodecaphonic compositions by
a French composer.  The Deux Pièces for piano, Op. 5
(1946), also date from 1946, and are likewise examples of
twelve-tone writing.  Occasionally a very impelling jazz
rhythm permeates the texture.

After a short period, Nigg desired to deliver himself
from the yoke of strict twelve-tone composition, and enter-
ed a long phase of experimentation.[61] In 1948, Nigg, Elsa
Barraine, and Roger Desormière founded the French branch
of the Association of Progressive Composers and Musicolo-
gists, engendered partly by a desire to move away from
the strictly disciplined approach to the Schoenberg method
as advocated by Leibowitz.

More recently Nigg has returned to what he describes as a natural or personal dodecaphonic technique,
freed from the constraint, abstractions, and formality of
preconceived ideas.[62]

Nigg considers his second piano sonata (pub. 1965),
which embraces this revision of his ideas, as his most
important twelve-tone piano work.  Written especially for
the piano contests at the Paris Conservatory, it frequently
demands virtuosity, particularly in the first movement.  The
second movement consists of a very free variation on the
row.  The last movement exploits the principle of non-retrogradable rhythms.

Piano Music

Deux Pièces, Op. 5 (1946).  Paris, Le Chant du Monde,
    1947.

Deuxième Sonate pour Piano.  Paris, Jobert, 1965.

Bibliography

Collaer, Paul.  A History of Modern Music.  Trans. Sally
    Ables.  New York, World, 1961.

Fremiot, Marcel.  "Nigg, Serge," Die Musik in Geschichte
    und Gegenwart, IX, 1527-28.

Goléa, Antoine.  Vingt Ans de Musique Contemporaine: de
    Messiaen à Boulez.  Paris, Seghers, 1962.

Leibowitz, René. Schoenberg and His School. Trans. Dika
    Newlin. New York, Philosophical Library, 1949.

"Nigg, Serge," Baker's Biographical Dictionary of Musicians.
    Fifth Edition with 1965 Supplement, 1162; 72.

Roy, Jean. Présences Contemporaines: Musique Française.
    Paris, DeBresse, 1962.

Searle, Humphrey. "Nigg, Serge," Grove's Dictionary of
    Music and Musicians (5th ed.), VI, 91.

## PAQUE, DESIRE

(b. Liège, May 21, 1867; d. Bessancourt, France,
November 20, 1939)

Désiré Pâque began composing as a youth, and later
received a musical training at the Liège Conservatory. A
considerable part of his large output was piano music.
Pâque remained an isolated experimenter in atonal and athematic music, most of his compositions remaining unpublished. As early as 1911, the year Arnold Schoenberg's twelve-
tone writing began to emerge in the Six Little Pieces for
piano, Pâque completed three atonal piano sonatas. He
coined the term "adjonction constante" (continual motivic
addition) to describe his style. The appearance of this
feature in his composition is interesting considering both
the prominent role of motivic writing in Schoenberg's discovery of a twelve-tone method and the important later adapt-
ations of motivic usage in serialism. However, although
Pâque featured a motivic principle in his writing from about
1908 to 1918, he did not fully exploit or transform its
character.

Piano Music

Sonatas, Op. 68, 69, 70 (1911). Paris, Simrock, n.d.

Bibliography

Austin, William W. Music in the 20th Century: From
    Debussy through Stravinsky. New York, Norton, 1966.

Eaglefield-Hull, A. A Dictionary of Modern Music and
    Musicians. London, Dent, 1924.

Lavoye, L. "Un Grand Méconnu: Désiré Pâque," Revue Musicale, XX (1938).

"Pâque, Désiré," Baker's Biographical Dictionary of Musicians (5th ed.), 1206.

Pâque, Désiré, "Classicisme," La Revue Musicale, XII (1931), 345.

_____. "L'Atonalité, ou Mode Chromatique Unique," La Revue Musicale, 107 (1930), 135.

_____. "Notre Esthétique," La Revue Musicale, XI (1930), 119.

Vander Linden, Albert. "M. J. L. Désiré Pâque," Die Musik in Geschichte und Gegenwart, X, 739-40.

Wangermee, R. La Musique Belge Contemporaine. Brussels, La Renaissance du Livre, 1959.

## PAZ, JUAN CARLOS

(b. Buenos Aires, August 5, 1897)
Address: Rincón 210 piso I B; Buenos Aires, Argentina

The first imposing figure who led to the adoption of twelve-tone techniques in South America was Juan Carlos Paz. Largely self-taught, except for some instruction from Constantino Gaito, his style evolved past a neo-romantic chromaticism. He composed a set of Piano Variations (1928) which contain tonal characteristics but also many features of twelve-tone writing. Since the mid 1930's Paz has employed twelve-tone writing almost exclusively, in a contrapuntal texture that adheres closely to the Schoenberg technique. The set of Diez Piezas Sobre una Serie en Los Doce Tonos (1936) is rather strict and simple, yet resourceful; in this work, the use of retrograde turns of row segments effectively exploits the potential harmonic colors of the series.

Paz has been active in the formation of agencies for the promotion of modern music. In 1929 he was one of the organizers of the Grupo Renovación. This group, opposed to

sterile tradition, had sought new expression by adherence
to the concepts of J. S. Bach, Hindemith, and Stravinsky,
but found Schoenberg's ideas approaching their aims more
closely. The group was reformed as the Nueva Música.
Through this organization, Paz and his associates initiated
a series of concerts in 1937, to promote contemporary
music in South America. Paz has also written extensively
on the history of twentieth-century music.

Piano Music

"Balada No. II de 'Canciónes y Baladas'," Op. 31, No. 2
   (1936) Latin-American Art Music for the Piano, Francisco Curt Lange, ed. New York, Schirmer, 1942.

"Diez Piezas Sobre una Serie en Los Doce Tonos" (1936),
   Boletin Latino-Americano de Música, Curt Lange, Dr.
   Tomo IV. Suplemento Musical. Montevideo, El Futuro
   Instituto Interamericano de Música.

Bibliography

Composers of the Americas. Vol. II. Washington, D.C.,
   Pan American Union, 1956.

Fraser, Norman. "Paz, Juan Carlos," Grove's Dictionary
   of Music and Musicians (5th ed.), VI, 602.

Paz, Juan Carlos. A Schönberg o el Fin de la Era Tonal.
   In preparation.

_____. Introducción a la Música de Nuestro Tiempo.
   Buenos Aires, Nueva Vision, 1955.

_____. La Música en los Estados Unidos. Mexico,
   Fondo de Cultura Economica, 1952.

"Paz, Juan Carlos," Baker's Biographical Dictionary of
   Musicians (5th Ed.), 1218.

Romano, Jacobo. "Paz, Kagel, Kropfl: Tres Revitaliza-
   dores de la Música Argentina Contemporanea," Sonda, I
   (October, 1967), 3-14.

PENTLAND; BARBARA
(b. Winnipeg, January 2, 1912)
Address: 4765 West 6th Ave., Vancouver 8; British Columbia

Barbara Pentland began her development as a
composer in Canada simultaneously with her training as a
pianist. Her musical studies were continued in Paris with
Cécile Gauthiez, who transmitted the influence of César
Franck to Pentland's early works. In 1939 Pentland received a scholarship enabling her to do graduate work at
Juilliard, mainly under Frederic Jacobi and Bernard Wagenaar. During the summers of 1941 and 1942 she studied
with Aaron Copland at Tanglewood. In 1942 she also came
into contact with John Weinzweig, the first twelve-tone
composer in Canada and in 1947 met Dika Newlin, a pupil
of Schoenberg. In developing her own contrapuntal technique, Pentland gradually evolved away from the cast of
traditional harmony and toward the styles of Schoenberg
and Webern. Her Wind Octet (1948) contains her first
clearly serial writing. Between 1955 and 1957, Pentland
lived mainly in Germany. This experience provided further
exposure, particularly at Darmstadt, to the post-Webern
trends and confirmed her own tendencies toward the use of
meaningful material in as thin a texture as possible in order
to heighten clarity of musical expression. The tone row is
not pre-constructed but arises from the initial musical ideas
and is then developed with considerable flexibility by the use
of numerous permutations and inter-relationships of the
various row forms.[63]

Two recent piano scores, Toccata (1958) and Fantasy
(1962), are very similar in compositional style, but the
Fantasy is more complex level. Whereas both works utilize
the full keyboard range, the Fantasy frequently employs
several registers simultaneously by strategic use of the
pedal, permitting the build-up of vertical structures containing as many as ten of the twelve tones. A more strident
dissonance is used in the linear sections, as well. While
the Toccata is not rhythmically complicated the Fantasy not
only imparts a more forceful sense of rhythmic drive but
contains involved oppositions of tempi and asymmetrical
rhythms.

Pentland has performed widely as a pianist. She
was a member of the faculty of the Royal Conservatory of
Music of Toronto in the early 1940's and of the University

of British Columbia from 1949 to 1963.

Piano Music

Sonata Fantasy (1947).   Unpub.   ms.

Dirge (1948).   Toronto, BMI Canada Ltd., n.d.

Sonatinas (1951).   Unpub.   ms.

Mirror Study (1952).   Unpub.   ms.

Two-Piano Sonata (1953).   Unpub.   ms.

Aria (1954).   Unpub.   ms.

Interlude (1955).   Unpub.   ms.

Toccata (1958).   Toronto, BMI Canada Ltd., 1961.

Duets After Pictures by Paul Klee (1958-59).   Unpub.   ms.

Fantasy (1962).   Toronto, BMI Canada Ltd., 1966.

Shadows (1964).   Unpub.   ms.

Caprice (1965).   Unpub.   ms.

Bibliography

Composers of the Americas.   Vol.   VI.   Washington, D.C.,
    Pan American Union, 1960.

Gillespie, John.   Five Centuries of Keyboard Music: An
    Historical Survey of Music for Harpsichord and Piano.
    Belmont, Calif., Wadsworth Pub. Co., 1965.

Kallman, Helmut.   "Pentland, Barbara," Die Musik in
    Geschichte und Gegenwart, X, 1020-21.

"Pentland, Barbara," 1965 Supplement to Baker's Bio-
    graphical Dictionary of Musicians (5th ed.), 101.

Thirty-four Biographies of Canadian Composers.   Montreal,
    Canadian Broadcasting Corp., 1964.

PERLE, GEORGE

(b. Bayonne, New Jersey, May 6, 1915)
Address: c/o ASCAP; 575 Madison Avenue, New York, N.Y.

George Perle acquired his musical training at DePaul
University, the American Conservatory of Music, and New
York University.  In addition he studied composition pri-
vately with Ernst Křenek.  He has taught widely in the
United States and is currently a member of the faculty at
Queens College in New York.  He has written extensively
on serial composition and is presently preparing a study
to be titled The Operas of Alban Berg.

Perle began composition in a free atonal style but
since 1939 he has used his own twelve-tone modal system
as well as strict twelve-tone and some tonal writing.  He
was reluctant to adopt serialism because of its seeming
lack of harmonic function but was challenged to seek the
existence of some functional principle in serial writing
equivalent to the functional harmony of the tonal system.[64]
One approach had been the use of serial procedures by a
number of composers predating Schoenberg's clarification
of his twelve-tone technique.  Some of his observations are
described in his Serial Composition and Atonality.[65]  A
main theory of this book is that a series is formed of
constituent parts and that this inherent segmentation of the
basic set should be exploited, whereby one or more segments provide the source of a set complex.  Perle's concept of segmentation is not to be equated with motivic
structuring, as a segment may or may not constitute a
motive, and vice versa.

The Six Preludes for piano are fully chromatic.
Portions of the twelve tones are relegated to thematic lines
in a manner suggestive of serial technique.  But the inter-
spersing of remaining tones is dictated by harmonic design
and a strict ordering of the complete twelve-tone scale is
not maintained.  Thus the pieces are a cross between
atonal and twelve-tone composition, representing Perle's
twelve-tone modal system, his own modification of the
Schoenberg method.

Piano Music

"Six Preludes, New Music for the Piano.  New York,
    Lawson-Gould, 1958.

Piano Sonata (1950).  New York, Southern Music, n. d.

Interrupted Story (1956).  Bryn Mawr, Pa., Theodore
    Presser, n. d.

Short Sonata (1964).  Bryn Mawr, Pa., Theodore Presser,
    n. d.

Bibliography

Austin, William W.  Music in the 20th Century: From
    Debussy through Stravinsky.  New York, Norton, 1966.

Chase, Gilbert.  America's Music: From the Pilgrims to
    the Present.  Rev. 2nd ed.  New York, McGraw-Hill,
    1966.

Custer, Arthur.  "Current Chronicle:  Philadelphia," The
    Musical Quarterly, LIII (April, 1967),  251-59.

Machlis, Joseph.  Introduction to Contemporary Music.  New
    York, Norton, 1961.

Perle, George.  "An Approach to Simultaneity in Twelve-
    Tone Music," Perspectives of New Music, III (1964),
    91-101.

_____.  "Atonality and the Twelve-note System in the
    United States," The Score, XXVII (July, 1960) 51-66.

_____.  "The Chansons of Antoine Busnois,"
    Musical Review, XI (May, 1950).

_____.  "Evolution of the Tone-Row: The 12-tone Modal
    System," Musical Review, II (1941),  273-87.

_____.  "The Harmonic Problem in 12-tone Music,"
    Musical Review, XV (1954),  253.

_____.  "Integrative Devices in the Music of Machaut,"
    The Musical Quarterly, XXXIV (April, 1948).

_____.  "Possible Chords in Twelve-Tone Music," The
    Score, IX (1954).

_____. Serial Composition and Atonality. 2nd ed.
Berkeley, Univ. of Calif. Press, 1968.

_____. "Theory and Practice in Twelve-Tone Music, "
The Score, XXVI (June, 1959), 58.

_____. "Twelve-Tone Tonality, " Monthly Musical
Record, LXXIII (October, 1943), 175.

_____. "Woyzeck and Wozzeck, " The Musical Quarterly,
LIII (April, 1967), 206-19.

"Perle, George, " Baker's Biographical Dictionary of
Musicians (5th ed.), 1228.

Ward, Martha Kingdon. "Perle, George, " Grove's Dictionary of Music and Musicians (5th ed.), VI, 672-73.

Weinberg, Henry. "The Music of George Perle, " American
Composers Alliance Bulletin, X (1962).


POUSSEUR, HENRI

(b. Malmédy, Belgium, July 23, 1929)
Address: 8 Croix de Chôdes; Malmédy, Belgium

    Henri Pousseur's interest in avant-garde trends
began to widen at Darmstadt from study with Pierre Boulez.
His continuing association with this musical center has led
to his collaboration with artists seeking to create a synthesis
of music and sculpture.  Pousseur is also an active member
of Variation, a group fostering avant-garde music in Liège,
and writes extensively on contemporary music.

    Pousseur's interest in electronic music and the
problems of form in contemporary music led to his composition entitled Scambi (1958), one of the first examples of
open form in the electronic media.

    Interest in Webern's concepts led Pousseur to de-
velop an analytical method for the study of Webern's melodic
lines.  He coined the term "organic chromaticism" to describe Webern's style.[66] Pousseur's system is based on the
tenet that each note is linked to its chromatic neighbors

by adjacent major 7ths or minor 9ths appearing in either
the melodic line or the vertical progressions.

The legacy of Webern is obvious in Pousseur's piano
scores of the last decade, particularly with regard to fragmentation.  Although the Variations II (1955-56) have a
thicker texture than typical of Webern pointillism, this is
not the  case with subsequent piano scores.  Mobile (1957-
58) and Caractères (1961) exemplify Pousseur's efforts to
exploit the possibilities for integrating the rhythmic element
more closely with the fragmented pitch sounds in order to
achieve a greater sense of space and time.  In these works,
an integral rhythm and thin texture with judicious chromaticism
stresses the linear movement.  Thus Pousseur avoids a
tendency toward a saturated chromaticism whereby the density of complex vertical structures stalls the momentum.
These scores utilize Pousseur's notational innovations, amply
described in their prefaces.  These annotations provide
considerable insight into his variety of indeterminate rhythms.

The less difficult Apostrophe et Six Réflexions (1964-
66) marks a change of pace.  Reverting to traditional notation, Pousseur seems to be seeking the limits within which
traditional melodic outlines and consonances can be absorbed
into a serial work.

Pousseur's piano scores demonstrate considerable
flexibility in his use of serial principles.

Piano Music

Exercices pour Piano: Variations I (1956).   Milan, Suvini
    Zerboni, n. d.

Exercices pour Piano: Impromptu et Variations II (1955-56).
    Milan, Suvini Zerboni, 1959.

Mobile pour Deux Pianos (1957-58).   Milan, Suvini Zerboni,
    1961.

Caractères (1961).  London, Universal Edition, 1962.

Miroir de Votre Faust (Caractères II) (1964).   London,
    Universal Edition, n. d.

Apostrophe et Six Réflexions (1964-66).   Unpub. ed.

Bibliography

Dibelius, Ulrich.  Moderne Musik 1945-1965.  Munich, R.
   Piper, 1966.

Goléa, Antoine.  Vingt Ans de Musique Contemporaine: de
   Boulez à l'Inconnu.  Paris, Seghers, 1962.

Hitchcock, H. Wiley.  "Current Chronicle: New York," The
   Musical Quarterly, LI (July, 1965), 530-40.

Karkoschka, Erhard.  Das Schriftbild der Neuen Musik.
   Celle, Germany, Hermann Moeck, 1966.

Koenig, Gottfried Michael.  "Henri Pousseur," Die Reihe
   IV (1960), 14-28.

Kohn, Karl.  "Current Chronicle: Los Angeles," The Musical Quarterly, XLIX (July, 1963), 360-69.

Pousseur, Henri.  "Da Schoenberg a Webern: una Mutazione,"
   trans. Vittorio Armanni, Incontri Musicali, I (December,
   1956), 3-39.

_____.  "Formal Elements in a New Compositional
   Material," Die Reihe, I (1958), 30-34.

_____.  "Music, Form and Practice (an Attempt to
   Reconcile Some Contradictions)," Die Reihe, VI (1964),
   77-93.

_____.  "Outline of a Method," trans. Leo Black, Die
   Reihe, III (1959), 44-88.

_____.  "The Question of Order in New Music," trans.
   David Behrman, Perspectives of New Music, V (1966),
   93-111.

_____.  "Scambi," Gravesaner Blätter, IV (1959),
   36-54.

_____.  "Webern's Organic Chromaticism," Die Reihe,
   II (1958).

"Pousseur, Henri," 1965 Supplement to Baker's Biographical Dictionary of Musicians (5th ed.), 104.

Prieberg, Fred K. Lexikon der Neuen Musik. Freiburg,
Karl Alber, 1958.

_____. Musica ex Machina. Berlin, Ullstein, 1960.

Von Lewinski, Wolf-Eberhard. "Pousseur, Henri," Die
Musik in Geschichte und Gegenwart, X, 1529-31.

Wörner, Karl H. "Current Chronicle: German," The
Musical Quarterly, XLVI (April, 1960), 270-75.


RAMOVS, PRIMOZ

(b. Ljubljana, Yugoslavia, March 20, 1921)
Address: Gorupova ul. 2; Ljubljana, Yugoslavia

Primož Ramovš graduated from the Musical Academy
in Ljubljana in 1941. His principal teacher was Slavko
Osterc. Following study in Italy with Alfredo Casella and
Goffredo Petrassi, he returned to his homeland. Presently
he is the librarian of the Library of the Slovene Academy
of Sciences and Arts in Ljubljana.

A lengthy list of compositions includes both chamber
and orchestral works. His former neo-classic style has
been increasingly replaced with contemporary styles. About
half of his piano scores employ dodecaphonic techniques.
The Variacije za Klavir (1959-60) are restricted to use of
the four basic forms of the pitch row without any transpositions. Three years later the Pentektasis za Klavir
(1963), in total serialization, employs five simultaneous
rows. Each series (of pitch, duration, dynamics, timbre,
and density, containing 12, 9, 8, 7, and 5 components,
respectively) is individually composed. New combinations
continually arise because each series has a different number
of components. The Dialogi (1962) for two pianos features
the simultaneous use of two pitch rows in the third part,
following their separate use in the preceding sections.

Three of his dodecaphonic piano works feature
motivic construction. Four-tone units provide the basic
material in Utrinki ob Bachovem imenu za Klavir (1963-64),

Mali nokturno za Klavir (1964), and (Ne)-Simetrija za Klavir
(1965). This last score also contains an aleatory element
and a unique notational format.

Ramovš has moved rapidly along a course of serial
experimentation. Since 1965 the principle of ordering, particularly of the pitch series, has been considerably relaxed.
Recent piano works, Konstanta in Sekvence (1965), Preludij
in Vrnitve (1966), and Ciklus (1966), reflect the channeling
of Ramovs' interest toward the device of perpetual development of his initial material although with frequent regress
to the original forms, in contrast with composers who prefer
to develop transformations ad infinitum. It is also indicative
of Ramovš' serial style that he has applied principles of
inversion or retrograde movement to all components of the
design, thus becoming a major factor in creating the musical form.

Piano Music

Variacije za Klavir (1959-60). Ljubljana, Silvester Orel,
    1961. Dialogi (2 Klavirs) (1962). Unpub.

Pentektasis za Klavir. Ljublána, Ramovš, 1963.

Utrinki ob Bachovem Imenu za Klavir (1963-64). Ljublana,
    n.p., 1965.

Mali Nokturno za Klavir. Ljublana, n.p., 1964.

(Ne)-Simetrija za Klavir (1965). Ljublana, n.p., n.d.

Konstanta in Sekvence (constant and sequences) 1965. Un-
    pub. ms.

Preludij in Vrnitve (preludes and returns) (1966). Unpub.
    ms.

Ciklus (Cyclus) (1966). Unpub. ms.

Bibliography

"Ramovš, Primož," 1965 Supplement to Baker's Biographic-
    al Dictionary of Musicians (5th ed.), 107.

RANDS, BERNARD

(b.  Sheffield, England, March 2, 1935)
Address: University College of North Wales; Bangor;
Caernarvonshire, North Wales

     Bernard Rands studied with Roman Vlad, Luigi
Dallapiccola, and Reginald Smith Brindle and has had some
association with Luciano Berio.  The Tre Espressioni, a
piano score written after study with Brindle and during
study with Dallapiccola, is based on a twelve tone series.
In it, Rands demonstrates an ability to balance freedom and
control within a serial language.

     In Espressione IV (1964) Rands exploits the physical
relationship of two pianos.[67] The musical material at a
given moment either stresses similar piano qualities in both
instruments, or exploits diverse sounds and effects obtainable by the pairing of the keyboards.

     There is no appreciable bibliography for Rands at
present.

Piano Music

Tre Espressioni.   London, Universal Edition, 1965.

Espressione IV (1964) for two pianos.   London, Universal
     Edition, 1965.

REYNOLDS, ROGER

(b.  Detroit, Michigan, July 18, 1934)
Address: c/o C. F. Peters Corp.; 373 Park Avenue South;
New York, New York 10016

     Roger Reynolds majored in engineering, receiving a
degree from the University of Michigan in 1957, and then
pursued his interest in music, obtaining a master's degree
in music in 1961.  As a Fulbright scholar he devoted the
year of 1962-63 to the study of electronic music at Cologne.
He has actively promoted avant-garde trends, and participated
in the founding of the ONCE festival at Ann Arbor.  In 1967

he was situated in Japan as a Fellow of the Institute of
Current World Affairs.

Stimulated by interest in the ideas of Roberto
Gerhard,[68] serial composition has played an important role
in his early works, although it has not been used in recent
works.  The development of his style, particularly in
electronic music, has also been affected by his knowledge
of mathematics and his interest in psychoacoustics.

Epigram and Evolution (1959), for the piano, alter-
nately develops a certain row in a strict and then in a
free manner.  A playful characteristic found throughout
other scores appears in several sections.  The Fantasy for
Pianist (1964), a more advanced work, is based on permutation of a segmental row (hexachords or tetrachords).
The serial concept is also extended to the time structure
of all four movements.  The method used to create this
proportional time structure derives the rhythmic patterns
from the row by numbering up by semi-tones from the
lowest tone of a transposition.[69]

Piano Music

Epigram and Evolution (1959).   New York, Peters, 1963.

Fantasy for Pianist.   New York, Peters, 1964.

Bibliography

Chase, Gilbert.   America's Music: From the Pilgrims to
    the Present.  Rev. 2nd ed.   New York, McGraw-Hill,
    1966.

Clarke, Henry Leland.  "Current Chronicle: Seattle," The
    Musical Quarterly, LI (July, 1965), 540-44.

Hitchcock, H. Wiley.  "Current Chronicle: Ann Arbor,"
    The Musical Quarterly, L (October, 1964), 515-19.

_____ .  "Current Chronicle: New York," The Musical
    Quarterly, LI (July, 1965), 540-44.

Mason, Colin.  "Gerhard, Roberto," Grove's Dictionary of
    Music and Musicians (5th ed.), 599-601.

"Reynolds, Roger," 1965 Supplement to Baker's Biographical
    Dictionary of Musicians (5th ed.), 109.

Schwartz, Elliott and Barney Childs (eds.). Contemporary
    Composers on Contemporary Music. New York, Holt,
    Rinehart, Winston, 1967.

Yates, Peter. Twentieth Century Music. New York,
    Pantheon, 1967.

## RIEGGER, WALLINGFORD

(b. Albany, Georgia, April 29, 1885; d. New York,
April 2, 1961)

        Wallingford Riegger emerged from the conservative
cast of American composers to assume a relatively radical
style.    Born into a musical family, Riegger began his
musical development early as a cellist.   He later became
associated with Leon Theremin in the development of electronic instruments and learned to play an electronic  cello.
Following graduation in 1907 from the Institute of Musical
Art in New York, where his major studies in composition
and theory were with Percy Goetschius, Riegger spent ten
years studying and conducting in Germany.    Most of his
teaching activity upon return to the States was in the New
York area where he participated in the efforts of many
early groups attempting to further interest in contemporary
music.    The years in Germany had stimulated Riegger's
interest in atonality and twelve-tone systems and led him to
make a thorough study of acoustics and the Schoenberg
technique.    By 1927, Riegger was experimenting with the
use of atonality in his works.   (Much of his work during
this period was published under a variety of pseudonyms).
During the 1930's he developed his use of tone-rows.
Henceforth a combination of atonality, tonality,  and free
and strict dodecaphony constituted his style, in a fabric
that was usually contrapuntal.   The twelve-tone writing is
Schoenbergian in many respects, as in the varied treatment of motivic figures derived from the row, but unorthodox as in the use of such features as tonality.   Tonal
centers are sometimes artificially established or derived,
but traditional tonality is incorporated on occasion.

        Intricate rhythmic patterns, frequently employing poly-

rhythms, assumed a distinctive style in his work. He
wrote several works for piano and drums in the 1930's,
during a phase in which he was preoccupied with rhythm.
Riegger's interest in rhythm was furthered by his association with modern dance. The piano four-hand works (later
orchestrated by the composer), Evocation (1933), The Cry
(1935), and New Dance (1935), formed a suite for three
dancers. These works represent Riegger's versatility in
both rhythmic and atonal writing. He introduced tonics and
dominants. Among the harmonic sounds, fourths predominate. Motivic figuration is exploited by what Riegger called
"cumulative sequence" (traditional repetition and accumula-
tive extension of motives carried to an extreme). The
driving rhythms are an integral part of the melodic and
harmonic events and point up the inventiveness of Riegger's
atonal writing.

     In the introduction to a collection of piano pieces
entitled New and Old (1947), Riegger emphatically states
his belief that a continuity of relationship always   exists
between the past and the new, no matter how radical the
changes. By isolating and exploiting each of a dozen
modern techniques in these pieces, Riegger provides some
illuminating insights into their possible combinations with
twelve-tone writing. Analytical notes describe his synthesis
of classical and modern idioms, demonstrating their compatibility and clarify pertinent aspects of recent musical development. A typical example is the combination of rhythms
characteristic of Bartók with a changing sequence pattern
suggestive of Boris Blacher's variable meter technique.

     Riegger continued to couple an extensive study of
acoustics with the use of ideas stemming from indigenous
and immigrant musical cross-currents in the United States.

Piano Music

Scherzo for Two Pianos, Op. 13a. New York, Peer
     International Corp., 1954.

Evocation (for two pianos or piano four hands), Op. 17.
     New York, Peer International Corp., 1953.

The Cry (for two pianos or piano four hands), Op. 22. New

York, Peer International Corp., 1953.

New Dance (for two pianos or piano solo). New York, Assoc. Music Pub., n.d.

New and Old: Twelve Pieces for Piano. New York, Boosey & Hawkes, 1947.

Variations (for two pianos), Op. 54a. New York, Assoc. Music Pub., n.d.

Bibliography

Austin, William W. Music in the 20th Century: From Debussy through Stravinsky. New York, Norton, 1966.

Carter, Elliott. "Wallingford Riegger," American Composers Alliance Bulletin, II (February, 1952), 3.

Chase, Gilbert. America's Music: From the Pilgrims to the Present. Rev. 2nd ed. New York, McGraw-Hill, 1966.

Eschmann, Karl. Changing Forms in Modern Music. Boston, Schirmer, 1945.

Gillespie, John. Five Centuries of Keyboard Music: An Historical Survey of Music for Harpsichord and Piano. Belmont, Calif., Wadsworth Pub. Co., 1965.

Glanville-Hicks, Peggy. "Riegger, Wallingford," Grove's Dictionary of Music and Musicians, VII, 162-63.

Goldman, Richard Franko. "Current Chronicle: New York," The Musical Quarterly, XLVII (July, 1961), 396-400.

_____. "The Music of Wallingford Riegger," The Musical Quarterly, XXXVI (January, 1950), 39-61.

_____. "Riegger, Wallingford," Die Musik in Geschichte und Gegenwart, IX, 476-77.

Machlis, Joseph. Introduction to Contemporary Music. New York, Norton, 1961.

Reis, Claire R.  Composers in America: Biographical
    Sketches of Contemporary Composers with a Record of
    their Works.  Rev. and enl. ed.  New York, Macmillan,
    1947.

"Riegger, Wallingford, " Baker's Biographical Dictionary of
    Musicians.  Fifth Edition with 1965 Supplement, 1341;
    110.

Salazar, Adolfo.  Music in Our Time: Trends in Music
    Since the Romantic Era.  Trans. Isabel Pope.  New
    York, Norton, 1946.


ROCHBERG, GEORGE


(b.  Paterson, New Jersey, July 5, 1918)
Address: c/o ASCAP; 575 Madison Avenue; New York,
New York 10022


        George Rochberg received a musical education at
the Curtis Institute, where he later taught.  Rochberg's
adoption of serial composition came about rather gradually
and was only temporary.  The Symphony No. 1 (1948)
is the first work in which he used a row.  In compositions
during the ensuing years he used a twelve-tone technique
but finally abandoned it in 1963, when the method no longer
seemed to serve his musical expression.[70]

        Twelve Bagatelles (1952) for piano is in the twelve-
tone idiom, with no particular complications in the application.  Influences of Schoenberg and Webern are obvious.
The Sonata-Fantasia (1956), on the other hand, is a very
complex realization of the potential freedom in a single row.
No single form is consistently employed and many kinds of
manipulation appear.  The harmonic structure of the work,
especially with regard to the use of hexachords, is true to
the theoretical principles on which Rochberg has written.

        Rochberg's theoretical writings have always followed
fact rather than posing hypothetical ideas about the potential of contemporary music.  He has specialized in the
study of the hexachordal division of a row.  His short study
on this single aspect of twelve-tone composition, The Hexachord and its Relation to the Twelve-tone Row (1955), was
one of the first efforts to delve exhaustively into a particular

facet of twelve-tone practice. Somewhat clumsy in eluci-
dating the mathematical relationship clearly, the monograph
nevertheless explores thoroughly the workings of mirror
inversion with regard to the hexachord in twelve-tone scores.
A later article, "The Harmonic Tendency of the Hexachord"
(1959), supplements this study. These studies outline how
Schoenberg, in the course of time, discovered the significance of the hexachord, within which single notes could be
freely rearranged without disturbing the inherent order of
the complete series, and thus perceived the harmonic potential in the combination of hexachord mirrors. This, of
course, amounts to a special type of alteration, but Rochberg is more concerned first, with the significance of the
hexachords to a chordal system associated with the twelve-
tone system and second, with the belief that this chordal
language is derived from symmetry, resulting from the
hexachord phenomena, which is to be understood as the
source of structural order. Rochberg also compares Schoenberg's use of the hexachord with Hauer's tropes and Babbitt's
source sets. Rochberg's conclusions are based on the study
of specific scores but it is questionable if his summary
emphasizes clearly enough that his generalizations apply only
to a specific, highly specialized type of structure, which,
for example, could not be an harmonic scheme underlying
an asymmetrical plan of manipulating a row.

Piano Music

Twelve Bagatelles for Piano (1952). Bryn Mawr, Pa.,
    Theodore Presser, 1955.

Sonata-Fantasia for Piano (1956). Bryn Mawr, Pa.,
    Theodore Presser, 1958.

Bibliography

Beckwith, John and Udo Kasemets (eds.). The Modern
    Composer and His World. Toronto, Univ. of Toronto
    Press, 1961.

Chase, Gilbert. America's Music: From the Pilgrims to
    the Present. Rev. 2nd. ed. New York, McGraw-Hill,
    1966.

Henahan, Donald J. "Current Chronicle: Chicago, " The
    Musical Quarterly, LIII (April, 1967), 246-50.

Machlis, Joseph. Introduction to Contemporary Music.
   New York, Norton, 1961.

Ringer, Alexander L. "Current Chronicle: Cleveland,"
   The Musical Quarterly, XLV (April, 1967), 230-34.

_____. "Current Chronicle: St. Louis," The Musical
   Quarterly, XLVII (January, 1961), 101-103.

_____. "The Music of George Rochberg," The Musical
   Quarterly, LII (October, 1966), 409-430.

_____. The Hexachord and its Relation to the Twelve-
   tone Row. Bryn Mawr, Pa., Theodore Presser, 1955.

_____. "The Harmonic Tendency of the Hexachord,"
   Journal of Music Theory, III (November, 1959), 208-230.

_____. "The New Image of Music," Perspectives of
   New Music, II (1963).

_____. "Webern's Search for Harmonic Identity,"
   Journal of Music Theory, VI (1962), 109-124.

"Rochberg, George," Baker's Biographical Dictionary of
   Musicians. Fifth Edition with 1965 Supplement, 1354;
   110.

Schwarz, Elliott. "Current Chronicle: Brunswick, Maine,"
   The Musical Quarterly, LI (January, 1965), 682.


SAKAC, BRANIMIR

(b. Zagreb, 1918)
Address: Meduliceys 27; Zagreb, Yugoslavia

     Branimir Sakač has gradually moved from a tradition-
al to a contemporary style dominated by serial and aleatoric
methods. The two piano works, Preludio Aleatorio (1961),
and Study II (1964) are each based on a 12-tone row and the
use of chance. The later work is much more radical in
that the chance element is much more prominent and that it
permits opportunity for striking contrasts between piano
effects to occur.

Sakač has been active in efforts to synthesize sound, motion, and spatial relationships in modern art. He has also been prominent in sponsoring contemporary music in Yugoslavia, particularly through his participation in the Muzicki Biennale, a major international music festival since 1961.

Piano Music

Preludio Aleatorio (1964).    Unpub.    ms.

Study II for Piano (1964).    Unpub.    ms.

Bibliography

Lück, Rudolf.   Contemporary Yugoslavian Piano Music. Vol. 2.   Cologne, Hans Gerig, n. d.


SCHAFFER, BOGUSLAW

(b.   Lvov, Poland (Now in USSR), June 6, 1929)
Address: Kolorowa 4; Nowa Huta, Poland

Boguslaw Schäffer received a degree in musicology from the Jagiellonian University in Cracow in 1953.   He studied composition with A. Malawski.   Schäffer's early scores included the first twelve-tone orchestral work written in Poland (1953).   Until 1958 he was active as an historian, theoretician, and critic of twentieth-century music.   Since 1959 he has devoted most of his time to composition and in 1963 became a faculty member at the State College of Music in Cracow.

The Polish folk idiom is prominent in much of his early work but Schäffer has gradually abandoned this element since his adoption of serial techniques.   His main interest has become the development of proportional rhythms. He has devised a graphic notation for portraying sound intensities, proportions of duration, and positioning of notes, through use of analytical geometry and, frequently, red and green colors.   This notation is employed in several of the pieces collected in Musica per Pianoforte (1949-1960). Except for the Sonata for Two Pianos (1952) the volume includes most of Schäffer's piano scores.   The pieces trace

his movement from a rather conservative style to a radical
one. A lengthy commentary facilitates understanding of his
graphic notation.

Piano Music

Musica per Pianoforte (1949-1960).  Warsaw, Przedstawicielstwo Wydawnictw Polskich, 1960.

Bibliography

Jarocinski, Stafan (ed.).  Polish Music.  Warsaw, Polish
Scientific Publishers, 1965.

Karkoschka, Erhard.  Das Schriftbild der Neuen Musik.
Celle, Germany, Hermann Moeck, 1966.

Lissa, Zofia.  "Schäffer, Boguslaw," Die Musik in
Geschichte und Gegenwart, IX, 1533.

Maegaard, Jan.  Musikalsk Modernisme 1945-1962.  Copenhagen, Stig Vendelkaers, 1964.

Salzman, Eric.  Twentieth-Century Music: An Introduction.
Englewood Cliffs, N.J., Prentice-Hall, 1967.

Schäffer, Boguslaw.  Almanac of Polish Contemporary Composers.  Cracow, n.p., 1956.

_____.  Nowa Muzyka.  Cracow, n.p., 1958.

"Schäffer, Boguslaw," 1965 Supplement to Baker's Biographical Dictionary of Musicians (5th ed.), 115.

SCHAT, PETER

(b.  Utrecht, June 5, 1935)
Address: O. Z. Voorburgwal 119; Amsterdam, The
Netherlands

       In addition to classes at The Hague Royal Conserva-
tory, Peter Schat studied with Mátyás Seiber and Pierre
Boulez.  Schat utilizes both serial and electronic idioms
in a wide variety of styles.

The Inscripties for piano contains a twelve-tone row
that is segmented into two asymmetrical parts. Each part
is further segmented to correlate with a basic rhythmic
pattern, also asymmetrically divided. A distinctive quality
is achieved from deviations in asymmetrical note groupings
placed in opposition to the almost ostinato repetition of
rhythmic motives. A brief opportunity for chance and
improvisation is permitted in the second of the three pieces.

Piano Music

Inscripties voor Piano. Amsterdam, Donemus, 1959.

Bibliography

"Schat, Peter," 1965 Supplement to Baker's Dictionary of
    Musicians (5th ed.), 115.

SCHIBLER, ARMIN

(b. Kreuzlingen, Switzerland, November 20, 1920)
Address: Wolfbachstrasse 33; 8023 Zürich, Switzerland

Armin Schibler studied composition with Willy Burkhard and others in Zürich. A wide variety of styles is
represented in his chamber, orchestral, and opera scores.
Schibler considers Vivaldi and Bach the major influences
in his neo-Baroque beginnings, especially in his works up
to Op. 13. His dodecaphonic phase occurred mainly in the
early 1950's. Only his chamber opera, Die Späte Süehne,
has a strict serial composition. Schibler wrote several
piano compositions during this time, employing what he
describes as "dodecaphonic tonality." He defines the term
as tonal equality of the twelve tones without the use of a
series.[71] Aphorismen für Klavier (1951) contains nine short
pieces, each compelling for its expressiveness. Although
the ordering of the twelve tones is not consistent, certain
lyrical motives recur in combination with rhythmic patterns
to provide a sense of unity. Contrast is provided with the
rhapsodic passages by the exploitation of specific sonority
in conjunction with a pervasive rhythm.

Piano Music

Aphorismen für Klavier, Op. 29.  Berlin, Ahn & Simrock,
    1960.

Ornamente, Op. 32.  Berlin, Ahn & Simrock, n.d.

Dodecaphonic Studies for Pedagogic Use.  Germany, Kahnt
    Lindan, n.d.

Bibliography

Mohr, Ernst.  "Schibler, Armin," Die Musik in Geschichte
    und Gegenwart, IX, 1692-94.

Reich, Willi.  "On Swiss Musical Composition of the
    Present," trans. Ernest Sanders, The Musical Quarterly,
    LI (January, 1965), 78-91.

"Schibler, Armin," Baker's Biographical Dictionary of
    Musicians.  Fifth Edition with 1965 Supplement, 1435;
    115.

Von Fischer, Kurt.  "Schibler, Armin," Grove's Dictionary
    of Music and Musicians (5th ed.), VII, 482.

Wörner, Karl H.  Armin Schibler; Werk und Persönlichkeit.
    Amriswil, Switzerland, n.p., 1953.


SEARLE, HUMPHREY

(b.  Oxford, England, August 26, 1915)
Address: 44 Ordnance Hill; London N.W. 8, England

        Humphrey Searle and Elisabeth Lutyens were the
first dodecaphonic composers in England.  Searle studied
composition with John Ireland and R. O. Morris in London
at the Royal College of Music.  In 1934 the first performance in England of Alban Berg's Wozzeck stimulated Searle's
use of atonal and twelve-tone music.  He acquired a scholarship to work with Webern in Vienna in 1937 and 1938.  His
study there concentrated on Schoenberg's harmonic theories
but when Searle's twelve-tone composition subsequently began
about 1939 or 1940 the influence of Webern was evident,
particularly in passages of thin texture, and by the frequency
of 7ths and 9ths in the melodic line.  Searle has stated, however, that he tends to join sounds rather than maintain the

isolated pointillism of Webern.[72] The romantic flavor of
Schoenberg has also been apparent and in Searle's later
works this kinship with Schoenberg style has increased.

Searle's compositions fluctuate between atonal and
serial styles. Among the piano scores, Threnos & Toccata
(1948), the Piano Sonata (1951),[73] and Prelude on a Theme
of Alan Rawsthorne (1965) are all twelve-tone works. Searle
has specialized in the study of Liszt and the piano sonata
utilizes both the Lisztian and the Schoenbergian ideas on
thematic transformation.[74] The Suite for Piano (1956) is
basically atonal and not serial, although in the third movement a long series and other applications of serial techniques are evident.

Searle's theoretical writing includes a volume entitled Twentieth-Century Counterpoint in which he has pro-
posed an all-purpose scheme for analyzing contemporary
music. His English translation of Rufer's book on Schoenberg's Structural Functions of Harmony are valuable contributions to musicology.

## Piano Music

Threnos & Toccata, Op. 14 (1948). London, Alfred Leng-
    nick, 1949.

Piano Sonata, Op. 21 (1951). London, Oxford Univ. Press,
    1952.

"Suite for Piano, Op. 29." Contemporary British Piano
    Music. London, Schott, 1956.

Prelude on a Théme of Alan Rawsthorne (1965). London,
    Faber & Faber, 1968.

## Bibliography

Lockspeiser, Edward. "Humphrey Searle," The Musical
    Times, (September, 1955).

Mason, Colin. "Searle, Humphrey," Grove's Dictionary of
    Music and Musicians (5th ed.), VII, 679-81.

Rayment, Malcom. "Searle, Humphrey," Die Musik in
    Geschichte und Gegenwart, XII, 440-42.

Reti, Rudolph.  Tonality in Modern Music.  New York,
    Collier, 1962.

Rufer, Josef.  Composition with Twelve Notes Related Only
    to One Another.  Trans.  Humphrey Searle.  London,
    Barrie and Rockliff, 1954.

Schafer, Murray.  British Composers in Interview.  London,
    Faber & Faber, 1963.

Searle, Humphrey.  "New Kinds of Music (Boulez's methods
    of Composition), Twentieth Century, 161 (May, 1957),
    480-83.

_____.  "A Note on 'Gold Coast Customs,'" Music
    Survey, III, 18-23.

_____.  Twentieth-Century Counterpoint.  London,
    Ernest Benn, 1954.

"Searle, Humphrey," Baker's Biographical Dictionary of
    Musicians.  Fifth Edition with 1965 Supplement, 1489;
    117.


## SEROCKI, KAZIMIERZ

(b.  Toruń, March 3, 1922)
Address: Piwarskiego 16/10; Warsaw 36, Poland

    Kazimierz Serocki began his musical career as a
concert pianist but gradually restricted himself to composition.  Following graduation from the State High School of
Music in Łódz in 1946, he studied with Nadia Boulanger
in Paris.  His output includes orchestral works, song cycles,
chamber music, and film scores.[75]

    The fourth, fifth, and sixth preludes in Serocki's
Suite of Preludes for piano (1952), represent the first dodecaphonic post-war writing in Poland.[76] The composer noted
that the Suite (as also the Sonate pour Piano of 1955) does
not fully comply with the Schoenberg practices.[77] The fourth
prelude is completely iterative, containing two distinct rows
which are alternated in one of their forms.  Other twelve-
note statements in the fifth and sixth preludes retain only
the basic shape of these two similar rows (both of which are

completely ascending forms).

In the Musica Concertante (1958), a cyclic symphonic form for chamber orchestra, Serocki made his first use of total serialization.[78]

A Piacere (1963) is described by the composer as an open-form, based technically on serial-statistic methods which utilize a determinate sound material. It is chance music only with regard to ordering and tempi. Each of the thirty short suggestions has been given an approximate duration in terms of seconds.

Serocki was a member of the group which organized the first Warsaw Autumn in 1956, one of the major contemporary music festivals today.

Piano Music

Suite of Preludes for Piano (1952). Cracow, Polskie Wydawnictwo Muzyczne, 1954.

Sonata na Fortepiano. Cracow, Polskie Wydawnictwo Muzyczne, 1955.

A Piacere. Cracow, Polskie Wydawnictwo Muzyczne, 1963.

Bibliography

Halski, Czeslaw R. "Serocki, Kazimierz," Grove's Dictionary of Music and Musicians. (5th ed.), VII, 710.

Jarocinski, Stefan (ed.). Polish Music. Warsaw, Polish Scientific Pub., 1965.

_____. "Polish Music after World War II," The Musical Quarterly, LI (January, 1965), 244-58.

Lissa, Zofia. "Serocki, Kazimierz," Die Musik in Geschichte und Gegenwart, XII, 567-68.

Schäffer, Boguslaw. Klasyvy Dodekafonii. 2 vols. Cracow, Polskie Wydawnictwo Muzyczne, 1961-64.

Schiller, Henryk. "Percussion in the Contemporary Polish Music," Res Facta, I (1967), 43-45.

"Serocki, Kazimierz," Baker's Biographical Dictionary of
    Musicians. Fifth Edition with 1965 Supplement, 1498;
    118.

Stone, Kurt. "Reviews of Records," The Musical Quarterly,
    L (April, 1964), 260-71.

SKALKOTTAS, NIKOS

(b. Chalcis, Greece, March 8, 1904; d. Athens,
September 19, 1949)

        Nikos Skalkottas, considered by Schoenberg to be one
of his outstanding students, began his career as a fine
violinist but abandoned this goal in 1925. The gold medal
and scholarship which he won upon graduation from the
Athens Conservatory as a violinist enabled him to go to
Germany in 1921. There, his interest turned to composition,
the winning of other prizes enabling him to remain for
about two decades. From 1927 until 1932 he studied with
Philipp Jarnach, Kurt Weill, Adolph Weiss, and Schoenberg.
The Nazi regime forced Skalkottas to return to his Greek
homeland in 1933.

        The main characteristics of a mature style in which
the use of tonality was abandoned were already evident in
the early works of Skalkottas between 1925 to 1927. Skalkottas initially employed serialism very strictly (1928 to
1938) but gradually displayed a considerable freedom. On
frequent occasions he used serial techniques without stating
a basic pitch row, but combined them with non-serial ideas
characteristic of the music of a Catholic mass of the Renaissance period. His style consequently held affinity with the
contrapuntal techniques of Webern as well as the dodecaphony of Schoenberg. But Skalkottas eventually revised the
original twelve-tone principles and created the first major
modification of the Schoenberg technique. His private
system, which remains largely undeciphered, is marked by
an individuality that sets him apart from his contemporaries.
The most striking feature is the association of two to eigh-
teen rows that form a basic complex, in which as many as
four rows may occur simultaneously. The extensive use
of simultaneity incurs an involved texture, so that although
retrograde forms occur occasionally, transposition and inversion are avoided. Variation techniques are seldom applied

to complete rows, but rather to segments of three or five notes. Such asymmetrical groupings were not yet in common use at the time Skalkottas employed them, although precedents can be found beginning with Schoenberg's early twelve-tone scores.

Skalkottas effectively demonstrated the possibility of combining modern techniques in a traditional form in Fifteen Little Variations (1927). This set of piano pieces was written in the year Skalkottas began study with Schoenberg. Many features of these variations foretold the nature of his mature style. Although a casual hearing might give the impression that the work imitates classical models, Skalkottas employed a modified twelve-tone technique. The group of chords that constitute the thematic material (reminiscent of Schoenberg's chordal beginnings in his Op. 33a) indicate the segmentation of two ten-note rows. Four segments supply the basic material for the succeeding variations in what is usually a clear-cut relationship to the basic thematic material, but occasionally is a complicated readjustment in the ordering. Similar segmental manipulation is characteristic throughout Skalkottas' later compositions. It becomes an involved technique, applied in a predominantly contrapuntal texture, with the simultaneous use of several rows becoming commonplace. This modification of the conventional row use whereby the structure contains a group of complexes is intended to facilitate audibility of twelve-tone music by stressing vertical sounds. Even though the writing is basically linear, Skalkottas was able to utilize harmonic color more fully, for the use of several simultaneous rows provides an enriched source. A listener's interest is caught immediately by having the theme announced as segments of sheer harmonic quality lacking association with tonal functions. In addition, the segmental treatment allows the motivic figures to be emphasized more readily by frequent repetitions in shorter spans of time, thereby reinforcing the unity of the thematic material.

The general styles of the third and fourth piano suites are similar, since both date from his middle period (1938 to 1945). The texture is, of course, much fuller than that of Fifteen Little Variations. Exploitation of chord sounds for color effects is highly developed in these years. Chords are frequently grouped to maintain the tension of sheer sound in what Papaioannou describes as a "neighborhood relationship.[79]

The predominance of fourth chords, frequently containing juxtaposed fifths (frequently diminished), and numerous 9th and 7th chords, suggest the quality of jazz. Syncopated rhythmic passages of a definite jazz character also occur in this middle period.

During his last ten years, Skalkottas tended to write works on a large scale. Passacaglia (1940) is from a set of 32 piano pieces only partially published. Asymmetrical rhythms have become increasingly predominant in this final period. Another provocative feature is the creation of a tonal sense without recognizable tonal functions. It would be misleading to consider this tonality in the traditional manner. Possibly it constitutes nothing more than the sense of unity that good twelve-tone writing can create, but it is not presumptuous to consider that Skalkottas was consciously in command of specific harmonic principles derived from Schoenberg's ideas. Skalkottas' ability to control set complexes was ahead of his time and demanded tremendous understanding of both vertical and horizontal structuring. It is conceivable in view of certain unique features they have in common, that Skalkottas and Schoenberg shared many theoretical discussions on harmonic principles of twelve-tone music during their close association.

Piano Music

Fifteen Little Variations (1927). London, Universal Edition, 1958.

Passacaglia (1940). London, Universal Edition, 1955.

Suite for Piano No. 3. London, Universal Edition, 1962.

Suite for Piano No. 4. (1941). London, Universal Edition, 1955.

Bibliography

Austin, William W. Music in the 20th Century: From Debussy through Stravinsky. New York, Norton, 1966.

Georgii, Walter. Klaviermusik. 2nd ed. Zürich, Atlantis, 1950.

Keller, Hans. "Nikos Skalkottas: An Original Genius," The
    Listener, LII (1954), 1041.

Papaioannou, John G. "Nikos Skalkottas," Music in the
    Twentieth Century, Howard Hartog, ed. New York,
    Praeger, 1957.

_____. "Skalkottas, Nikos," Die Musik in Geschichte
    und Gegenwart, XII, 744-47.

Schoenberg, Arnold. Style and Idea. New York, Philosophi-
    cal Library, 1950.

"Skalkottas, Nikos," Baker's Biographical Dictionary of
    Musicians (5th ed.), 1523.

Slonimsky, Nicolas. "New Music in Greece," The Musical
    Quarterly, LI (January, 1965), 225-235.

Taylor, Kendall. "Skalkottas, Nicos," Grove's Dictionary
    of Music and Musicians (5th ed.), VII, 827-28.

## SREBOTNJAK, ALOJZ

(b. Postojna, Yugoslovia, June 27, 1931)
Address: Celovska 97; Ljubljana, Yugoslavia

      Alojz Srebotnjak studied music in Yugoslavia, Italy,
London, and Paris. His first compositions were marked by
neo-classic and expressionistic traits, but Srebotnjak proceeded to adopt serial techniques in the 1960's. The Invenzione Variata per Pianoforte (1961) is a forceful example of
twelve-tone writing. In his use of the classical twelve-tone
style, Srebotnjak displays considerable individuality. For
example, pointillistic effects are achieved within thick as
well as thin textures. Strong dissonances and driving
rhythms suggest a unique combination of the styles of
Schoenberg and Charles Ives.

Piano Music

Invenzione Variata per Pianoforte (1961). Ljubljana,
    Yugoslavia, Drustvo Slovenskih Skladateljev, 1961.

## Bibliography

Andreis, et al.   Historijski Razvoj Musičke Kulture u
    Jugoslaviji.   Zagreb, Skolska Knjiga, 1962.

Cvetko, Dragotin.   Histoire de la Musique Slovène.
    Zagreb, Založba Obzorja Maribor, 1967.

Helm, Everett.   "Music in Yugoslavia," The Musical
    Quarterly, LI (January, 1965), 215-224.

"Srebotnjak, Aloiz," 1965 Supplement to Baker's Biographical
    Dictionary of Musicians (5th ed.), 123.

"Srebotnjak, Alojz," Musička Enciklopedija, II, 626.

## STOCKHAUSEN, KARLHEINZ

(b. Mödrath, Germany, August 22, 1928)
Address: Meister-Johann Strasse 6; 5 Cologne-Braunsfeld,
West Germany

Karlheinz Stockhausen received musical training at
the Music High School in Cologne and Cologne University.
He began composition as a strict serial composer.   Following study with Darius Milhaud, Olivier Messiaen, and Pierre
Schaeffer in Paris, Stockhausen continued to develop a style
of composition allied with twelve-tone writing and electronic
music.   The music of Webern has also been a major
influence on Stockhausen's development.   Association with
Boulez brought him prominence in France.   Stockhausen
became the key figure in the transference of French ideas
on total serialization to German soil and his writings on
rhythm are among the most penetrating studies on the
subject.

Stockhausen has become a leader among twentieth-
century composers experimenting with new concepts of space
and time that began during the post-Webern movement.   The
style of his earlier music can be described as continually
interrupted cadence but his mature style requires a different
definition, for his music has become an expression of
continuous movement.   This later style is the more successful of the two trends, which in general represent the two
main approaches to rhythm in this century.   Each is concern-

ed with expressing musical space and time as motion and
attempting to understand the relationships between motion
and form.    These two approaches to rhythm are at the roots
of contemporary musical concepts, demanding development
of understanding of the very essence of form itself and the
processes by which it is perceived.

In 1954 Stockhausen planned a cycle of twenty-one
piano pieces, of which eleven have been completed.   The
first ten pieces are interchangeable if performed either as
a cycle or in groups, but may be performed separately.
No. XI contains nineteen units to be performed at random,
but the composition is to end whenever a single unit has
been uttered for the third time.

So far the set is very pianistic.   No drastic change
in style has yet occurred although the form has become
increasingly open and the internal structures have become
more integrated.   This becomes more noticeable in No. V,
for in this piece Stockhausen emphasized the great range of
the keyboard to heighten the sense of space, and used silence
more effectively to accentuate the sense of motion.   Throughout the pieces the pedals are utilized to exploit the effects of
the overtones.   The texture is usually pointillistic, with
vertical structures frequently inserted for a specific effect
on the rhythmic movement, such as a cadential suggestion,
or to exploit an intervallic complexity.   The most distinctive
of the pieces to date is No. IX.   A single chord is reiterated
ad infinitum, incorporating the six modes of attack that
Stockhausen derived from his electronic effects, and then
serves as the source for the remainder of the composition.
Again the pedal provides a means for releasing the full
potential of the sounds inherent in a specific vertical structure.    The work is a tour de force in the exploitation of a
single sonority.

Stockhausen has become an important theoretician of
serial and electronic music, seeking to relate musical
expression to acoustics and perception.   Furthermore, he is
a theorist who utilizes his theories in practice; for example,
his rhythmic principles are built on the theory that a person's
perception of a proportional rhythm is most natural and
he has capitalized on qualities of visual perception of the
performer in creating his time-fields.   In his writings he
continues to develop the extension of all parameters of musical expression, just as he does in his music.

Stockhausen and Henry Eimert have been the co-editors of Die Reihe, one of the main periodicals devoted to contemporary music.

Piano Music

Klavierstücke I-IV.  London, Universal Edition, 1954.

Klavierstücke V (1954), VI (1955), VII (1954), VIII (1954). London, Universal Edition, 1965.

Klavierstücke IX & X.  London, Universal Edition, 1967.

Klavierstücke XI.  London, Universal Edition, 1957.

Bibliography

Ashley, Robert, Larry Austin, and Karlheinz Stockhausen. "Conversation," Source, I (1967), 104-107.

Austin, William W.  Music in the 20th Century: From Debussy through Stravinsky.  New York, Norton, 1966.

Boehmer, Konrad.  Zur Theorie der Offenen Form in der Neuen Musik.  Darmstadt, Tonos, 1967.

Cadieu, Martine.  "Duo avec Stockhausen," Nouvelles Littéraires, (June 15, 1961), 9.

Craft, Robert.  "Boulez and Stockhausen," The Score, XXIV, (November, 1958), 54-62.

Dallin, Leon.  Techniques of Twentieth Century Composition. 2nd ed.  Dubuque, Iowa, Wm. C. Brown, 1964.

Dibelius, Ulrich.  Moderne Musik 1945-1965.  Munich, R. Piper, 1966.

Eco, Umberto.  "L'Opera in Movimento e la Coscienza dell' Epoca," Incontri Musicali, III (August, 1959), 32-54.

Galli, Hans.  Moderne Musik-Leicht Verständlich.  Munich, Francke, 1964.

Gillespie, John.  Five Centuries of Keyboard Music: An

Historical Survey of Music for Harpsichord and Piano. Belmont, Calif., Wadsworth Pub. Co., 1965.

Goléa, Antoine. Vingt Ans de Musique Contemporaine: de Boulez à l'Inconnu. Paris, Seghers, 1962.

Hansen, Peter S. An Introduction to Twentieth Century Music. Boston, Allyn and Bacon, 1961.

Hartog, Howard (ed.). European Music in the Twentieth Century. New York, Praeger, 1957.

Helm, Everett. "Current Chronicle: France," The Musical Quarterly, XLIV (October, 1958), 520-21.

_____. "Current Chronicle: Germany," The Musical Quarterly, XLV (January, 1959), 100-104.

Hodeir, André. Since Debussy: A View of Contemporary Music. Trans. Noel Burch. New York, Grove, 1961.

Hutcheson, Ernest. The Literature of the Piano: A Guide for Amateur and Student. 3rd ed. rev. Rudolph Ganz. New York, Knopf, 1964.

Karkoschka, Erhard. Das Schriftbild der Neuen Musik. Celle, Germany, Hermann Moeck, 1966.

Kirby, F. E. A Short History of Keyboard Music. New York, The Free Press, 1966.

Lindlar, Heinrich. "Stockhausen, Karlheinz," Die Musik in Geschichte und Gegenwart, XII, 1368-9.

Luening, Otto. "Karlheinz Stockhausen," The Juilliard Review, VI (Winter, 1958-59), 10-11.

Machlis, Joseph. Introduction to Contemporary Music. New York, Norton, 1961.

Maegaard, Jan. "Karlheinz Stockhausen," Nordisk Musik-kultur, VII (March, 1958), 11-14.

_____. Musikalsk Modernisme 1945-1962. Copenhagen, Stig Vendelkaers, 1964.

Manzoni, Giacomo. "Profili di Musicisti Contemporanei;
    Karlheinz Stockhausen," Musica d'Oggi, I, (April, 1958),
    229-233.

Marquis, G. Welton. Twentieth Century Music Idioms.
    Englewood Cliffs, N. J., Prentice-Hall, 1964.

Metzger, Heinz-Klaus. "John Cage o della Liberazione,"
    trans. Sylvano Bussotti, Incontri Musicali, III (August,
    1959), 16-31.

Mitchell, Donald. The Language of Modern Music. New
    York, St. Martin's, 1966.

Nono, Luigi. "Die Entwicklung der Reihentechnik," trans.
    Willi Reich, Darmstädter Beiträge zur Neuen Musik, I,
    (1958), 25-37.

Pade, Else Marie, and Anker Blyme. "Efter Stockhausen
    ...," Dansk Musiktidsskrift, XXXIII (April, 1958), 48-9.

Porena, Boris. "L'Avanguardia Musicale di Darmstadt,"
    Rassegna Musicale, XXVIII (September, 1958), 208-14.

Prieberg, Fred K. "Erste Elektronische Partitur," Neue
    Zeitschrift für Musik, CXVIII (April, 1957), 241.

_____. Musica ex Machina: Uber das Verhältnis von
    Musik und Technik. Berlin, Ullstein, 1960.

Rohwer, Jens. Neueste Musik: Ein Kritischer Bericht.
    Stuttgart, Ernst Klett, 1964.

Salzman, Eric. Twentieth-Century Music: An Introduction.
    Englewood Cliffs, N. J., Prentice-Hall, 1967.

Schaeffer, Pierre. Vers une Musique Expérimentale.
    Paris, Richard-Masse, 1957.

Scherchen, Hermann. "Stockhausen und die Zeit: zur
    Geschichte einer Geschichte," Gravesaner Blätter, IV
    (1959), 29-31.

Schnebel, Dieter. "Karlheinz Stockhausen," trans. Leo
    Black, Die Reihe, IV (1960), 121-35.

Stockhausen, Karlheinz. "Actualia," trans. Leo Black,
___ Die Reihe, I (1958), 45-51.

_____. "The Concept of Unity in Electronic Music,"
trans. Elaine Barkin, Perspectives of New Music, I
(Fall, 1962), 39-48.

_____. "Two Lectures: I Electronic and Instrumental
Music; II Music in Space," trans. Ruth Koenig, Die Reihe,
V (1961), 59-82.

_____. "Une Expérience Electronique," La Musique et
Ses Problèmes Contemporains. Jean Louis Barrault, ed.
Paris, Juilliard, 1954.

_____. "For the 15th of September, 1955," trans. Leo
Black, Die Reihe, II (1958), 37-9.

_____. ". . . How Time Passes . . .," trans.
Cornelius Cardew, Die Reihe, III (1959), 10-40.

_____. "Kadenzrhythmik bei Mozart," Darmstädter
Beiträge zur Neuen Musik, IV (1961), 38-72.

_____. Momente. Cologne, n. p., 1963.

_____. "Music und Graphik," Darmstädter Beiträge zur
Neuen Musik, III (1960), 176.

_____. "Music and Speech," trans. Ruth Koenig, Die
Reihe, VI (1964), 40-64.

_____. "Musique dans l'Espace," Revue Belge de Musi-
cologie, XIII (1959), 76.

_____. "Notes on Mixtur (1964)," trans. William
Sylvester, Electronic Music Review, I (January, 1967),
16-17.

_____. "Structure and Experiential Time," trans. Leo
Black, Die Reihe, II (1958), 64-74.

_____. Texte zu Eigenen Werken zur Kunst Anderer
Aktuelles: Aufsätze 1952-1962 zur Theorie des Kom-
ponierens. B. 1. Cologne, M. DuMont Schauberg, 1963;

Texte zu Eigenen Werken zur Kunst Anderer Aktuelles: Aufsätze 1952-1962 zur Musikalischen Praxis. B 2. 1964.

"Stockhausen, Karl Heinz," Baker's Biographical Dictionary of Musicians. Fifth Edition with 1965 Supplement, 1574-5; 124.

Vlad, Roman. Storia della Dodecafonia. Milan, Suvini Zerboni, 1958.

Von Lewinski, Wolf-Eberhard. "The Variety of Trends in Modern German Music," trans. Donald Mintz, The Musical Quarterly, LI (January, 1965), 166-79.

Wörner, Karl H. "Current Chronicle: Germany," The Musical Quarterly, XLV (April, 1959), 237-39.

_____. "Current Chronicle: Germany," The Musical Quarterly, XLVI (April, 1960), 270-75.

_____. "Current Chronicle: Germany," The Musical Quarterly, XLVII (April, 1961), 243-47.

_____. "Karlheinz Stockhausen: Werk + Wollen, 1950-1962," Kontrapunkte, VI (1963), 5-142.

Yates, Peter. Twentieth Century Music: Its Evolution from the End of the Harmonic Era into the Present Era of Sound. New York, Pantheon, 1967.

Zillig, Winifried. Variationen über Neue Musik. Munich, Nymphenburger, 1959.


TAL, JOSEPH

(b. Poznań, Poland, September 18, 1910)
Address: Devora Hanevia 3; Jerusalem, Israel

Joseph Tal received his musical training in Germany at the Hochschule für Musik in Berlin. Tal has become noted as a pianist and a conductor, as well as a composer and teacher. In 1937 he joined the faculty of the Israel Conservatory of Music and Dramatic Arts, as a teacher of piano and composition. He later became head of this institution, serving until 1954.

Tal's Exodus II (1958) was the first electronic composition in Israel. The Center for Electronic Music in Israel
was organized under his direction in 1961.

The Dodecaphonic Episodes for Piano (1963) are based
on a twelve-tone row and use many of the 48 forms. The
first episodes also introduce a rhythmic series with its R
and I forms. In the second episode the rhythmic row is
developed according to Boris Blacher's variable meter system, the form being dependent on the continuous time flow
thus created. The third episode features motivic exploitation.
The fourth and last permits improvisation which is controlled by the rhythmic proportions derived from the pitch row.

Tal tends to avoid a strict twelve-tone idiom and uses
improvisation as one means for providing freedom. He
restricts improvisatory variations on the parts within the
whole, in order to loosen but not weaken the framework.

Piano Music

Dodecaphonic Episodes for Piano (1963). Tel Aviv, Israel
    Music Institute, 1966.

Bibliography

Beckwith, John and Udo Kasemets (eds.). The Modern
    Composer and His World. Toronto, Univ. of Toronto
    Press, 1961.

Gradenwitz, Peter. Music and Musicians in Israel: A Com-
    prehensive Guide to Modern Israeli Music. Rev. and
    enl. ed. Tel Aviv, Israeli Music Publications, 1959.

_____. "Tal, Joseph," Grove's Dictionary of Music
    and Musicians (5th ed.), VIII, 293.

Ringer, Alexander L. "Musical Composition in Modern
    Israel, The Musical Quarterly, LI (January, 1965),
    282-297.

"Tal, Joseph," Baker's Biographical Dictionary of Musi-
    cians (5th ed.), 1613.

## TOKUNAGA, HIDENORI

(b.    Kagoshima, Japan, March 25, 1925)
Address: 6--3 Itayado-cho; Suma-ku; Kobe-shi, Japan

Following private instruction, Hidenori Tokunaga
studied at the Tokyo Music Academy from 1943 to 1946.    The
main influences from his exposure to Western Music during this
period were the rhythmic ideas of Olivier Messiaen and Béla
Bartók and the tone cluster usage of Henry Cowell.    Tokunaga
maintained a close contact with Cowell during the latter's remaining years.    The evolution of Tokunaga's style has been
drastic although the influence of Japanese folk art in his
childhood has largely been retained in the creation of his
thematic lines.    Most recently Tokunaga has been attracted
by the music and theories of Karlheinz Stockhausen to the aspect of autonomy in serial and electronic music. [80]

Three Interludes for Piano (1958) is based on a
twenty-four and not a twelve-tone series in keeping with
Tokunaga's theory as to the importance of considering the
row and its retrograde form as a single unit, thereby providing the basis for an inversion principle that affords
clarity in serial composition.    He considers three acoustical
elements: traction, repulsion, and synthesis, as having a
fusional relationship within the original twenty-four tone
series.    He views this phenomena as the result of the shift
of sound quality during movement through the vertical piles.
These changes are to be controlled by the horizontal movement if the retrograde form is to be an essential part of a
series.    Development comes from a chain reaction stimulated
by the bass line of vertical piles. [81]

Tokunaga was among the group that organized Elan
in 1958 to promote contemporary music in Japan.    He has
also been active in other contemporary music societies in
his country.    Presently he teaches in Kobe.    There is no
appreciable bibliography for this composer.

Piano Music

Short Poetical Works for Piano: "Botanical Garden" by Kyuko
    Kawaji (1943).    Unpub.  reprod.

Three Interludes for Piano (1958).    Bryn Mawr, Pa.,
    Theodore Presser, 1963.

Some Pieces from "Note for Pianoforte." (1959).   Unpub.
   reprod.

Three Sections for Pianoforte from Paul Klee's Tableaus
   (1960).   Unpub.  reprod.

## URBANNER, ERICH

(b.  Innsbruck, Austria, 1936)
Address: Gumpendorferstrasse 63E/II/8; Vienna, Austria

       Erich Urbanner studied composition at the Academy
of Music in Vienna from 1955 to 1961.  His principal
teachers were Karl Schiske and Hanns Jelinek.  His early
scores won him immediate recognition in several competitions
during this period.  Urbanner considers the imagination and
improvisatory prowess of the composer to be better stimulated by developing a basic series than extending the serial
principles.[82]  Personal experience has led him to renounce
total serialization, which he regards as sterile and inaudible.
The lyrical Elf Bagatellen für Klavier (1959) are characterized by extreme clarity.  Their simplicity belies the
considerable ingenuity employed in their construction.  The
set was written while Urbanner was a student of Jelinek, as
a contribution to a series of teaching pieces, Libelli Dode-
caphonici. Three other recent piano works employ the classical twelve-tone technique at a more advanced level.

       Urbanner has been a professor at the Vienna Academy
since 1961.  As yet, no significant bibliography can be
supplied for him.

Piano Music

Elf Bagatellen für Klavier (1959).   Vienna, Universal
   Edition, 1961.

Five Pieces for Piano (1965).   Austria, Alfred Peschek, n.d.

Meditation for Piano (1966).   Vienna, Doblinger, n.d.

Improvisation II for two pianos (1966).   Austria, Alfred
   Peschek, n.d.

## VALEN, FARTEIN

(b.  Stavanger, Norway, August 25, 1887;
d.  Haugesund, Norway, December 14, 1952)

The most extensive efforts in Scandinavia to develop a twelve-tone style were those of Fartein Valen.  Valen spent his youth in Madagascar where his father was a missionary.  He later majored in languages at the University of Oslo, but interest in music led him to Berlin to study at the Hochschule für Musik from 1909 to 1913.  As a result of this experience, three influences became dominant on his composition: Palestrina, J. S. Bach, and Schoenberg.  Valen returned to Norway to teach and compose and he developed a twelve-tone style very similar to Schoenberg's.  However, he did not stimulate interest among his contemporaries, and his music has remained relatively unknown.  Valen Societies in Norway and England have recently publicized his work.

Valen's twelve-tone writing begins with the Trio for Violin, Cello, and Piano, Op. 5 (1923).  In his piano solo works after 1935 the twelve-tone technique exists in a well-developed style.  Both Bjarne Kortsen[83] and Humphrey Searle[84] have noted an important distinction between Valen and Schoenberg with regard to harmony apparent in the piano music.  Valen does not rely on the series as a source of his vertical structure.  Homophonic chords are, in fact, infrequent in his work.  His use of polyphonic structures does, however, bear some relationship to a tonal style.

## Piano Music

Four Piano Pieces, Op. 22 (1935).  Ms.

Variations for Piano, Op. 23 (1936).  Ms.

Gavotte and Musette, Op. 24 (1936).  Oslo, Harald Lyche, 1948.

Prelude and Fugue, Op. 28 (1937).  Ms.

Prelude, Op. 29, No. 1.  Oslo, Harald Lyche, 1948.

Prelude, Op. 29, No. 2.  Oslo, Harald Lyche, 1948.

Intermezzo, Op. 36 (1939).  Ms.

Piano Sonata No. 2 (The Hound of Heaven), Op. 38 (1941).
Ms.

Bibliography

Austin, William W.  Music in the 20th Century: From
    Debussy through Stravinsky.  New York, Norton, 1966.

Gurvin, Olav.  Fartein Valen, en Banebryter: i Nyere Norsk
    Musikk.  Drammen and Oslo, n. p., 1962.

Friskin, James, and Irwin Freundlich.  Music for the Piano.
    New York, Rinehart, 1954.

Horton, John.  "Valen, Fartein," Grove's Dictionary of
    Music and Musicians, VIII, 651.

Kortsen, Bjarne.  Studies of Form in Fartein Valen's Music.
    Oslo, n. p., 1961.

Searle, Humphrey.  Twentieth-Century Counterpoint.  London,
    Ernest Benn, 1954.

"Valen, Fartein," Baker's Biographical Dictionary of
    Musicians.  Fifth Edition with 1965 Supplement, 1682; 132.

VAN VLIJMEN, JAN

(b.  Rotterdam, October 11, 1935)
Address: Nachtegaalaan 19; Hoevelaken, The Netherlands

        Jan Van Vlijmen is one of the younger Dutch com-
posers who has incorporated dodecaphonic techniques in most
of his writing.  He studied at the Utrecht Conservatory,
where Kees van Baaren was his principal teacher.  From
1961 to 1967 Van Vlijmen directed the Amersfoort School of
Music and since 1965 has taught theory at the Utrecht Conservatory.  His compositions are mainly for chamber groups.

        Van Vlijmen's Costruzioni per Due Pianoforti (1960)
constitutes a major work of considerable complexity.  All
48 forms of the row are used, with retrograde and inverted
forms prominently featured.  Furthermore, the entire structure is controlled by principles of retrogression and inver-

sion. Thus the first movement is a retrograde movement.
The second of the two movements, set within two slow sections, is a canon in which the rhythmic movement becomes
progressively compact. The second piano part is an inversion of the first. The music does not alternate the main
events between the two pianos, but continues them in an
integrated texture. The interplay between the two pianos is
thus reminiscent of Boulez's Structures. As in the Boulez
work, the audibility of the details of some of the elaborate
dynamic markings is not high yet these details contribute
to the over-all effect of tension and release. The linear
design, combined with these dynamic subtleties, creates an
even stronger sense of forward momentum than does the
Boulez work. The entire range of the keyboard is exploited
to great advantage by use of such features as wide pointillistic leaps and the use of striking sonorities derived from
widely spaced intervals. The intricate patterns of rhythmic
design move rapidly through the relatively thin and extremely
pointillistic texture of this piece. The driving rhythmic
momentum of widely spaced sounds creates a space-time relationship that unifies the entire musical structure.

Piano Music

Costruzioni per Due Pianoforti (1960). Amsterdam, Donemus,
    1961.

Bibliography

"Vlijmen, Jan Van," 1965 Supplement to Baker's Biographical
    Dictionary of Musicians (5th ed.), 134.

Wouters, Jos. "Dutch Music in the 20th Century," The
    Musical Quarterly, LI (January, 1965), 97-110.

VLAD, ROMAN

(b. Cernauti, Rumania, December 29, 1919)
Address: Via XXIV Maggio 51; Rome, Italy

        One of the first Italians to write twelve-tone music,
Roman Vlad began to adopt the Schoenberg technique in 1939.[85]
Vlad was born in Rumania, where he graduated from the
Cernauti Conservatory in 1933. He settled in Italy in 1938
and after studying with Alfred Casella, his association with

Frank Martin and Luigi Dallapiccola stimulated his use of
twelve-tone techniques.  In the Cinque Exercizi Dodecafonici
per Pianoforte (1943), later rechristened as the Studi Dodecafonici, a segment of the basic row recurs in the transpositions so frequently that it provides a source of structural
unity.  Vlad frequently creates a complex of two rows; at
such times this recurring segment of the basic row is
conspicuous.

Vlad derived the twelve-tone rows for two piano
works from traditional themes.  The Variazioni Concertanti
(1954-55) for two pianos (with or without orchestra) uses
a twelve-tone series extracted from Mozart's Don Giovanni.
Variazioni Intorno all'Ultima Mazurka di Chopin (1964)
employs a row constructed from the initial bars of the
Chopin mazurka in F flat major.[86]

Vlad's use of contemporary ideas is broad and experimental.  For example, he has worked with electronic music
since 1957.  Regardless of the idiom, his music is characterized by a fusion of tonal and non-tonal elements.

Vlad is also well-known for his writings on contemporary music.  These include an important monograph on
Stravinsky and a comprehensive history, Storia della Dodecafonia (1958), that is one of the most valuable sources for
information on twelve-tone music.

Piano Music

Studi Dodecafonici per Pianoforte (1943).  Milan, Suvini
     Zerboni, 1958.

Variazioni Concertanti.  Milan, Suvini Zerboni, n.d.

Variazioni Intorno all'Ultima Mazurka di Chopin (1964).
     Milan, Suvini Zerboni, n.d.

Bibliography

Austin, William W.  Music in the 20th Century: From
     Debussy through Stravinsky.  New York, Norton, 1966.

Gatti, Guido M.  "Vlad, Roman," Grove's Dictionary of
     Music and Musicians (5th ed.), IX, 33.

Graziosi, G.  "Roman Vlad, " Rassegna Musicale.
     (January, 1953).

Hartog, Howard (ed.).  European Music in the Twentieth
     Century.  New York, Praeger, 1957.

"Vlad, Roman, " Baker's Biographical Dictionary of Mu-
     sicians.  Fifth Edition with 1965 Supplement, 1719; 134.

Vlad, Roman.  Modernità e Tradizione nella Musica Contem-
     poranea.  Turin, n.p., 1955.

_____.  Storia della Dodecafonia.  Milan, Suvini Zerboni,
     1958.

_____.  Stravinsky.  Trans.  Frederick and Ann Fuller.
     London, Oxford Univ. Press, 1960.


VOGEL, WLADIMIR RUDOLFOVICH


(b.  Moscow, February 29, 1896)
Address: Oetlisbergstrasse 7-8053; Zürich, Switzerland

     Wladimir Vogel, of German and Russian descent, was
raised in Russia, but eventually settled in Switzerland.
His main compositional studies with Ferruccio Busoni (1920
to 1924) resulted in a classical style.[87] Philosophy in general
and the music of Scriabin were also important influences on
his work.  His interest in twelve-tone writing developed
about 1936 from lectures by Willi Reich.  Vogel was stimulated to study books by Ernst Křenek, Erwin Stein, Josef
Rufer and others, and the music scores of Schoenberg.  He
then became the first Swiss twelve-tone composer.

     Vogel has made a comparison of the basic concepts
of the Schoenberg School with his own adaptation.[88] The
Schoenbergians, according to Vogel, lacked sufficient concern
for the sound quality of their polyphony because of their
preoccupation with the motivic character of the polyphonic
structure.  On the other hand, Vogel considers his modification of the method as utilizing a wider range within the
tone space, and also representing a loosening of the polyphonic treatment of the series.  Vogel also comments that
his philosophy of music approaches the static tone constel-
lation of Hauer.

Two piano works bear relation to serial composition, the Variêtude (1931) and the Epitaffio (1936). The Variétude contains chaconne-like repetitions of the principal theme, suggestive of a rhythmic series. Vogel describes the Epitaffio (dedicated to Alban Berg) as a specialized use of row technique, which is not the use of twelve tones related to one another in the Schoenberg sense. Rather, the basic series arises from the soggetto (or, "subject") in the manner of the old musical practice as employed, for example, by J. S. Bach. A long series of 23 tones using nine pitches, derived from the phrase Alban Berg aufs Grab Friede!, constitutes the passacaglia theme. Vogel evolves ever-changing motives to ornament this continuous thread, in effect using a combination of perpetual variation and motivic development from the initial idea. The brilliance of much of the figuration is typical of Vogel's style. The work is an effective example of application of serial writing to a traditional form.

Both expressionist and advanced twelve-tone styles have appeared throughout Vogel's compositions, among which choral works are the most prevalent.

Piano Music

Variêtude (1931). New York, Boosey & Hawkes, 1947.

Epitaffio per Alban Berg (1936). Milan, Ricordi, 1954.

Bibliography

Austin, William W. Music in the 20th Century: From Debussy through Stravinsky. New York, Norton, 1966.

Collaer, Paul. A History of Modern Music. Trans. Sally Abeles. New York, World, 1961.

Corbet, August. "Vogel, Vladimir (Rudolfovich)," Grove's Dictionary of Music and Musicians (5th ed.), IX, 34.

Lindlar, Heinrich (ed.). "Wladimir Vogel," Musik der Zeit, X (1955), 71.

Oesch, Hans. "Vogel, Wladimir," Die Musik in Geschichte und Gegenwart.

_____ . Wladimir Vogel. Sein Weg zu Einer Neuen
Musikalischen Wirklichkeit.  Bern, Francke, 1967.

_____ . "Wladimir Vogels Werke für Klavier, "
Schweizerische Musikzeitung, XCVIII (1957), 51.

Reich, Willi.  "On Swiss Musical Composition of the Present,"
The Musical Quarterly, LI (January, 1965), 78-91.

Rognoni, Luigi.  "Porträt Wladimir Vogel, " Melos, XXII
(1955), 165.

Vogel, Wladimir.  "Der Moderne Sprechchor, " Neue Zeitschrift für Musik, X (1960).

_____ . "Grundsätzliches zum Dramma Oratorio, "
Schweizerische Musikzeitung, CVI (1966).

_____ . "Il Coro Parlato, " Musica d'Oggi, III (1960),
354.

_____ . "Nachwort zum Dramma Oratorio, "
Schweizerische Musikzeitung, CVII (1967).

_____ . "Uber Busonis Dr. Faust, " Schweizerische
Musikzeitung, CVI (1966)

_____ . "Zu Meiner Modigliani-Kantate, " Schweizerische
Musikzeitung, CII (1962), 78.

"Vogel, Wladimir, " Baker's Biographical Dictionary of Musicians.  Fifth Edition with 1965 Supplement, 1720; 134.


WAGNER-REGENY, RUDOLF


(b. Szasz-Régen, Transylvania, Hungary [now Rumania],
August 28, 1903)
Address: Adlergestell 255; Berlin Adlersdorf; Germany

During the early 1920's, Rudolf Wagner-Régeny
resided in Germany and studied music in both Leipzig and
Berlin for a period of about three years.  Since that time
a major portion of his compositions have been operas and
ballets.  Attracted by its individuality, he began to adopt

features of dodecaphonic writing in 1946.    His own description of his experiments with the incorporation of Blacher's variable meter system with the use of pitch series is included in Rufer's Composition with Twelve Notes Related Only to One Another.89 Zwei Tanze für Palucca (1950) and Fünf französische Klavierstücke (1951) are examples of Wagner-Régeny's twelve-tone writing.    In these relatively uncomplicated piano pieces tonal features are in evidence throughout.    The use of tone rows is secondary to the rhythm, yet they contribute a vital component to the effectiveness of the variable meters.

Each of the Sieben Klavierfugen is dedicated to the composer who is being imitated.

Piano Music

Zwei Tänze für Palucca (1950).  Vienna, Universal Edition, 1951.

Fünf Französische Klavierstücke (1951).  Berlin, Bote & Bock, 1952.

Sieben Klavierfugen (1953).  Berlin, Bote & Bock, 1954.

Bibliography

Redlich, Hans F.  "Wagner-Régeny, Rudolf, " Grove's Dictionary of Music and Musicians (5th ed.), IX, 90-91.

Rufer, Josef.  Composition with Twelve Notes Related Only to One Another.  Trans. Humphrey Searle.  New York, Macmillan , 1954.

"Wagner-Régeny, Rudolf, " Baker's Biographical Dictionary of Musicians.  Fifth Edition with 1965 Supplement, 1744; 136.

WEBER, BEN BRIAN

(b.  St. Louis, July 23, 1916)
Address: 418 Central Park West, Apt. 99; New York, New York

Ben Weber studied medicine at the University of

Illinois, but transferred to DePaul University to study
music. Weber was attracted both by atonalism and the
Schoenberg idiom and adopted the twelve-tone technique in
1938, being largely self-taught in its use. He believes
adequate freedom in twelve-tone writing is obtainable within
the scope of the method and is never hampered by an implied
strictness. He has demonstrated his thought processes as
completely geared to working with a basic twelve-note
row and its forms.[90] The O and I forms, and transpositions
he intends to incorporate, are determined in the planning
stage of a composition. His frequent pivots from a common
tone facilitate progression to another row form. Weber
feels that the frequent inference that his music is tonal
results from the fact that he usually designs his row so
that certain chords are predetermined by the harmonies
inherent in the serial ordering. This sometimes causes
tonally-associated harmonies to occur automatically. Thus
any tonal associations are chance occurrences in the relationship between the series and its own harmonic potential
and do not constitute a type of synthesis of twelve-tone
and tonal writing. Weber's wry comment, ". . . [there is]
enough chance involved with serialism as it is . . .,"[91]
is his explanation as to why he has not chosen to write
chance music per se.

Some of Weber's favorite devices for attaining freedom within the procedures of the Schoenberg technique are
described as follows. In the manner of Alban Berg, Weber,
on occasion, may derive an alternate row from the original
series by the use of alternate numbers, one of the simplest
means of permutation. Thus the succession from 1 through
12 becomes 1 3 5 7 9 11 2 4 6 8 10 12. This derived row
may be obtained with the O and its forms, or be the thematic basis for other movements. However, there is no consis-
tency in Weber's writing as to whether or not the same,
related, or new rows are used in the movements of a single
composition.

Weber does not hesitate to juggle the ordering and
interrupt the flow of succession at any time in order to
develop a motivic idea. He may use neighbor tones as an
expansion device, enabling the addition of notes to either
linear or vertical structures.

Weber's first twelve-tone compositions, adhering
closely to the Schoenberg technique, were for piano, the

Five Bagatelles, Op. 2 (1938). Another early example of
Weber's twelve-tone writing occurs in the set of Three
Piano Pieces, Op. 23 (1946). The first and second pieces
are based on free references to twelve-tone rows. The
third (the first to be composed) is atonal.

Weber has written several other piano works during
the last two decades and all employ serial techniques. The
most recent, Suite for Piano Four-hands, Op. 56 (1964), in
comparison with the earlier works, reveals a thinner texture, more counterpoint, and more asymmetry and freedom
in the rhythmic movement. But the most significant development is that in Weber's mature style a greater complexity
of control absorbs the atonal and serial techniques so that
they are not obvious.

Piano Music

Five Bagatelles, Op. 2 (1938). Bryn Mawr, Pa., Theodore
    Presser, n.d.

Three Piano Pieces, Op. 23 (1946). Hillsdale, N.Y.,
    Bomart Music Pub., 1953.

Episodes, Op. 26a (rev. 1957). New York, Composers
    Facsim. Edition, 1957.

Piano Suite No. 2, Op. 27 (1948). New York, Composers
    Facsim. Edition, 1952.

"Humoreske," Op. 49. New Music for the Piano. New
    York, Lawson-Gould, 1963.

"Lyric Piece," Op. 40a. American Composers of Today.
    New York, Marks, 1956.

Suite for Piano Four-hands, Op. 56. New York, Composers
    Facsim. Ed., 1964.

Bibliography

Edmunds, John and Gordon Boelzner. Some Twentieth
    Century American Composers. A Selective Bibliography.
    2 vols. New York, N.Y. Pub. Lib., 1959 & 1960.

Glanville-Hicks, Peggy. "Weber, Ben," Grove's Dictionary
   of Music and Musicians (5th ed.), IX, 222.

Machlis, Joseph. Introduction to Contemporary Music.
   New York, Norton, 1961.

"Weber, Ben," Baker's Biographical Dictionary of Musicians.
   Fifth Edition with 1965 Supplement, 1758-9; 137.

"Weber, Ben," Bulletin of American Composers Alliance, II
   (1955).

WEINZWEIG, JOHN

(b. Toronto, March 11, 1913)
Address: 107 Manor Road East; Toronto 7, Ontario

     John Weinzweig, born in Canada of Polish parents,
developed a love of music during his youth in a Toronto
neighborhood where folk music of many ethnic cultures was
frequently heard. He eventually undertook serious music
study at the University of Toronto. In his freshman year
he organized and conducted the University of Toronto
Symphony Orchestra. He completed his musical training at
the University of Rochester, where contact with the music[92]
of Alban Berg led him to adopt the twelve-tone technique.
The prime attraction that twelve-tone composition held for
Weinzweig was its potential for melodic control and thematic
extension. He considered this potential not fully exploited
in the music of Berg and Schoenberg. Weinzweig's concern
for melodic unity led him to use the row as a complete
entity, rather than to exploit motivic or segmental treatment.
Furthermore, he tended to invent a new row for each movement of a score. However, he has stated that recent works
have utilized the harmonic implications of a row and, except
for minor adjustments of the second hexachord, that he intends to use a single row and its transpositions for complete
works. With regard to tonality, he makes no effort to
avoid "islands of polarity."[93]

     Dirgeling and Themes with Variable are both twelve-
tone piano works dating from 1939, the year he introduced
the Schoenberg technique to Canada. In 1950 the following
short twelve-tone piano pieces were published: Berceuse
(uses a five-note series), Toccata Dance, and Conversation

Piece.   A piano concerto has just been oompleted, in which
jazz and blues styles are incorporated with a twelve-tone
series.

        Weinzweig joined the faculty of the Royal Conserva-
tory of Music in Toronto in 1939 and since 1952 has taught
at the University of Toronto.

Piano Music

Dirgeling (1939).   Facsim.

Themes with Variable (1939).   Facsim.

Berceuse (1950).   London, Oxford Univ. Press, n.d.

Toccata Dance (1950).   London, Oxford Univ. Press, n.d.

Conversation Piece (1950).   London, Oxford Univ. Press,
        n.d.

Bibliography

Thirty-four Biographies of Canadian Composers.   Montreal,
        Canadian Broadcasting Corp., 1964.

"Weinzweig, John, " Baker's Biographical Dictionary of
        Musicians.   Fifth Edition with 1965 Supplement, 1774;
        137.

WEISS, ADOLPH ANDREAS

(b.   Baltimore, September 12, 1891)
Address: c/o American Composers Alliance; 170 West 74th
Street; New York, New York   10023

        The initial efforts to introduce the Schoenberg tech-
nique into the United States were undertaken by Adolph
Weiss.   In 1924 he went abroad and studied with Schoenberg,
both in Austria and in Germany, and gained great enthusiasm
for twelve-tone writing.   Upon returning to the States in
1927 he not only continued to compose in the twelve-tone
idiom but became an active member of the Pan-American
Society of Composers.   Through this organization he promoted concerts of contemporary music and thereby strongly inter-

ested some Americans in the Schoenberg concepts. However, in general, the results of his efforts to publicize
this new music were discouraging. He finally settled in
California, where he devoted his time mainly to composition
and playing the bassoon in various orchestras. His piano
works are fully chromatic, and obviously influenced by
impressionism as well as the expressionism of Schoenberg.

Piano Music

Piano Sonata (1932). Unpub. ms.

Pulse of the Sea (1944). New York, Composers Facsim.
    Edition, n. d.

Protest for Two Pianos (1945). Unpub. ms.

Bibliography

Chase, Gilbert. America's Music: From the Pilgrims to
    the Present. Rev. 2nd ed. New York, McGraw-Hill,
    1966.

Cowell, Henry (ed.). American Composers on American
    Music. Stanford, Calif., Stanford Univ. Press, 1933.

Hutcheson, Ernest. The Literature of the Piano: A Guide
    for Amateur and Student. 3rd ed., rev. Rudolph Ganz.
    New York, Knopf, 1964.

Reis, Claire R. Composers in America: Biographical
    Sketches of Contemporary Composers with a Record of
    their Works. Rev. and enl. ed. New York, Macmillan,
    1947.

Weiss, Adolph. "Autobiographical Notes," American
    Composers Alliance Bulletin, VII (1958), 2.

"Weiss, Adolph," Baker's Biographical Dictionary of Musi-
    cians. (5th ed.), 1775.

WOLFF, CHRISTIAN


(b. Nice, France, March 8, 1934)

Address: 36 Sparks Street; Cambridge, Massachusetts
02138

Christian Wolff was born in France but has lived in
the United States since childhood. He received a Ph. D.
in comparative literature from Harvard in 1963. He has
been mainly self-taught in music. He became associated
with the group around John Cage and studied with Cage for
about a month. Cage encouraged Wolff to analyze the Symphony, Op. 21, by Webern. Wolff's observations of the
spatial concepts achieved by Webern's arrangement of a
series according to both serial and contrapuntal consider-
ations stimulated experimentation with many ideas in his
own composition.[94] With Webern as a point of departure,
and using Cage's concept of rhythmic structure based on
proportional sequences, Wolff established a musical form
on the basis of rhythmic continuity. He felt that multiplica-
tion of a basic rhythmic series by its components successively provides an additional series which is comparable to the
transformations of a tone-row; the number of components
determine the number of sequences, or phrases, and the
number of sections. Further, the sum of the components
in the initial series constitutes the square root of the total
structure.[95] The ordering of the initial series may be dependent on some systematized plan or may be a random selection.
Execution of such a rhythmic design may incorporate the
element of chance but the composer limits the performer's
selectivity to the boundaries predetermined by the original
series.

Wolff's compositions date from the 1950's. For
Piano I (1952), in spite of its early date and less involved
structure, typifies the essential nature of Wolff's subsequent composition. The pitches, durations, and dynamics
are each based on a pattern of nine components, repeated
with such re-ordering and over-lapping as is necessary to
compensate for a structural length of sixteen beats.

Piano Music

Duet I. New York, C. F. Peters, n. d.

Duo for Pianists I. New York, C. F. Peters, n. d.

Duo for Pianists II. New York, C. F. Peters, n. d.

For Pianist. New York, C. F. Peters, n.d.

For Piano I (1952). New York, C. F. Peters, 1963.

For Piano II. New York, C. F. Peters, n.d.

Suite I for Prepared Piano. New York, C. F. Peters, n.d.

Bibliography

Wolff, Christian. "On Form," Die Reihe, VII (1965), 26-31.

_____ . "On Movement," Die Reihe, II (1959), 61-63.

"Wolff, Christian," 1965 Supplement to Baker's Biographical
   Dictionary of Musicians (5th ed.), 140.

WOLPE, STEFAN

(b. Berlin, August 25, 1902)
Address: 217 West 70th Street; New York, New York

        Stefan Wolpe studied music at the Berlin Academy
where his teachers included Paul Juon, Franz Schreker,
Ferruccio Busoni, and briefly, Anton Webern. From 1923
to 1933 his output was mainly atonal works for symphonic
and chamber mediums. Such influences as the rhythms
of Stravinsky, the melodic and harmonic ideas of Bartók,
and jazz elements, particularly in the style of Kurt Weill,
are evident. The war forced Wolpe to move to Israel in
1933, where he taught composition at the Jerusalem Conservatory and studied with Hermann Scherchen. It was in Israel
that Four Studies in Structure (1936), which includes the Passacaglia for piano, was written. This set represents a
major stage in Wolpe's mature development; from that time
his serial technique has continually sought to expand the
serial potential. The Passacaglia is based on the progressive
use of all intervallic relationships. Eleven counter-themes
constructed on twelve-tone successions of each interval constitute its linear design. [96] Edward Levy has noted the
significance of this work to Wolpe's later development.[97]

        In 1939, Wolpe settled in the United States, where the
bulk of his serial compositions have been written. In 1948

he founded the Contemporary Music School in New York.
He has held several teaching positions on the East Coast.

    Form for piano (1959) exemplifies the change in
Wolpe's serial technique in recent years. (Unfortunately,
this score and several of Wolpe's other piano scores are
not in print.) His typical complexity is maintained, but
with more economical means of expression, so that a sense
of space is emphasized by the thinner, open texture. Levy
discusses the refinement of Wolpe's use of intervallic relationships.[98] A lecture given by Wolpe in the year that
Form was completed, elaborates on the evolution of basic
serial concepts. He stresses the structural significance
inherent in the unifying power of a twelve-tone, all-chromatic
circuit. He concludes with a provocative classification of
basic types of organic modes.[99]

Piano Music

Early Piece for Piano (1924).  New York, McGinnis & Marx,
    1955.

Passacaglia (1936).  Unpub.  ms.

"Pastorale, " U.S.A.  Vol. II.  New York, Leeds, n.d.

Zemach Suite (1939).  London, Hargail, n.d.

Toccata in Three Movements.  Unpub.  ms.

Battle Piece.  Unpub.  ms.

Two Studies for Piano (Part Two) (1948).  New York,
    McGinnis & Marx, 1955.

Enactments for 3 Pianos (1951-53).  Unpub.  ms.

Form (1959).  Unpub.  ms.

Bibliography

Austin, William W.  Music in the 20th Century: From
    Debussy through Stravinsky.  New York, Norton, 1966.

Bauer, Marion.  "Stefan Wolpe, " Modern Music, XVII (1939).

French, Richard F. "Current Chronicle: New York, " The
   Musical Quarterly, XLVIII (July, 1962), 387-92.

Levy, Edward. "Stefan Wolpe: (For his Sixtieth Birthday), "
   Perspectives of New Music, II (Fall-Winter, 1963), 51-65.

Machlis, Joseph. Introduction to Contemporary Music. New
   York, Norton, 1961.

Tudor, David. Jacket notes, Stefan Wolpe, Esoteric recording ES-530.

Wolpe, Stefan. "Thinking Twice," Contemporary Composers
   on Contemporary Music. Elliott Schwarz and Barney
   Childs, eds. New York, Holt, Rinehart and Winston, 1967.

"Wolpe, Stefan, " Baker's Biographical Dictionary of Musicians. (5th ed.), 1818.


WOYTOWICZ, BOLESŁAW


(b. Dunajowice, Poland, December 5, 1899)
Address: Kilinskiego 50; Katowice, Poland

     Bolesław Woytowicz completed training as a concert
pianist in Warsaw at the Frederick Chopin College of Music.
He studied mathematics and law, and received a Ph. D.
from Warsaw University in Russian philology. From 1930 to
1932 he studied in Paris with Nadia Boulanger.

     Woytowicz employs serial techniques, but not exclu-
sively. In fact, he tends to use many other contemporary
ideas as well and his works also have romantic, neo-classic
and atonal characteristics. Each work is concerned primarily with structure and is usually polyphonic.

     Woytowicz wrote two sets of piano etudes, one in
1948 and the other in 1960. They were intended as graded
studies in various aspects of contemporary music. In the
second set, the 9th, 6th and 10th pieces constitute a triptych
in the twelve-note technique.

     These etudes are the only piano compositions in which
Woytowicz has employed twelve-tone writing. He considers

mastery of the technique essential and expects all of his students to learn it but preferably not to use it in piano pieces. His experience has led him to consider that the system is a bit one-sided and that only the exceptional composer can develop his individuality through its use.[100]

## Piano Music

Ten Studies for Piano (1960). Warsaw, Przedstawicielstwo Wydawnictw Polskich, 1961.

## Bibliography

Halski, Czesław R. "Woytowicz, Bolesław," Grove's Dictionary of Music and Musicians (5th ed.), IX, 369-70.

Jarocinski, Stefan (ed.). Polish Music. Warsaw, Polish Scientific Pub. 1965.

"Woytowicz, Bolesław," Baker's Biographical Dictionary of Musicians (5th ed.), 1824-25.

## ZIMMERMANN, BERND ALOIS

(b. Bliesheim, Germany, March 20, 1918)
Address: 5021 Grosskönigsdorf; Zur Mühle 20, West Germany

Bernd Zimmermann emerged from the traditional teaching of Philipp Jarnach, Wolfgang Fortner, and René Leibowitz to widen his range of interest regarding contemporary forms and styles. His early works, containing prominent folk-rhythms, show an affinity with the romantic atonalism of Schoenberg, as well as the influence of Béla Bartók. The German ability to employ powerful fugal writing is evident in all of Zimmermann's writing. His first twelve-tone compositions are quite strict. Retaining a flavor of Schoenberg, he moved quickly through a free twelve-tone phase to the total serialization characteristic of his writing in the last decade.

Zimmermann's earliest published piano work is Enchiridion (1951). The score emphasizes no particular contemporary idiom. Elements of Hindemith, Bartók, and Schoenberg are the most evident influences. In Konfigurationen (1956) Zimmermann had already moved past his period

of strict twelve-tone writing. The dominant feature in this
work is not serialism but the exploitation of dynamics.
Reinhold Schubert has made an extensive analysis of Perspektiven,[101] also composed in 1956, an intricately structured
and totally serial work conceived as an imaginary ballet.
The Monologe (1960-64), for two pianos with or without
orchestra, constitutes a contemporary medley incorporating
familiar themes of Debussy, Bach, Messiaen, and Mozart.

Zimmermann has achieved relatively little renown,
but some of his recent works support Hartog's prophecy
that he may yet assume the stature of a major German composer.[102] Like so many of the Germans, Zimmermann
devotes much time to composing opera. He has been a
member of the faculty of the Cologne Conservatory.

Piano Music

Enchiridion (1951). London, Schott, 1954.

Konfigurationen: Acht Stücke für Klavier (1956). Mainz,
   Schott, 1957.

Perspektiven: Musik zu Einem Imaginären Ballett für Zwei
   Klaviere. Mainz, Schott, 1956.

Monologe für Zwei Klaviere (1960-64). Mainz, Schott, 1964.

Bibliography

Hartog, Howard (ed.). European Music in the Twentieth
   Century. New York, Praeger, 1957.

Lewinski, Wolf-Eberhard von. "Current Chronicle: Germany,"
   The Musical Quarterly, LI (July, 1965), 555-58.

Schubert, Reinhold. "Bernd Alois Zimmermann," Die Reihe
   IV (1960), 103-113.

"Zimmermann, Bernd A.," Baker's Biographical Dictionary
   of Musicians. Fifth Edition with 1965 Supplement, 1848;
   143.

# Notes

1. Gilbert Amy, letter to the author, Aug. 24, 1966.

2. Milton Babbitt, letter to the author, June 19, 1966.

3. An analysis of the first composition appears in Charles Burkhardt, Anthology for Musical Analysis (New York, Holt, Rinehart, and Winston, 1964), pp. 371-78.

4. The theories of Schoenberg, Babbitt, and Křenek are discussed and compared by George Perle, Serial Composition and Atonality (2nd ed. Berkeley, Univ. of Calif. Press, 1968).

5. Joseph Machlis, Introduction to Contemporary Music (New York, Norton, 1961), pp. 618-19.

6. Ramón Barce, "Nuevo Sistema Atonal," Atlántida, 21 (May-June, 1966), 329-43.

7. Ramón Barce, letter to the author, July 8, 1966.

8. André Hodeir, Since Debussy: A View of Contemporary Music, trans. Noel Burch (New York, Grove, 1961), pp. 161-203.

9. Jürg Baur, letter to the author, July 25, 1966.

10. Ibid.

11. Luciano Berio, letter to the author, June 18, 1966.

12. Cf. Arnold Elston, "Some Rhythmic Practices in Contemporary Music," The Musical Quarterly, XLII (July, 1956), 318-29.

13. Cf. Hodeir, op. cit., pp. 97-123.

14. Further comparisons are made by Richard Franko Goldman, "Current Chronicle: New York," The Musical Quarterly, XLVII (April, 1961), 233-39.

15. Norman Demuth, French Piano Music: A Survey with Notes on its Performance (London, Museum Press, 1959), pp. 152-56.

16. The relationship Boulez develops between these two techniques has been described by György Ligeti, "Some Remarks on Boulez' 3rd Piano Sonata," Die Reihe, V (1961), 56-58.

17. Cf. Antoine Goléa, "French Music Since 1945," trans. Lucile H. Brockway, The Musical Quarterly, LI (January, 1965), 22-37.

18. György Ligeti, "Pierre Boulez," Die Reihe, IV (1960), 36-62.

19. Earle Brown, letter to the author, Feb. 21, 1968.

20. Earle Brown, jacket notes, Earle Brown and Morton Feldman, Time recording 58007.

21. Earle Brown, letter to the author, Feb. 21, 1968.

22. Gilbert Chase, American Composers on American Music (Baton Rouge, Louisiana State Univ. Press, 1966), pp. 298-305.

23. Earle Brown, letter to the author, February 21, 1968. One of the major concert pianists of contemporary music, David Tudor was a key figure in transporting aleatoric concepts of the Cage group from the United States to Europe in the 1950's.

24. Cf. Julia Smith, Aaron Copland (New York, Dutton, 1955), pp. 128-33.

25. Ibid., pp. 230-35.

26. Cf. Wilfred Mellers, Music and Society: England and the European Tradition, 2nd ed. (London, Dennis Dobson, 1950), pp. 205-208.

27. Cf. Arthur Berger, "Aaron Copland's 'Piano Fantasy'," Juilliard Review, V (1957), 13.

28. Cf. Hugo Cole, "Aaron Copland (II)," Tempo, 77 (Summer, 1966), 9-15.

29. Arthur Berger, "The Music of Aaron Copland," The
    Musical Quarterly, XXXI (October, 1945), 420-471.

30. Guido M. Gatti, "Casella, Alfredo," Grove's
    Dictionary of Music and Musicians (5th ed.), II,
    106-108.

31. Cf. Roman Vlad, Luigi Dallapiccola, trans. Cynthia
    Jolly (Milan, Suvini Zerboni, 1957), pp. 46-52.

32. Norman Demuth, French Piano Music (London,
    Museum Press, 1959), pp. 63-65.

33. Cf. Jos. Wouters, "Ton de Leeuw," Sonorum Speculum,
    XIX (1964), 1-28.

34. Cf. Arthur Custer, "Contemporary Music in Spain,"
    The Musical Quarterly, LI (January, 1965), 44-60.

35. Luis de Pablo, letter to the author, June 17, 1966.

36. Franco Donatoni, letter to the author, August 2, 1966.
    Latter work also given as Tre Improvisazioni per
    Pianoforte.

37. Peter Racine Fricker, letter to the author, July 8,
    1966.

38. Ibid.

39. Cristobal Halffter, letter to the author, June 24,
    1966.

40. Cf. Arthur Custer, "Contemporary Music in Spain,"
    The Musical Quarterly, LI (January, 1965), 48.

41. Johann Wolfgang von Goethe, Farbenlehre (Leipzig,
    Insel, 1926), pp. 83-105.

42. A detailed summary of Hauer's theories is provided
    by Karl Eschmann, Changing Forms in Modern
    Music (Boston, Schirmer, 1945), pp. 83-105.

43. Correspondence regarding unsuccessful efforts to
    achieve a collaboration between these two men can
    be found in Erwin Stein (ed.), Arnold Schoenberg

Letters, trans. Eithne Wilkins and Ernst Kaiser (New York, St. Martin's, 1965).

44. Zwölftonschrift: eight stave lines and three clefs employed in such a manner that accidentals are unnecessary. See sample in Eschmann, op. cit.

45. A melodic electrophone capable of producing quarter tones and eighth tones.

46. Ellis B. Kohs, letter to the author, March 6, 1968.

47. Cf. Ernst Křenek, Studies in Counterpoint, (New York, Schirmer, 1940), pp. vii-ix.

48. Glenn Gould, jacket notes on Berg, Schoenberg, Křenek, Columbia recording ML 5336.

49. Cf. Křenek, op. cit., pp. 19-25.

50. Wilbur Lee Ogdon, "Series and Structure: An Investigation Into the Purpose of the Twelve-Note Row in Selected Works of Schoenberg, Webern, Křenek and Leibowitz" (unpub. doctoral dissertation, Indiana Univ., Bloomington, 1955) p. 247.

51. Cf., André Hodeir, Since Debussy: A View of Contemporary Music, trans. Noel Burch (New York, Grove, 1961), pp. 105-109.

52. Donald Lybbert, letter to the author, July 7, 1966.

53. Cf., Willi Reich, "On Swiss Musical Composition of the Present," trans. Ernest Sanders, The Musical Quarterly, LI (January, 1965), 78-91.

54. Mrs. Martin, letter to the author, Nov. 11, 1966.

55. Donald Martino, letter to the author, July 18, 1966.

56. Donald Martino, "The Source Set and its Aggregate Formations, Journal of Music Theory, V (November, 1961), 224-74.

57. Pavle Merku, letter to the author, July 4, 1966.

58. Hodeir, op. cit., op. 97-123.

59. In France, as elsewhere, neither the achievements of several Americans, notably Milton Babbitt, nor anticipatory steps by other composers in the extension of serial principles, had been recognized at this time.

60. René Leibowitz, Schoenberg and His School, trans. Dika Newlin (New York, Philosophical Library, 1949), p. 230.

61. Serge Nigg, letter to the author, July 18, 1966.

62. Ibid.

63. Barbara Pentland, letter to the author, July 28, 1966.

64. Gilbert Chase, America's Music: From the Pilgrims to the Present (rev. 2nd ed., New York, McGraw-Hill, 1966), pp. 614-15.

65. George Perle, Serial Composition and Atonality (2nd ed, ; Berkeley, Univ. of Calif. Press, 1968).

66. Cf. Henri Pousseur, "Webern's Organic Chromaticism," Die Reihe, II (1958), 51-60.

67. Bernard Rands, letter to the author, June 22, 1966.

68. Gerhard, who had studied with Schoenberg, was particularly interested in combining traditional harmony and the twelve-tone technique into a twelve-tone tonality, in which, for example, he equated segmentation and inversion. Cf. Colin Mason, "Gerhard, Roberto, " Grove's Dictionary of Music and Musicians (5th ed.), 599-601.

69. Karen Reynolds, letter to the author, July 20, 1966.

70. George Rochberg, letter to the author, July 18, 1966.

71. Armin Schibler, letter to the author, November, 1966.

72. Murray Schafer, British Composers in Interview (London, Faber & Faber, 1963), pp. 125-36.

73. Cf. Rudolf Reti, Tonality in Modern Music (New York, Collier, 1962), p. 72.

74. Cf. Josepf Rufer, Composition with Twelve Notes Related Only to One Another, trans. Humphrey Searle (London, Barrie and Rockliff, 1954), pp. 194-5.

75. Stefan Jarocinski (ed.), Polish Music (Warsaw, Polish Scientific Pub., 1965), pp. 251-52.

76. Boguslaw Schäffer, Classics of Dodecaphony I (Cracow, Polskie Wydawnictwo Muzyczne, 1964), p. 157.

77. Kazimierz Serocki, letter to the author, July 2, 1966.

78. Ibid.

79. Cf. John G. Papaioannou, "Nikos Skalkottas," European Music in the Twentieth Century, Howard Hartog, ed. (New York, Praeger, 1957), p. 326.

80. Hidenori Tokunaga, letter to the author, August 27, 1966.

81. Ibid.

82. Erich Urbanner, letter to the author, August 10, 1966.

83. Bjarne Kortsen, Studies of Form in Fartein Valen's Music (Oslo, n.p., 1961).

84. Humphrey Searle, Twentieth-Century Counterpoint (London, Ernest Benn, 1954).

85. Roman Vlad, letter to the author, November 2, 1966.

86. Ibid.

87. Wladimir Vogel, letter to the author, July 8, 1966.

88. Ibid.

89. Josef Rufer, Composition with Twelve Notes Related Only to One Another, trans. Humphrey Searle (New York, Macmillan, 1954), pp. 198-200.

90. Ben Weber, conversation with the author, July, 1966.

91. Ibid.

92. John Weinzweig, letter to the author, July 23, 1966.

93. Ibid.

94. Christian Wolff, letter to the author, August 6, 1966.

95. Cf. Christian Wolff, "On Form," Die Reihe, II (1959), 61-63.

96. David Tudor, jacket notes, Stefan Wolpe, Esoteric recording ES-530.

97. Edward Levy, "Stefan Wolpe: (For his Sixtieth Birthday)," Perspectives of New Music, II (Fall-Winter 1963), 56.

98. Ibid., 57-61.

99. Stefan Wolpe, "Thinking Twice," Contemporary Composers on Contemporary Music, Elliott Schwarz and Barney Childs, eds. (New York, Holt, Rinehart & Winston, 1967), pp. 274-307.

100. Bolesław Woytowicz, letter to the author, July 1, 1966.

101. Reinhold Schubert, "Bernd Aloïs Zimmermann," Die Reihe IV (1960), 103-113.

102. Howard Hartog (ed.), European Music in the Twentieth Century (New York, Praeger, 1957), p. 201.

Chapter III

A Geographical Survey

The assimilation and spread of serial composition began with Schoenberg and his immediate students. For example, Nikos Skalkottas carried the twelve-tone method back to his Greek homeland in the 1930's. Wladimir Vogel settled in Switzerland and became the first twelve-tone composer in that country. Hans Apostel and Hanns Jelinek remained in Vienna, and have continued to be major exponents of twelve-tone writing in Austria. Apostel has tended to exert modifications upon the Schoenberg technique while Jelinek has remained a stalwart advocate of strict twelve-tone writing.

A general decline in musical activity in Austria followed the great period of the Schoenberg School, largely due to the emigration of Schoenberg, Ernst Křenek, and many others. But recently there has been a rejuvenation of avant-garde trends stimulated by the extended visits of György Ligeti and Roman Haubenstock-Ramati.

Cross-influences between native and immigrant composers played an important role in the development of twentieth-century music throughout the American continents. Schoenberg's twelve-tone technique was first transplanted from Europe by Juan Carlos Paz of Argentina. Many features of twelve-tone writing appeared in his Piano Variations (1928), forecasting the adoption of a fully twelve-tone style in his work and that of others in South America.

The initial efforts at importing the technique of the twelve-tone row to the United States were undertaken by Adolph Weiss. In 1924 he went abroad and studied with Schoenberg. Upon returning to the States in 1927, while continuing to utilize the twelve-tone idiom in his own composition, he became a leading member of the Pan-American Society for Composers. This organization promoted concerts of contemporary music and interested some Americans in the Schoenberg concepts. The League of Composers began publication of Modern Music to circulate both complete scores

199

and articles about the new music. Aaron Copland, Roger
Sessions, and Henry Cowell were prominent in the movement beginning in the late 1920's to sponsor contemporary
performances. However, in general the results of these
efforts to promote new music were discouraging. In the
immediate pre-war years the opponents of contemporary
music undermined these projects.[1]  Fortunately the institu-
tions of higher learning in the States began to expand their
music curricula about this time and many composers acquired teaching positions and a haven for the dissemination
of their ideas and performance of their compositions.

Weiss had initiated interest in twelve-tone writing
in the States but a more effective impact was the immigration
of Arnold Schoenberg and Ernst Křenek. The war also
brought other important composers to the States, many of
whom maintained strong connections with European musical
trends.  A wealth of ideas from such composers as Béla
Bartók,[2] Paul Hindemith,[3] and Igor Stravinsky[4] was received
with mixed feelings by a people whose craving for creative
independence was weakened by conservative tendencies.  The
Schoenberg technique, in particular, met with considerable
antagonism and only sporadic adoption ensued.

Yet several composers experimented with concepts
related in varying degree to the twelve-tone concept.  Henry
Cowell's use of tone-clusters can be cited as an important
influence on harmonic structuring,[5] and is symbolic of the
American tendency to be preoccupied with harmonic aspects
of composition.  This fact has had considerable influence on
twelve-tone music in this country.  Charles Ives (1874-1954),
an almost exact contemporary of Schoenberg, clearly indicated
a path for the emancipation of rhythm by his use of poly-
rhythms, his lack of symmetry, and his elimination of
regular bar lines and time signatures.  The significance
of his achievements with regard to rhythm has only recently
been properly evaluated.[6]  Although not primarily a twelve-
tone composer, he does use dodecaphony sporadically in
his highly chromatic writing.

Wallingford Riegger was another member of the older
American generation who paid particular attention to rhythmic innovations.  Riegger demonstrated a great originality
in utilizing ideas stemming from the cross-currents between
native and immigrant composers in the United States in the
1930's.  His work is a prototype of the so-called American

individualism, a neutral quality of style which the melting-
pot nature of this country could more easily nourish than
the national styles of Europe.

Post-war dodecaphony in the United States continued,
with few exceptions, to reflect a basically conservative
attitude. Antagonism[7] was counteracted by Milton Babbitt's
vehement support of strict serial composition. Between
these two extremes came the use of the serial technique
as a stepping-stone to other ideas, such as the chance and
aleatoric music of John Cage,[8] and the acceleration of
American participation in electronic music.[9] Babbitt's
initial efforts in rhythmic serialization did not immediately
stimulate the prominent role for total serialization that the
French and German avant-garde brought about in Europe,
but nevertheless his prophetic work laid foundations for a
later development of electronic music in the States.

In Canada[10] as elsewhere in the Americas the facets
of twelve-tone writing were shaped by dual influences: the
characteristic styles of its native composers and the ideas
brought by immigrants during and just before the turbulent
war years. The serial principles were introduced into
Canada by John Weinzweig, who came into contact with them
during his studies at the University of Rochester. Canada
has maintained a considerable interest in twelve-tone and
serial composition.

A third stage of the serial concept followed the
transitional period of early use of the Schoenberg technique:
extension of the twelve-tone row principle to the parameter
of rhythm, making total serialization possible. Composers
from several countries participated, notably the United
States, but France was the main spawning grounds for this
extension of the serial concept.

René Leibowitz, the composer-theorist who emigrated
from Poland to France as a youth, was a principal influence
in transplanting the Schoenberg technique to France. France
had several among her own composers, such as Charles
Koechlin and Abel Decaux,[11] who contributed to the establishment of a musical climate receptive to new ideas. Although
he is not noted as a serial composer, Olivier Messiaen became a major link in the chain of serial evolution through
the rhythmic innovations he expounded in his teaching and
applied in his piano études. In the circle of students around

Messiaen the dominant figure was Pierre Boulez. He
combined the ideas of Messiaen and Schoenberg to effect
a notable extension of serial principles to any or all musical elements. Boulez also stimulated the realization that
freedom was available within the use of total serialization
just as it was within the strict dodecaphony of Schoenberg.

The contacts between Pierre Boulez and Karlheinz
Stockhausen were crucial factors in the development of
Cologne and Darmstadt as international centers for experimentation with avant-garde music. Stockhausen is not only
a key figure in Germany but has become internationally
prominent for his theoretical writings and his compositions
utilizing both serial and electronic potential.

Alliance of the twelve-tone technique of Schoenberg
with the German contrapuntal heritage produced a wide
variety of styles and forms. Both radical and conservative
trends in the use of serial methods were represented, but
the divergence of serial techniques to electronic music in
Germany has played a major role in the evolution of both
serial and electronic expression.

The theories and music of Paul Hindemith, which
incorporated German traditions with his own twelve-tone
system, had their effect on Germans experimenting with
the Schoenberg technique. Although Hindemith left Germany
for the United States in 1939, his influence in his homeland
remained strong.

A comparison of American, German, and French
serial composition at mid-century reveals two important
trends changing their function. The conservative and radical
poles were no longer centered respectively around harmony
versus twelve-tone writing but had moved together in a
liberal direction and now centered around strict versus free
twelve-tone practice. The strict twelve-tone adherents became the conservative faction opposing the radical attitude
that advocated a free application of the twelve-tone principles
and their extension. The innovations of Arnold Schoenberg
were assuming the status of a traditional twelve-tone system.
The radical viewpoint held that strict dodecaphony was an
exhausted technique, whereas the conservative viewpoint felt
that the style lost its identity when license was taken. Strict
dodecaphony floundered because with the lack of published

documentation many misconceptions regarding the original
formulation arose. Rufer's publication of an explication of
the method, begun in collaboration with Schoenberg, was not
until 1952. Meanwhile composers discovered a variety of
ways to expand the initial concepts. The extension of the
serial principles throughout the musical elements and the
expanded potential for musical expression provided by the
merger of electronic and serial music initiated a new phase
of serial composition.

The introduction of the twelve-tone idiom of Schoenberg into England about 1940 by Humphrey Searle and
Elisabeth Lutyens was not immediately followed by a flurry
of activity. But as serialism touched the relatively conservative trends in English music during the post-war period it
splintered into trends which have recently become identifiable.

Three general groups are convenient for categorizing
this course of events. To the first belong those composers
who stimulated more than a casual interest in dodecaphonic
writing in a generally conservative style. Herein the tendency was to concur with the strict Schoenberg style. By
the mid-fifties the strict twelve-tone style became increasingly widespread and also a flirtation with Webern pointillism began, which was rather incongrously combined with
English block harmonicism. Those in the second category,
which included the New Manchester Group, tended to incorporate many post-Webern ideas while maintaining much of
the classical twelve-tone style. Finally, in more recent
years, several English composers, and some from other
parts of the British Isles, succeeded in breaking the shack-
les of conservatism and are now taking a significant part in
experimentation. England is a country addicted to fads and
early in the 1960's her interest in contemporary music reached a peak. Although this interest subsided after a brief
period, the effects on composers were longer-lived and served
both to break the tendency toward a conservative use of
serialism and to establish serial writing on a firm basis of
mature regard by both public and composers. The result
is a more comfortable grasp of contemporary idioms in the
1960's as compared to the relatively conservative and
frequently stilted application of the 1950's.

The first Italian composers to demonstrate a strong
interest in the Schoenberg technique before World War II
were Camillo Togni, [12] who completed the first Italian serial

score in 1942, Luigi Dallapiccola, and Roman Vlad. Italian
interest in dodecaphonic writing emerged slowly, as certain
influences tended to suppress it temporarily in the period
between the world wars. The influence of the prominent
teacher-composer, Alfred Casella (1883-1947), inhibited
composers in their attitude toward dodecaphony, for Casella
sought to repress extreme chromaticism. Although Casella
was extremely active in promoting the music of young composers, the Schoenberg style was not included in Casella's
enthusiasm for new music. Casella counteracted the interest
in twelve-tone writing cultivated in the early 1940's by the
students of Togni, Dallapiccola, and Vlad.

Goffredo Petrassi (b. 1904),[13] who had initially suc-
cumbed to this negative attitude of Casella's proceeded to
exploit and extend the use of chromaticism in his writing.
By 1951 his use of twelve-tone devices was pronounced.
Retaining some classical features from Casella and Hindemith, Petrassi first fused certain elements from Stravinsky
(notably his characteristic sonorities) as well as modal, poly-
tonal, and both tonal and atonal ideas. Thus whereas
Casella suppressed twelve-tone writing, Petrassi, another
influential teacher, served as the antithesis to this influence,
and made many of the younger generation in Italy aware of
dodecaphonic possibilities.

In recent years Italy has yielded a preponderance of
composers who are energetically exploiting the potentials of
serial composition. This country is one of the most interesting areas of activity in contemporary music today. The
Italians adopted and subsequently modified the serial idiom
with rapidity. They have shown a particular inclination for
the use of permutation techniques.

Furthermore, the so-called "destruction types" [14]
have been popular as a basis for new extremes of freedom
and originality in the construction of musical forms. For
example, "permeability," the simultaneous employment of
varying musical textures, is a favorite device.

The Italian serial composition of the 1950's is particularly important because of concern for linear structure,
which elsewhere had been somewhat buried as interest had
turned toward investigation of rhythm and vertical sonorities.
Dallapiccola's success in his dodecaphonic writing with
maintaining lyricism renewed interest generally in Italy in

this aspect. A new variety of a free chromaticism in Italy, alleviating rigidity in serial composition, is nowadays replacing the more ambiguous chromaticism of late romanticism that yielded the strict twelve-tone technique as its own self-discipline.

Several nations that have been late starters in the use of contemporary idioms for reasons of smaller size, peripheral location, or political pressures, have made rapid strides and significant contributions to twelve-tone and serial music.

Though not in the foreground themselves, the older generation in the Netherlands includes several composers, such as William Pijper and Henk Badings, who have consciously and effectively guided their students into the mainstreams of avant-garde music. [15] Among the younger generation Henri Pousseur is particularly well-known. He has also collaborated with major artists in experiments seeking to synthesize kinetic sculpture and sound imparted by electronic music.

Until recently Poland had a limited participation in contemporary music because of her political confinement. The efforts of Josef Koffler in the 1940's to interest his countrymen in twelve-tone music were not successful. Rediscovery of the Schoenberg technique through the compositions of Webern by Bolesław Szabelski in the late 1950's stimulated a strong wave of enthusiasm. Poland has now become the scene of one of the major international music festivals, Automne de Varsovie, in which her own composers are prominent, particularly Lutold Lutosławski. [16]

Probably the most extensive efforts to explore the potential of the twelve-tone style in Scandinavia were those of Fartein Valen. However, he did not stimulate interest generally in that area and his music has remained relatively unknown. Since World War II interest in modern music has grown in Scandinavia but is confined for the most part to the larger cities, where it has been encouraged by foreign visitors such as György Ligeti, in connection with various concert series of modern music. His influence has strengthened ties between Poland and Sweden, which have been a main source for stimulus toward the use of contemporary idioms. [17]

It should be noted that Scandinavia may well by-pass
a phase in which twelve-tone or serial writing predominates
and move on into the field of electronic music, using serial
features most selectively. Modern Nordic composers seem
to be preoccupied with the exploitation of sound for sound's
sake. An electronic studio currently nearing completion
under the direction of Knut Wiggen is being designed to
provide a technical potential for electronic music rivalling
other studios already in existence. Wiggen has collaborated
extensively with others, Stockhausen in particular, in the
effort to construct a first-rate studio. Continuance of this
sort of cooperative relationship should foster a further ex-
change of ideas between Scandinavia and the rest of Europe
and revitalize the annual international festival in Stockholm
which sporadically emphasizes contemporary music.

Spain is one of the most recent converts to contemporary trends. Although serial techniques have not been
employed by a great number of composers, there has been
no hesitation on the part of a few to pursue daring experimentation, such as the search for a twelve-tone tonal center.
Interest in progressive trends has already led to the publication of an important new periodical, Sonda, sponsorship
of numerous contemporary concerts, and extensive radio
programming of avant-garde music.

The international climate of Switzerland creates a
stimulating cultural atmosphere unusually receptive to new
ideas. This country partook early of twelve-tone procedures
in the work of Frank Martin and Wladimir Vogel. However,
the lack of a serious, indigenous Swiss musical tradition has
encouraged a rare brand of eclecticism and Swiss originality
is sometimes stifled by over-saturation of a score with
compatible ideas. Many members of the younger generation
have effectively employed serial principles in a variety of
synthetic styles.

Even the Oriental countries have exchanged ideas
about contemporary musical idioms with the West. Serial
practice is particularly limited only in the Iron Curtain
countries, and even in these areas it is beginning to emerge
in spite of an ideology inhospitable to abstract artistic
expression.

The flexibility of serial techniques allows their adaptation to almost any national style and indeed these character-

istics so vital in serial composition, flexibility and adaptability, have introduced twelve-tone and serial composition throughout the world. The starting point for the Schoenberg technique was the use of the twelve chromatic tones in a series. Fundamental to the choice of a serial ordering was basic consideration of a musical shape. The Schoenberg twelve-tone technique has undergone considerable metamorphosis, yet its fundamental concepts, of a basic series and a musical shape, have continued adequately to embrace all extensions made of it. Although Schoenberg's formulation did not specifically state how the basic principles could be extended, he possessed a strong intuition that his technique held a vast potential for exploitation in a variety of styles and he in fact nurtured highly diverse styles in his first students, Berg and Webern.

The present study of the development of serial composition has divided the exploitation of Schoenberg's basic idea into six stages: formulation, assimilation, extension, re-evaluation, broadening, and diversification. A retrospective view will probably simplify the first five categories of this division into a single phase and consider them as the formative period of serial composition. The present stage of diversification, the development of which seems to have originated during the 1960's, represents a growing awareness among composers working in all national styles that employing a serial organization within all conceivable traditional and avant-garde compositional techniques can enrich their own individual style and at the same time link their compositions to one of the mainstreams of twentieth-century music. The serial technique is but one of many stylistic forces active in music today, but one cannot deny that this technique is the most widespread of compositional devices in the last half of the twentieth century. Moreover, the apparent gravitational force of this technique seems to be drawing an ever increasing number of composers from all geographical and stylistic poles.

Thus the principle of serial organization appears to be unifying the infinitely diverse musical movements and styles developed in the early part of this century, and the web of relationships which are just now coming into view will require further study. Each extension of serial techniques has developed further understanding of underlying serial functions and considerable efforts have been made to comprehend the determining factors of serial structuring, not only by musicians but scholars from other fields. Many aspects of sound itself and the perception thereof have been the subject of studies by scientists and philosophers: but the results of these efforts appear in widely scattered sources and require evaluation and correlation. There is a pressing need for comparative studies of the theory and practice related to serial composition, studies which will clarify the terminology and notational devices employed in this tradition, distinguish and define the various streams which have been opened by the present diversification, indicate the extraneous features in various modifications of serial compositions, and establish the essential functional principles inherent in serial organization today.

## Notes

1. A candid discussion of this appears in the introduction to the study by Wilbur Lee Ogdon, "Series and Structure: An Investigation into the Purpose of the Twelve-Note Row in Selected Works of Schoenberg, Webern, Křenek, and Leibowitz" (unpub. doctoral dissertation, Indiana Univ., Bloomington, 1955).

2. Cf. Halsey Stevens, The Life and Music of Béla Bartók (New York, Oxford Univ. Press, 1953) which includes an extensive discussion of his works and a lengthy bibliography.

3. The principal biography of Hindemith is that by Heinrich Strobel, Paul Hindemith (Mainz, n.p., 1948).

4. See Eric Walter White, Stravinsky: The Composer and His Works (Berkeley, Univ. of Calif. Press, 1966).

5. Cowell's study of acoustics is summarized in his statement of his prophetic theory of new music. One of the most interesting aspects of his work is presented in the introduction, wherein he affirms that unconscious perception was in accord with natural law. Henry Cowell, New Musical Resources (New York, Knopf, 1930).

6.  See the study by Henry and Sydney Cowell, Charles
    Ives and His Music (New York, Oxford Univ. Press,
    1955).

7.  In practice, one of the most striking antitheses to a
    dodecaphonic theory was the composition of the
    French-born Edgard Varèse. He completely
    eliminated any concern for thematic material of any
    sort and based his composition entirely on audibility
    of sounds. An extensive bibliography is contained
    in a recent study completed by one of his former
    students. Fernand Ouellette, Edgard Varèse (Paris,
    Seghers, 1966).

8.  Bibliography and other information on Cage can be
    found in the annotated catalog, handled by C. F.
    Peters, John Cage (New York, Henmar, 1962).
    Cage has become known as the champion of chance
    techniques. Since the merger of serial and elec-
    tronic music, the bridge between serial and chance
    or aleatoric techniques is shortening. Several
    recent composers have taken tangent paths incorpor-
    ating both techniques. In a letter to this author,
    July 18, 1966, Cage clarified his relationship to
    twelve-tone and serial composition. He came close
    to a serial style in his early chromatic writing,
    his nearest approach probably occurring in unpublish-
    ed dance accompaniments in which he sought to
    employ a diatonic twelve-tone style and in some
    of his experimentation with rhythm in percussion
    pieces. "Finally, my use of charts for the
    Concerto for Prepared Piano and Chamber Orchestra
    involved, as method, a "series" of identical moves
    (as in the magic square)."

9.  The field of electronic music has been dominated by
    the activities in France at Radiodiffusion Français,
    in Germany at the West German Radio (Cologne),
    and in America at Columbia University. A concise
    summary of the work at these studios appears in
    Joseph Machlis, Introduction to Contemporary
    Music (New York, Norton, 1961), pp. 425-429.
    Also useful is the chronology from 1897-1962,
    contained in William W. Austin, Music in the 20th
    Century: From Debussy through Stravinsky (New

York, Norton, 1966), pp. 378-380. Complete cover-
age of this subject is available in the history by
Fred K. Prieberg, Musica ex Machina (Berlin,
Ullstein, 1960).

10. Information on Canadian composers can be found in
Thirty-Four Biographies of Canadian Composers
(Montreal, Canadian Broadcasting Corp., 1964).

11. A fascinating account of twentieth-century piano composition in France can be found in the final chapters
of Norman Demuth's French Piano Music: A Survey
with Notes on its Performance (London, Museum
Press, 1959), pp. 115-158.

12. Camillo Togni (b. 1922) adopted a twelve-tone style
in the 1940's, following a period of study with
Casella. He has written several piano works in
this style. Very little has been written about this
composer's work, other than a short discussion by
Roman Vlad, Storia della Dodecafonia (Milan, Suvini
Zerboni, 1958), p. 265.

13. Consult the collection of essays devoted to Petrassi
and his work by Guido M. Gatti (ed.), "L'Opera
di Goffredo Petrassi," Quaderni della Rassegna
Musicale, I (1964).

14. These are discussed by György Ligeti, "Metamorphoses of Musical Form," Die Reihe, VII (1965)
12-14.

15. For information on Pijper, Badings, and other Dutch
composers see Eduard Reeser (ed.), Music in
Holland: A Review of Contemporary Music in the
Netherlands, trans. Ian F. Finlay (Amsterdam,
Meulenhoff, 1959). An informative study of Belgian
contemporary music is by Robert Wangermee, La
Musique Belge Contemporaine (Brussels, La Renais-
sance du Livre, 1962).

16. For supplementary information see Stefan Jarocinski
(ed.), Polish Music (Warsaw, Polish Scientific Pub.,
1965).

17. In addition to John Horton, Scandinavian Music: A
    Short History (London, Faber & Faber, 1963),
    several volumes on contemporary music in individual
    Scandinavian countries are listed in the bibliography.

# BIBLIOGRAPHY

Abendroth, Walter. Selbstmord der Musik?: Zur Theorie, Ideologie und Phraseologie des Modernen Schaffens. Berlin, Hesses, 1963.

Abraham, Gerald. A Hundred Years of Music. 3rd ed. Chicago, Aldine, 1964.

_____. This Modern Stuff. London, Search Publications, 1933.

Armitage, Merle (ed.). Schönberg. New York, Schirmer, 1937.

Arnheim, Rudolph. Toward a Psychology of Art: Collected Essays. Berkeley, Univ. of Calif. Press, 1966.

Austin, William W. Music in the 20th Century: From Debussy through Stravinsky. New York, Norton, 1966.

Babbitt, Milton. "Set Structure as a Compositional Determinant," Journal of Music Theory, V (1961), 72.

_____. "Some Aspects of Twelve-tone Composition," The Score, 12 (June, 1955), 53-61.

_____. "Twelve-Tone Invariants as Compositional Determinants," The Musical Quarterly, XLVI (April, 1960), 246-59.

_____. "Twelve-Tone Rhythmic Structure and the Electronic Medium," Perspectives of New Music, I (1962), 49-79.

Barce, Ramón, "Nuevo Sistema Atonal," Atlántida, 21 (May-June, 1966), 329-43.

Basart, Ann Phillips. Serial Music: A Classified Bibliography of Writings on Twelve-Tone and Electronic Music. Berkeley, Univ. of Calif. Press, 1961.

Bauer, Marion.  Twentieth Century Music.  New York,
    Putnam, 1947.

Beck, G.  Compositeurs Contemporaines.  Paris, Huegel
    & Cie, 1960.

Beckwith, John, and Udo Kasemets (eds.).  The Modern
    Composer and His World.  Toronto, Univ. of Toronto
    Press, 1961.

Bekku, Sadao, et al.  Music East and West.  Tokyo, n.p.,
    1962.

Bengtsson, Ingmar (ed.).  Modern Nordish Musik.  Fjorton
    Tonsättare om Egna Verk.  Stockholm, n.p., 1958.

Blom, Eric (ed.).  Grove's Dictionary of Music and Musi-
    cians.  10 vols.  5th ed.  New York, St. Martin's,
    1960.

Blume, Friedrich (ed.).  Die Musik in Geschichte und
    Gegenwart.  12 vols.  Kassel, Bärenreiter, 1949-.

Boehmer, Konrad.  Zur Theorie der Offenen Form in der
    Neuen Musik.  Darmstadt, Tonos, 1967.

Boulez, Pierre.  "Musikdenken Heute 1," Darmstädter
    Beiträge zur Neuen Musik, V (1963), 7-123.

_____.  Relevés d'Apprenti.  Paris, Seuil, 1966.

Brainard, Paul.  "A Study of the Twelve-Tone Technique."
    Unpub. master's thesis, Eastman School of Music,
    Univ. of Rochester, 1951.

Briggs, Gilbert A.  Pianos, Pianists and Sonics.  Stamford,
    Conn., Hermann Pub. Serv., 1951.

Brindle, Reginald Smith.  Serial Composition.  London,
    Oxford Univ. Press, 1966.

Brown, Earle.  "Form in New Music," Source, I (1967), 48-
    51.

Bull, Storm.  Index to Biographies of Contemporary Com-
    posers.  New York, Scarecrow, 1964.

Busoni, Ferruccio. The Essence of Music and Other
    Papers. Trans. Rosamond Ley. New York, Dover,
    1957.

Cage, John. Silence. Cambridge, M.I.T. Press, 1966.

Carmi, Avner, and Hannah. The Immortal Piano. New
    York, Crown, 1960.

Carner, Mosco. A Study of Twentieth-Century Harmony.
    4th ed. London, Williams, 1942.

Chase, Gilbert. The American Composer Speaks: A
    Historical Anthology, 1770-1965. Baton Rouge, Louisiana
    State Univ. Press, 1966.

_____. America's Music: From the Pilgrims to the
    Present. Rev. 2nd ed. New York, McGraw-Hill, 1966.

_____. The Music of Spain. 2nd rev. ed. New York,
    Dover, 1959.

Chávez, Carlos. Musical Thought. Cambridge, Mass.,
    Harvard Univ. Press, 1961.

_____. Toward a New Music. Trans. Herbert
    Weinstock. New York, Norton, 1937.

Coeuroy, André. La Musique Française Moderne. Paris,
    n.p., 1922.

_____. Panorama de la Musique Contemporaine. Paris,
    n.p., 1928.

Cohn, Arthur. Twentieth-century Music in Western Europe,
    the Compositions and the Recordings. Philadelphia,
    Lippincott, 1965.

_____. The Collector's 20th Century Music in the
    Western Hemisphere. Philadelphia, Lippincott, 1961.

Collaer, Paul. A History of Modern Music. Trans. Sally
    Abeles. New York, World, 1961.

Composers of the Americas. 11 vols. Washington, D.C.,
    Pan American Union, 1955-1965.

Cone, Edward T. "Beyond Analysis," Perspectives of New
    Music, VI (Fall-Winter, 1967), 33-51.

Cooper, Grosvenor W., and Leonard B. Meyer. The
    Rhythmic Structure of Music. Chicago, Univ. of
    Chicago Press, 1960.

Cooper, Martin. French Music: From the Death of Berlioz
    to the Death of Fauré. London, Oxford Univ. Press,
    1961.

Coopersmith, J. M. Music and Musicians of the Dominican
    Republic. Washington, D.C., Pan American Union,
    1949.

Copland, Aaron. Copland on Music. New York, Norton,
    1963.

_____. Music and Imagination. New York, New
    Amer. Lib. of World Lit., 1952.

_____. The New Music. Rev. ed. New York, Norton,
    1968.

Cowell, Henry. American Composers on American Music.
    Palo Alto, Calif., Stanford Univ. Press, 1933.

_____. New Musical Resources. New York, Knopf,
    1930.

Cowell, Henry and Sydney. Charles Ives and His Music.
    New York, Oxford Univ. Press, 1955.

Crocker, Richard L. A History of Musical Style. New
    York, McGraw-Hill, 1966.

Cross, Lowell M. (comp.). A Bibliography of Electronic
    Music. Toronto, Univ. of Toronto Press, 1967.

Davies, Hugh (comp.). International Electronic Music Cata-
    log. Electronic Music Review, II-III (April-July, 1967),
    1-330.

Deliège, Célestin. "Bibliographie de la Musique Atonale et Serielle . . . Textes Parus Depuis la Publication des Ouvrages de Leibowitz," Revue Belge de Musicolo - gie, XIII (1959), 132-148.

Demuth, Norman. French Piano Music: A Survey with Notes on its Performance. London, Museum Press, 1959.

_____. Musical Trends in the 20th Century. London, Rockliff, 1952.

Dent, Edward J. The Future of Music. London, Pergamon, 1965.

Dallin, Leon. Techniques of Twentieth Century Composition. 2nd ed. Dubuque, Iowa, Wm. C. Brown, 1964.

Dibelius, Ulrich. Moderne Musik 1945-1965. Munich, R. Piper, 1966.

Eaglefield-Hull, A. (ed.). A Dictionary of Modern Music and Musicians. 2 vols. London, Dent, 1924.

Edmunds, John, and Gordon Boelzner. Some Twentieth Century American Composers. A Selective Bibliography. 2 vols. New York, New York Pub. Lib., 1959-60.

Edwards, Arthur C. The Art of Melody. New York, Philosophical Library, 1956.

Eimert, Henry, and Karl-Heinz Stockhausen (eds.). Anton Webern. 2nd rev. ed. Bryn Mawr, Pa., Theodore Presser, 1959.

_____. Die Reihe, 8 vols. 1955-1962.

Eimert, Herbert. Grundlagen der Musikalischen Reihen- technik. Vienna, Universal Edition, 1964.

_____. Lehrbuch der Zwölftontechnik. Wiesbaden, Breitkopf & Härtel, 1966.

Elston, Arnold. "Some Rhythmic Practices in Contemporary Music," The Musical Quarterly, XLII (July, 1956), 318-29.

Epperson, Gordon. The Musical Symbol: A Study of the
    Philosophic Theory of Music. Ames, Iowa, Iowa State
    Univ. Press, 1967.

Erickson, Robert. The Structure of Music: A Listener's
    Guide. New York, Noonday Press, 1955.

_____. "Time Relations," Journal of Music Theory,
    VII (1963), 174-93.

Eschmann, Karl. Changing Forms in Modern Music.
    Boston, Schirmer, 1945.

Feldman, Morton. "Conversations Without Stravinsky,"
    Source, II (1967), 42-45.

Ferguson, Donald N. Music as Metaphor: The Elements of
    Expression. Minneapolis, Univ. of Minnesota Press,
    1960.

Fletcher, H., E. D. Blackman, and R. Stratton. "Quality
    of Piano Tones," Journal of the Acoustical Society of
    America, XXXIV (1962), 749-61.

Fiore, Mary Emma. "The Formation and Structural Use
    of Vertical Constructs in Selected Serial Composition."
    Unpub. doctoral dissertation, Indiana Univ., Bloomington,
    1963.

Forte, Allen. "Context and Continuity in an Atonal Work:
    A Set-theoretic Approach," Perspectives of New Music,
    I (Spring, 1963), 72-82.

_____. "Schenker's Conception of Musical Structure."
    Journal of Music Theory, III (1959), 1-30.

_____. "A Theory of Set-Complexes for Music,"
    Journal of Music Theory, VIII (1964), 136-83.

_____. Tonal Harmony in Concept and Practice.
    New York, Holt, Rinehart and Winston, 1962.

_____. Contemporary Tone Structures. New York,
    Columbia Univ. Teachers College, 1955.

Friedheim, Philip. "Rhythmic Structure in Schoenberg's Atonal Compositions," Journal of the American Musicological Society, XIX (1966), 59-72.

Friskin, James, and Irwin Freundlich. Music for the Piano. New York, Rinehart, 1954.

Galli, Hans. Moderne Musik-leicht Verständlich. Munich, Francke, 1964.

Gardavsky, Cenek (ed.). Contemporary Czechoslovak Composers. Prague, Panton, 1965.

Gatti, Guido M. (ed.). "L'Opera di Goffredo Petrassi," Quanderni della Rassegna Musicale, I (1964).

Georgii, Walter. Klaviermusik. 2nd ed. Zürich, Atlantis, 1950.

Gillespie, John. Five Centuries of Keyboard Music: An Historical Survey of Music for Harpsichord and Piano. Belmont, Calif. Wadsworth Pub. Co., 1965.

Goléa, Antoine. Esthétique de la Musique Contemporaine. Paris, Presses Universitaires de France, 1954.

_____. Vingt Ans de Musique Contemporaine: de Boulez à l'Inconnu. Paris, Seghers, 1962.

_____. Vingt Ans de Musique Contemporaine: de Messiaen à Boulez. Paris, Seghers, 1962.

Gradenwitz, Peter. Music and Musicians in Israel: A Comprehensive Guide to Modern Israeli Music. Tel Aviv, Israeli Music Publications, 1959.

Gurney, Edmund. The Power of Sound. New York, Basic Books, 1966.

Hansen, Peter S. An Introduction to Twentieth Century Music. Boston, Allyn and Bacon, 1961.

Hanson, Howard. Harmonic Materials of Modern Music; Resources of the Tempered Scale. New York, Appleton-Century-Crofts, 1960.

_____. Music in Contemporary American Civilization.
Lincoln, Neb., Univ. of Neb., 1951.

Hartog, Howard (ed.). European Music in the Twentieth
Century. New York, Praeger, 1957.

Hauer, Josef Matthias. Zwölftontechnik, Die Lehre von den
Tropen. Vienna, Universal Edition, 1926.

Henning, Roslyn Brogue. "The Use of Contrapuntal Techniques by Contemporary Composers." Unpub. doctoral
dissertation. Cambridge, Mass., Radcliffe College,
1957.

Henze, Hans Werner. Essays. Mainz, n. p., 1964.

Herzfeld, Friedrich. Musica Nova; Die Tonwelt Unseres
Jahrhunderts. Berlin, Ullstein, 1954.

Hill, Richard S. "Schönberg's Tone-Rows and the Tonal
System of the Future," The Musical Quarterly, XXII
(1936), 14-37.

Hiller, Jr., Lejaren A., and Leonard M. Isaacson.
Experimental Music: Composition with an Electronic
Computer. New York, McGraw-Hill, 1959.

Hindemith, Paul. A Composer's World. Cambridge, Mass.,
Harvard Univ. Press, 1952.

_____. Craft of Musical Composition. 2 vols. Trans.
Arthur Mendel. New York, Assoc. Music Pub., 1942.

Hines, Robert Stephan. The Composer's Point of View:
Essays on Twentieth-Century Choral Music by Those
Who Wrote It. Norman, Okla., Univ. of Oklahoma
Press, 1963.

Hodeir, André. Since Debussy: A View of Contemporary
Music. Trans. Noel Burch. New York, Grove, 1961.

Horton, John. Scandinavian Music: A Short History. London,
Faber & Faber, 1963.

Hutcheson, Ernest. The Literature of the Piano: A Guide
    for Amateur and Student. 3rd ed., rev. Rudolph Ganz.
    New York, Knopf, 1964.

Irvine, Demar (ed.). Anton von Webern: Perspectives.
    Seattle, Univ. of Wash. Press, 1966.

Jarocinski, Stefan (ed.). Polish Music. Warsaw, Polish
    Scientific Pub., 1965.

Jelinek, Hanns. Anhang zu Hanns Jelinek Anleitung zur
    Zwölftonkomposition: Tabellen und Kompositionsbeispiele
    von Schoenberg, Webern und Jelinek. 2 vols. Vienna,
    Universal Edition, n. d.

_____. Anleitung zur Zwölftonkomposition Nebst Allerlei
    Paralipomena: Appendix zu "Zwolftonwerk" Op. 15. 2
    vols. Vienna, Universal Edition, 1952, 1958.

John Cage. New York, Henmar Press, 1962.

Johnston, Ben. "Proportionality and Expanded Musical
    Pitch Relations," Perspectives of New Music, V (Fall-
    Winter, 1966), 112-120.

Judd, F. C. Electronic Music and Musique Concrete.
    London, Neville Spearman, 1961.

Kappel, Vagn. Contemporary Danish Composers against
    the Background of Danish Musical Life and History.
    2nd rev. ed. Denmark, Danske Selskab, 1950.

Karkoschka, Erhard. Das Schriftbild der Neuen Musik.
    Celle, Germany, Hermann Moeck, 1966.

Kassler, Michael. "A Sketch of the Use of Formalized Lan-
    guages for the Assertion of Music," Perspectives of
    New Music, I (Spring, 1963), 83-94.

_____. "Toward a Theory That is the Twelve-Note-
    Class System," Perspectives of New Music, V (Spring-
    Summer, 1967), 1-80.

Katz, Adele T. Challenge to Musical Tradition: A New
    Concept of Tonality. London, Putnam, 1947.

Keil, Charles M. H. "Motion and Feeling through Music, " The Journal of Aesthetics and Art Criticism, XXIV (1966), 337-49.

Kelly, Robert. Theme and Variations: A Study of Linear Twelve Tone Composition. Dubuque, Iowa, Wm. C. Brown, 1958.

Kepes, György (ed.). The Nature and Art of Motion. New York, Braziller, 1965.

Kirby, F. E. A Short History of Keyboard Music. New York, The Free Press, 1966.

Klammer, Armin. "Webern's Piano Variations, Op. 27, 3rd Movement, " Die Reihe, II (1958), 81-92.

Koechlin, Charles. Traité de l'Harmonie. 3 vols. Paris, Eschig, 1925-30.

Kostelanetz, Richard (ed.). New American Arts. New York, Horizon, 1965.

Křenek, Ernst. Exploring Music. Trans. Margaret Schenfield & Geoffrey Skelton. London, Calder & Boyars, 1966.

_____. "A Composer's Influences, " Perspectives of New Music, III (Fall-Winter, 1964), 36-41.

_____. "Extents and Limits of Serial Techniques, " The Musical Quarterly, XLVI (April, 1960), 210-32.

_____ (ed.). Hamline Studies in Musicology. 2 vols. Minneapolis, Burgess Pub. Co., 1945-47.

_____. "Is the Twelve-tone Technique On the Decline?" The Musical Quarterly, XXXIX (October, 1953), 513-27.

_____. Music Here and Now. New York, Norton, 1939.

_____. Studies in Counterpoint. New York, Schirmer, 1940.

Lambert, Constant. Music Ho! A Study of Music in Decline. London, Faber & Faber, 1966.

Lang, Paul Henry. "An Evaluation of Dodecaphony at Mid-Century," The Musical Quarterly, XLIV (October, 1958), 503-10.

_____ (ed.). Problems of Modern Music: The Princeton Seminar in Advanced Musical Studies. New York, Norton, 1962.

Lang, Paul Henry, and Nathan Broder (eds.). Contemporary Music in Europe. New York, Norton, 1965.

Lange, Kristian, and Arne Ostvelt. Norwegian Music: A Brief Survey. London, Dennis Dobson, 1958.

Langer, Susanne K. Feeling and Form: A Theory of Art. New York, Scribner, 1953.

_____. Philosophy in a New Key. New York, The Amer. Lib., 1942.

_____ (ed.). Reflections on Art: A Source Book of Writings by Artists, Critics, and Philosophers. New York, Oxford Univ. Press, 1961.

Layton, B. J. "The New Liberalism," Perspectives of New Music, III (Spring-Summer, 1965), 137.

Leibowitz, René. Introduction à la Musique de Douze Sons. Paris, L'Arche, 1949.

_____. L'Evolution de la Musique, de Bach à Schonberg. Paris, Correa, 1951.

_____. Schoenberg and His School. Trans. Dika Newlin. New York, Philosophical Library, 1949.

Leichentritt, Hugo. Music, History, and Ideas. Cambridge, Mass., Harvard Univ. Press, 1958.

_____. Musical Form. Cambridge, Mass., Harvard Univ. Press, 1951.

Leirend, Charles. Belgian Music. New York, Belgian
    Gov. Inform. Center, 1955.

Lenormand, René. A Study of Twentieth-Century Harmony.
    Trans. Herbert Antcliffe. London, Williams, 1913.

Lewin, Harold Frederick. "Aspects of the Twelve-Tone
    System: Its Formation and Structural Implications."
    Unpub. doctoral dissertation, Indiana Univ., Blooming-
    ton, 1964.

Lewin, David. "On Certain Techniques of Re-Ordering in
    Serial Music," Journal of Music Theory, X (1966),
    276-87.

_____. "A Theory of Segmental Association in Twelve-
    Tone Music," Perspectives of New Music, I (1962),
    89-116.

Ligeti, György. "Metamorphoses of Musical Form," Die
    Reihe, VII (1956), 12-14.

Lindlar, Heinrich. Musik der Zeit: Eine Schriftenreihe zur
    Zeitgenössischen Musik. Bonn, Boosey & Hawkes, 1955.

Lissa, Zofia. "On the Evolution of Musical Perception,"
    trans. Eugenia Tanska, The Journal of Aesthetics and
    Art Criticism, XXIV (1965), 273-286.

Lowinsky, Edward E. Secret Chromatic Art in the Nether-
    lands Motet. Trans. Carl Buchman. New York,
    Russell & Russell, 1946.

Lundin, Robert W. An Objective Psychology of Music. 2nd.
    ed. New York, Ronald Press, 1967.

Machlis, Joseph. Introduction to Contemporary Music. New
    York, Norton, 1961.

Maegaard, Jan. Musikalsk Modernisme 1945-1962. Copen-
    hagen, Stig Vendelkaers, 1964.

Mäkinen, Timo, and Seppot Nummi. Musica Fennica.
    Trans. Kingsley Hart. Helsinki, Helsingissä Kustan-
    nusosakeyhtiö Otava, 1965.

Mandelbaum, Mayer Joel. "Multiple Division of the Octave
    and the Tonal Resources of 19-Tone Temperament."
    Unpub. doctoral dissertation. Indiana Univ., Blooming-
    ton, 1961.

Marquis, G. Welton. Twentieth Century Music Idioms.
    Englewood Cliffs, N. J., Prentice-Hall, 1964.

Martino, Donald. "The Source Set and Its Aggregate Forma-
    tions," Journal of Music Theory, V (1961), 204-23.

Masterpieces of Contemporary Japanese Music 1960.  Tokyo,
    Ongaku-no-tomo-sha, 1960.

Mason, Colin. "Gerhard, Roberto," Grove's Dictionary of
    Music and Musicians, (5th ed.), 599-601.

Mellers, Wilfred. Caliban Reborn: Renewal in Twentieth-
    Century Music. New York, Harper & Row, 1967.

_____. Music and Society: England and the European
    Tradition. 2nd ed. London, Dennis Dobson, 1950.

_____. Music in a Newfoundland: Themes and Develop-
    ments in the History of American Music. New York,
    Knopf, 1965.

_____. Studies in Contemporary Music. London,
    Dennis Dobson, 1947.

Messiaen, Olivier. The Technique of My Musical Language.
    Trans. John Satterfield. 2 vols. Paris, Alphonse
    Leduc, 1956.

_____. Traité du Rythme. Paris, n. p., 1954.

Meyer, Leonard B. Emotion and Meaning in Music.
    Chicago, Univ. of Chicago Press, 1956.

Michel, François (ed.). Encyclopédie de la Musique.
    3 vols. Paris, Fasquelle, n. d.

Miller, Horace Alden. New Harmonic Devices: A Treatise
    on Modern Harmonic Problems. Bryn Mawr, Pa.,
    Oliver Ditson, 1930.

Mitchell, Donald. "The Emancipation of the Dissonance: A
    Selected Bibliography," Hinrichsen's Music Year Book,
    VII (1952), 141.

_____. The Language of Modern Music. New York,
    St. Martin's, 1966.

Mitchell, William J., and Felix Salzer (eds.). The Music
    Forum. Vol. I. New York, Columbia Univ. Press,
    1967.

Moles, A. Les Musiques Expérimentales. Paris, Cercle
    D'Art Contemporain, 1960.

Mooser, R. -Aloys. Aspects de la Musique Contemporaine
    1953-1957. Geneva, Lahor et Fides, 1958.

_____. Panorama de la Musique Contemporaine 1947-
    1953. Geneva, Rene Kister, 1954.

_____. Regards sur la Musique Contemporaine 1921-
    1946. Neuchatel, Switzerland, Griffon, 1947.

_____. Visage de la Musique Contemporaine 1957-
    1961. Paris, Julliard, 1962.

Morgenstern, Sam (ed.). Composers on Music: An Anthology
    of Composer's Writings from Palestrina to Copland.
    New York, Bonanza, 1966.

Morthenson, Jan W. Nonfigurative Musik. Trans. Hans.
    Eppstein. Stockholm, Wilhelm Hansen, 1966.

Myers, Rollo H. (ed.). Twentieth Century Music. London,
    John Calder, 1960.

Music of Latin America. Washington, D.C., Pan American
    Union, 1963.

Newlin, Dika. Bruckner, Mahler, and Schoenberg. New
    York, Philosophical Library, 1949.

Nielsen, Tage. Danish Music after Carl Nielsen. Sweden,
    A. W. Henningsen, n.d.

Norman, Gertrude & Miriam Shrifte (eds.). Letters of
    Composers. New York, Grosset & Dunlap, 1946.

Ogdon, Wilbur Lee. "Series and Structure: An Investigation
    into the Purpose of the Twelve-Note Row in Selected
    Works of Schoenberg, Webern, Křenek, and Leibowitz."
    Unpub. doctoral dissertation, Indiana Univ., Blooming-
    ton, 1955.

Ouellette, Fernand. Edgard Varèse. Paris, Seghers, 1966.

Partch, Harry. Genesis of a Music. Madison, Wisc.,
    Univ. of Wisconsin Press, 1949.

Paz, Juan Carlos. Introducción a la Música de Nuestro
    Tiempo. Buenos Aires, Editorial Nueva Vision, 1955.

_____. La Música en los Estados Unidos. Mexico,
    Fondo de Cultura Economica, 1952.

Percy, Gösta (ed.). Swedish Music: Past and Present.
    Trans. Dick Litell. Stockholm, n.p., 1966.

Perle, George. "An Approach to Simultaneity in Twelve-
    Tone Music," Perspectives of New Music, III (Fall-
    Winter, 1964), 91-101.

_____. "Atonality and the Twelve-note System in the
    United States," The Score, XXVII (July, 1960), 51-66.

_____. "Evolution of the Tone-Row: The Twelve-
    Tone Modal System," Music Review, II (1941), 273-87.

_____. "The Harmonic Problem in 12-tone Music,"
    Musical Review, XV (1954), 253.

_____. "Possible Chords in Twelve-Tone Music,"
    The Score, IX (1954).

_____. Serial Composition and Atonality, 2nd ed.
    Berkeley, Univ. of Calif. Press, 1968.

_____. "Theory and Practice in Twelve-Tone Music,"
    The Score, XXVI (June, 1959), 58.

_____. "Twelve-Tone Tonality," Monthly Musical
    Record, LXXIII (October, 1943), 175.

Persichetti, Vincent. Twentieth-Century Harmony: Creative
    Aspects and Practice. New York, Norton, 1961.

Pfrogner, Hermann. Die Zwölfordnung der Töne. Zürich,
    Amalthea, 1953.

Pike, Alfred. "The Theory of Unconscious Perception in
    Music: A Phenomenological Criticism," The Journal of
    Aesthetics and Art Criticism, XXV (1967), 395-400.

Pleasant, Henry. The Agony of Modern Music. New York,
    Simon & Schuster, 1955.

Plebe, Armando. La Dodecafonia: Documenti e Pagine
    Critiche. Bari, Italy, Laterza, 1962.

Pousseur, Henri. "Da Schoenberg a Webern: una Mutazione,"
    Incontri Musicali, I (December, 1956), 3-39.

_____. "Formal Elements in a New Compositional
    Material," Die Reihe, I (1958), 30-34.

_____. "Music, Form and Practice (an Attempt to
    Reconcile Some Contradictions)," Die Reihe, VI (1964),
    77-93.

_____. "The Question of Order in New Music,"
    Perspectives of New Music, V (Fall-Winter, 1966),
    93-111.

Prieberg, Fred K. Lexikon der Neuen Musik. Freiburg,
    Karl Alber, 1958.

_____. Musica ex Machina: Uber das Verhältnis von
    Musik und Technik. Berlin, Ullstein, 1960.

Reeser, Eduard (ed.). Music in Holland: A Review of Con-
    temporary Music in the Netherlands. Trans. Ian F.
    Finlay. Amsterdam, Meulenhoff, 1959.

Regener, Eric. "Layered Music-Theoretic Systems,"
    Perspectives of New Music, VI (Fall-Winter, 1967),
    52-62.

Reich, Willi.  Alban Berg.  Trans.  Cornelius Cardew.
     New York, Harcourt, Brace, and World, 1965.

_____ (ed.).  Anton Webern: The Path to the New Music.
     Bryn Mawr, Pa., Theodore Presser, 1963.

Reis, Claire R.  Composers, Conductors, and Critics.
     New York, Oxford Univ. Press, 1955.

_____ .  Composers in America: Biographical Sketches
     of Contemporary Composers with a Record of their
     Works.  Rev. and enl. ed.  New York, Macmillan,
     1947.

Reti, Rudolph.  The Thematic Process in Music.  New
     York, Macmillan, 1951.

_____ .  Tonality in Modern Music.  New York,
     Collier, 1962.

Rochberg, George.  "The Harmonic Tendency of the Hexa-
     chord, " Journal of Music Theory, III (1959), 208-230.

_____ .  The Hexachord and its Relation to the 12-Tone
     Row.  Bryn Mawr, Pa., Theodore Presser, 1955.

_____ .  "The New Image of Music, " Perspectives of
     New Music, II (Fall-Winter, 1963), 1-10.

Rognoni, Luigi.  Expressionismo e Dodecaphonia.  Milan,
     Guilio Einaudi, 1954.

Rohwer, Jens.  Neueste Musik: Ein Kritischer Bericht.
     Stuttgart, Ernst Klett, 1964.

Rostand, Claude.  French Music Today.  Trans.  Henry
     Marx.  New York, Merlin Press, 1958.

Rothgeb, John.  "Some Uses of Mathematical Concepts in
     Theories of Music, " Journal of Music Theory, X
     (1966), 200-15.

Roy, Jean.  Présences Contemporaines: Musique Française.
     Paris, DeBresse, 1962.

Rufer, Josef. Composition with Twelve Notes Related
Only to One Another. Trans. Humphrey Searle.
London, Barrie and Rockliff, 1954.

Salazar, Adolfo. Music in Our Time: Trends in Music
Since the Romantic Era. Trans. Isabel Pope. New
York, Norton, 1946.

Salzman, Eric. "Modern Music in Retrospect," Perspectives
of New Music, II (Spring-Summer, 1964), 14-20.

_____. Twentieth-Century Music: An Introduction.
Englewood Cliffs, N.J., Prentice-Hall, 1967.

Sartori, Claudio (ed.). Dizionario Ricordi della Musica e
dei Musicisti. Milan, Ricordi, 1959.

Schafer, Murray. British Composers in Interview.
London, Faber & Faber, 1963.

Schäffer, Bogusław. Klasycy Dodekafonii. Cracow,
Polskie Wydawnictwo Muzyczne, 1961-64.

Schillinger, Joseph. The Mathematical Basis of the Arts.
New York, Philosophical Library, 1948.

_____. The Schillinger System of Musical Composition.
2 vols. New York, Carl Fischer, 1946.

Schloezer, Boris de, and Marina Scriabine. Problèmes de
la Musique Moderne. Paris, Editions de Minuit, 1959.

Schoenberg, Arnold. Style and Idea. New York, Philosophical Library, 1950.

_____. Models for Beginners in Composition. New
York, Schirmer, 1943.

_____. Theory of Harmony. Trans. Robert D. W.
Adams. New York, Philosophical Library, 1948.

_____. Structural Functions of Harmony. New York,
Norton, 1954.

_____. Harmonielehre. Vienna, Universal Edition,
1922.

Schuh, Willi, Hans Ehinger, Pierre Meylan, and Hans
    Schanzlin (eds.). Schweizer Musiker-Lexikon: Diction-
    naire Des Musiciens Suisses. Zürich, Atlantis, 1964.

Schuller, Gunther. "Conversation with Steuermann, "
    Perspectives of New Music, III (Fall-Winter, 1964),
    22-35.

Schwartz, Elliott, and Barney Childs (eds.). Contemporary
    Composers on Contemporary Music. New York, Holt,
    Rinehart and Winston, 1967.

Searle, Humphrey. Twentieth Century Counterpoint.
    London, Ernest Benn, 1954.

Sechter, Simon. Die Grundsätze der Musikalischen
    Komposition. 3 vols. Vienna, n.p., 1853-54.

Semmler, Rudolpf. Vom Eigenklang der Reihen. Zürich,
    Artemis, 1954.

Sessions, Roger. The Musical Experience of Composer,
    Performer, Listener. Princeton, N.J., Princeton
    Univ. Press, 1950.

Shattuck, Roger. The Banquet Years: The Origins of the
    Avant-Garde in France 1885 to World War I. New
    York, Doubleday, 1961.

A Short Survey of Music in Sweden. Trans. Claude
    Stephenson. Stockholm, Swedish Institute, 1962.

Slonimsky, Nicolas (ed.). Baker's Biographical Dictionary
    of Musicians. Fifth Edition with 1965 Supplement.
    New York, Schirmer, 1958; 1965.

_____. Music of Latin America. New York,
    Crowell, 1945.

_____. Music Since 1900. Boston, Coleman-Rose,
    1949.

Smither, Howard. "The Rhythmic Analysis of 20th Century
    Music, " Journal of Music Theory, VIII (1964), 54-88.

Spinner, Leopold.  A Short Introduction to the Technique
    of Twelve-Tone Composition.  London,  Hawkes,  1960.

Stadlen, Peter.  "Serialism Reconsidered, " The Score,
    XXIV (February,  1958),  12.

Stein, Erwin (ed. ).  Arnold Schoenberg Letters.  Trans.
    Eithne Wilkins and Ernst Kaiser.  New York,  St.
    Martin's, 1965.

_____ .  Musik: Form und Darstellung.  Munich, R.
    Piper,  1964.

_____ .  Orpheus in New Guises.  London,  n. p.,  1953.

Stein, Leonard.  "The Performer's Point of View, "
    Perspectives of New Music, I (Spring,  1963),  62-71.

Stevens, Halsey.  The Life and Music of Béla Bartók.
    New York,  Oxford Univ.  Press,  1953.

Stevenson, Robert.  Music in Mexico: A Historical Survey.
    New York,  Crowell,  1952.

Stockhausen, Karlheinz.  Momente.  Cologne,  n. p.,  1963.

_____ .  Texte zu Eigenen Werken zur Kunst Anderer
    Aktuelles.  2 vols.  Cologne,  M.  DuMont Schauberg,
    1963.

Stone, Kurt.  "Problems and Methods of Notation, "
    Perspectives of New Music,  I (Spring,  1963),  9-31.

Stravinsky, Igor.  The Poetics of Music in the Form of Six
    Lessons.  Trans.  Arthur Knodel & Ingolf Dahl.  New
    York, Vintage Books,  1956.

Strobel, Heinrich.  Paul Hindemith.  Mainz,  n. p.,  1948.

Stuckenschmidt, H. H.  Schoenberg.  New York,  Grove,
    1960.

_____ .  "Synthesis and New Experiments: Four Con-
    temporary German Composers, " trans.  Abram Loft,
    The Musical Quarterly,  XXXVIII (July,  1952),
    353-68.

Szabolcsi, Bence. A Concise History of Hungarian Music.
Trans. Sára Karig and Florence Knepler. London,
Barrie and Rockliff, 1964.

_____. A History of Melody. Trans. Cynthia Jolly
and Sára Karig. London, Barrie and Rockliff, 1965.

Teitelbaum, Richard. "Intervallic Relations in Atonal
Music," Journal of Music Theory, IX (1965), 72-128.

Thirty-Four Biographies of Canadian Composers. Montreal,
Canadian Broadcasting Corp., 1964.

Thomson, Virgil. The Art of Judging Music. New York,
Knopf, 1948.

_____. Music Reviewed 1940-1954. New York,
Vintage Books, 1967.

Thomson, William. "Hindemith's Contribution to Music
Theory," Journal of Music Theory, IX (1965), 52-71.

Toch, Ernst. The Shaping Forces of Music. New York,
Criterion Music Corp., 1958.

Ulehla, Ludmila. Contemporary Harmony: Romanticism
through the Twelve-Tone Row. New York, The Free
Press, 1966.

Vallas, Leon. The Theories of Claude Debussy: Musicien
Français. Trans. Maire O'Brien. New York, Dover,
1967.

Varèse, Edgard. "The Liberation of Sound," Perspectives
of New Music, V (Fall-Winter, 1966), 11-19.

Verrall, John. "A Method for Finding Symmetrical
Hexachords in Serial Form," Journal of Music Theory,
VI (1962), 277-82.

Vlad, Roman. Modernità e Tradizione Nella Musica Contemporanea. Turin, n.p., 1955.

_____. Storia della Dodecafonia. Milan, Suvini
Zerboni, 1958.

Wangermee, Robert. La Musique Belge Contemporaine.
    Brussels, La Renaissance du Livre, 1962.

White, Eric Walter. Stravinsky: The Composer and His
    Works. Berkeley, Univ. of Calif. Press, 1966.

Wildgans, Friedrich. Anton Webern. Trans. Edith Temple
    Roberts and Humphrey Searle. London, Calder &
    Boyars, 1966.

Winckel, Fritz. Music, Sound and Sensation: A Modern
    Exposition. New York, Dover, 1967.

Wouters, Jos. Netherlands Composers. Hilversum,
    The Netherlands, Radio Nederland, n. d.

Wuorinen, Charles. "Notes on the Performance of Contem-
    porary Music, " Perspectives of New Music, III (Fall-
    Winter, 1964), 10-21.

Wylie, Ruth. "Musimatics: A View from the Mainland, "
    The Journal of Aesthetics and Art Criticism, XXIV
    (1965), 287-94.

Xenakis, Iannis. Musiques Formelles. Paris, Richard-
    Masse, 1963.

Yasser, Joseph. A Theory of Evolving Tonality. New
    York, Amer. Lib. of Musicology, 1932.

Yates, Peter. An Amateur at the Keyboard. New York,
    Pantheon, 1964.

_____. Twentieth Century Music: Its Evolution from
    the End of the Harmonic Era into the Present Era of
    Sound. New York, Pantheon, 1967.

Zuckerkandl, Victor. Sound and Symbol: Music and the Ex-
    ternal World. Trans. Willard R. Trask. New York,
    Pantheon, 1956.